FROM ELVISH TO KLINGON

FROM ELVISH TO KLINGON

Exploring Invented Languages

MICHAEL ADAMS

OXFORD
UNIVERSITY PRESS

OXFORD
UNIVERSITY PRESS

Great Clarendon Street, Oxford OX2 6DP

Oxford University Press is a department of the University of Oxford.
It furthers the University's objective of excellence in research, scholarship,
and education by publishing worldwide in

Oxford New York

Auckland Cape Town Dar es Salaam Hong Kong Karachi
Kuala Lumpur Madrid Melbourne Mexico City Nairobi
New Delhi Shanghai Taipei Toronto

With offices in

Argentina Austria Brazil Chile Czech Republic France Greece
Guatemala Hungary Italy Japan Poland Portugal Singapore
South Korea Switzerland Thailand Turkey Ukraine Vietnam

Oxford is a registered trade mark of Oxford University Press
in the UK and in certain other countries

Published in the United States
by Oxford University Press Inc., New York

British Library Cataloguing in Publication Data
Data available

Library of Congress Cataloging in Publication Data
Data available

Typeset in Minion by Cenveo, Bangalore, India
Printed in Great Britain
on acid-free paper by
Clays Ltd, St Ives plc

ISBN 978–0–19–280709–0

10 9 8 7 6 5 4 3 2 1

Contents

Contents

~ 1 ~

The Spectrum of Invention

MICHAEL ADAMS

Every year, thousands of English professors in the United States, perhaps around the world, receive a circular offering them 'Shakespeare in the original language'—Klingon, the invented language of a warrior race in the invented future world of the television and film franchise, *Star Trek*. There are scholars of Klingon: they have written grammars and lexicons of the language, as well as translations, and they communicate with one another in refereed journals, one of them written entirely in Klingon (see Appendix 5). They treat Klingon as though it were a natural language, like English or Chinese, but Klingonists had to invent the language in order to write about it. To many of the circular's recipients, the enterprise of translating great literature into a 'fake' language seems plain silly; they probably believe the scholars responsible for it are inhabitants of a lunatic fringe.

Language, the kind in which we speak and write every day, began as a biological and social phenomenon in prehistory. From that hypothetical point forward, almost all of the world's languages have developed from the proto-language. Every new 'natural' language, when it *was* new, was a fresh sprig from an ancient root. One might think the plethora of naturally developed languages sufficient for human purposes, but invented languages suggest otherwise: inventing a language is intimidating work; no one would attempt to invent one unless driven by a serious purpose or aspiration.

And also by a sense that the language we have isn't always the language we want. As Suzanne Romaine writes later in this book (Chapter 8), 'A similarity of purpose and motivation drives inventors of all new languages whether in the real or fictional world. The perceived need for them arises from dissatisfaction with the current linguistic state of affairs. Recognition that language can be used for promoting or changing the social, cultural, and political order leads to conscious intervention and manipulation of the form of language, its status, and its uses.' Natural languages are themselves responsible for the dissatisfaction. As Arika Okrent notes in her excellent, partially participatory account, *In the Land of Invented Languages*, 'The primary motivation for inventing a new language has been to improve upon natural language, to eliminate its design flaws, or rather the flaws it has developed for lack of conscious design'. Looked at that way, invented languages almost seem inevitable: 'Why not build a better language?'. It is no surprise that 'the urge to invent languages is as old and persistent as language itself' (Okrent 2009, 11–12).

Invented languages are curious artefacts of culture and may be worth investigating on that basis alone. But they are really much more than curiosities. For one thing, there are many more invented languages than one might guess—we know about nearly a thousand around the world and throughout history, in fact, and we can only guess at how many schemes ended up in the fire or a mouse's nest. Okrent (2009, 298–314) provides a splendid, comprehensive list, but it is incomplete nonetheless, because people insist on inventing yet more languages. For instance, a Parisian under the pseudonym Frédéric Werst recently published *Ward* (2011), a novel in Wardwesân (with a parallel French translation), a language over which he has laboured for decades (Sage 2011). When everything is counted up, there have been roughly as many invented languages as there are natural ones, though, of course, the invented languages occasion relatively little use. Klingon is not alone, in other words, and many other invented languages are also culturally significant, with magnitude of significance in the eye of the beholder: Modern Hebrew, Esperanto, Orwell's Newspeak, and the languages of Tolkien's Middle-earth come to mind. In such company, and for good reasons, Klingon appears less silly, its speakers at least somewhat less crazy.

The origin and development of each invented language illustrates its inventor's sense of language, what it is, and what it should do, in linguistic and historical terms; each also implies its inventors' and users' dissatisfactions with the language(s) already available to them. As Okrent suggests, this mirroring justifies a second, informed look at invented languages, because 'language refuses to be cured and ... it succeeds, not in spite of, but because of the very qualities that the language inventors have tried to engineer away' (2009, 17). But invented languages do much more than scratch the itch of natural language: each expresses one or more among a wide range of purposes and aspirations—political, social, aesthetic, intellectual, and technological. Each invention originates in a complex human motive. Even more than natural languages, invented languages both reflect and urge the cultures in which they are proposed, appreciated, and occasionally even used.

Recovering the language of Adam

Language—you can't live with it and you can't live without it. Dissatisfaction with natural language is really a psychopathological dissatisfaction with being human, because language's design flaws, not to mention the mutual unintelligibility of the world's many languages, are OUR FAULT. At least, that's how the story goes. As the literary historian Russell Fraser puts it, 'In the Garden of Eden, Adam spoke a language in which one word conveyed the root meaning of one thing without the possibility of confusion. His language was semiotic' (1977, ix). Or, perhaps we should say it was 'onomastic', a language of names, for 'out of the ground the Lord God formed every beast of the field and every bird of the air, and brought them to the man to see what he would call them; and whatever the man called every living creature, that was its name' (Genesis 2:19). We still exercise this prerogative (see Appendix 8).

Though fallen from grace and expelled from Eden, humankind apparently continued to speak this language of one-to-one correspondences between words and things, but this linguistic purity, like all terrestrial purity, was too good to last. Our presumptuous ancestors attempted to build a tower to Heaven, and a jealous God was displeased:

> Now the whole earth had one language and few words ... And they said, 'Come, let us build ourselves a city, and a tower with its top in the heavens, and let us make a name for ourselves '... And the Lord came down to see the city and the tower which the sons of men had built. And the Lord said, 'Behold, they are one people, and they have all one language; and this is only the beginning of what they will do; and nothing that they propose to do will now be impossible for them. Come, let us go down and there confuse their language, that they may not understand one another's speech'. So the Lord scattered them abroad from there over the face of all the earth, and they left off building the city. Therefore its name was called Babel, because there the Lord confused the language of all the earth. (Genesis 11:1–9)

Ever since, language engineers have attempted to build not just a better language, but the original language, in order to unify the peoples of the world and, let's be honest, to regain Eden and our innocence, to reach a perfect human state by means of unambiguous speech and clear communication. Inventing the perfect language, however, is a lot like building a tower to Heaven—enterprising, yes, but already proscribed, history doomed to repeat itself, so we shouldn't expect success any time soon.

This impeccable logic has not deterred language inventors. Recovering the language of Adam, after all, would make a career—a sort of linguistic alchemy, it is the ultimate, elusive challenge. In the seventeenth century, it was an intellectual preoccupation of scholars across Europe, who pursued, as Arden Smith explains later in this book (see Chapter 2), 'what was called a "real character": a universal written language that could be understood by speakers of all tongues'. People who harbour this ambition aren't crazy, exactly, but, as Fraser puts it, 'They are profoundly optimistic' (1977, x). And though no one, not the seventeenth-century scholars nor the inventors of twentieth-century logical languages like Loglan (see Appendix 1), has ever reconstructed Adam's language or convinced any great number of people that they have, the attempt to purge language of ambiguity has produced valuable by-products. Fraser points out that 'the mathematical research of John Wallis anticipates the discovery of the differential calculus' (1977, 82), and we wouldn't want to do without the differential calculus or ∞, the symbol Wallis invented to mean 'infinity'. Inventing languages, even if they don't turn out as we hope they will, is hardly a waste of time.

Are all invented languages essays in the language of Adam, or at least in linguistic perfection? Arguably, no, yet the myth is often at least in the backs of the inventors' and users' minds. Its presence is felt most strongly in the creation of International Auxiliary Languages (IALs) like Esperanto, Volapük, Spokil, and many others, which directly address the 'interlinguistic problem' of mutual unintelligibility, whether God confounded human language or it got confusing all on its own (see Chapter 2 and Appendix 2). But when a community is first dispersed and then relocated (as in the case of Jews and Israel), or when a minority language is overwhelmed by the hegemony of an authorized one (as in the case of Cornish and English), then reconstruction (of languages like Modern Hebrew and Cornish) shares some purposes with the quest for Adam's lost language (see Chapter 8).

The languages Tolkien invented for the peoples of Middle-earth, especially the Elves, are not attempts to recover or even to imitate Adam's language, but they are aspirational, in two senses that correspond to the centuries-old search for it. First, Tolkien laboured for decades at his Elvish languages, and even if he didn't intend them to represent universally perfect language, he wanted them perfect in themselves, and he clearly thought they were beautiful, as do many of his readers (see Chapter 4). Second, Tolkien also enjoyed the challenge of doing something inconceivable to most people; for him, inventing languages was as irresistible as Everest to the mountain-climber. He loved English and other natural languages, but he thought he could make something as good, maybe better, because 'a living language … is not constructed', so is misaligned with our linguistic needs, 'and only by rare felicity will it say what we wish it to' (Tolkien 1983, 218). I guess that amounts to one sort of dissatisfaction Romaine and Okrent have in mind. In *The Lord of the Rings*, the Elves are about to return to Valinor from their exile in Middle-earth, a paradise regained. Perhaps there is a whiff of the Garden of Eden about Elvish after all.

In the dystopian worlds of George Orwell's *Nineteen Eighty-Four* and Anthony Burgess's *A Clockwork Orange*, invented language functions in an anti-language of Adam. Burgess's anti-hero, Alex, glibly distracts us and himself from the violence he perpetrates with his Nadsat, the criminal argot of teens in his time. Alex's England is no other Eden, demi-paradise, nor his language, the language invented for him, Eden's language; rather, both are dark, moralized consequences of Babel, the mutual unintelligibility and anti-sociality of people living on the same street. Where the language of Adam is unambiguous, transparent, Orwell's Newspeak is deliberately obscure, a language of prevarication, not the one with which Adam delved and called a spade a spade. Yet without the very notion of the language of Adam, would its antithesis be possible? The language of Adam may figure, however minutely, in many an invented language, but even as it serves as a unifying theme, we must consider the variety of invented languages as well.

The spectrum of invention

We continually create new words in order to fill lexical gaps, where there are things or concepts not yet covered by words: we encounter new species of flora or fauna, new physical entities (*quark*), political and financial institutions change (*freedom fries* 'French fries' [see Chapter 8], *euro* 'unit of currency'), we create new products and services and so also create brand names and trademarks for them. In the journal *American Speech*, the column 'Among the New Words', currently written by Ben Zimmer and Charles Carson, is a quarterly chronicle of this phenomenon, though it captures only a tiny fraction of new words, many of which are coined on the fly, for specific but ephemeral purposes. While natural languages depend on (relatively) stable structures, their vocabulary is constantly renewed, but what we do naturally and inevitably, even when it's creative, is not usually classified as 'invention'.

A good bit of new vocabulary, the ephemeral part of it, is slang. Slang is interesting in the current context because it lies at one end of the spectrum of linguistic invention. As I argue in *Slang: The People's Poetry* (2009), slang is 'inevitable' in a sense: social animals, we are always more or less simultaneously attempting to fit in and stand out, and slang is a means of doing so. It's a mode of performance that identifies us, marks affiliation with one group but not another, and amounts to poetry in everyday speech. As Barry J. Blake observes, 'Language is a means of communication, but a good deal of language use', including slang, 'is deliberately obscure' (2010, 1). We can be vague in everyday speech in our familiar natural language, but 'deliberation' is a step towards 'invention'.

According to Blake, 'Slang expressions tend to be self-consciously inventive, but some are rather forced and probably too clever to achieve wide circulation or longevity' (2010, 203). 'Self-consciously inventive' is obviously a step beyond mere 'invention'. Surely, it is the linguistic attitude of the genius at SlangSite.com who invented the word *accipurpodentally* 'accidentally on purpose', who doubtless revelled in the pleasures of *lexifabricography*, another item included in SlangSite's dictionary. Slang is itself 'accipurpodental', and the focus of 'lexifabricography' is on fabrication. Slang is inventive language and is usually invented, though many common items are used without speakers retaining any sense of that invention—it is not *an* invented language, however, though, like slang, some kinds of invented languages are 'forced and probably too clever to achieve wide circulation'.

According to Paul Baker, Polari is 'a secret language mainly used by gay men and lesbians, in London and other UK cities with an established gay subculture, in the first 70 or so years of the twentieth century' (2002, 2), an amalgam of criminal cant, theatre jargon, back and rhyming slang, Romani, Yiddish, and many other elements, with some unique grammatical features. Baker provides the following example: 'Well hello ducky, it's bona to vada your dolly old eek again. Order to your mother dear. Take the lattie on wheels did you? Fantabuloas! Oh vada that cod omee-palone in the naff goolie lally drags. Vada her gildy ogle fakes! Get dooey versa! I've nanti dinarly!' (2002, 2).

Most people would consider Polari a specific slang, but it is, from a structural point of view, wonderfully complex. As Baker concludes, 'In reference to Polari, I have also had to consider the question "What is a language?" carefully. Although some speakers used Polari in a complex and creative way that meant it was mutually unintelligible to outsiders, others merely employed it as a limited lexicon', so 'Polari cannot be called a language in the same way that English, French, Italian etc. are languages' (2002, 154). But among well-versed speakers and at the peak of its development, Polari was more than just words; slang is not *a* language but is sometimes a step closer to one than 'mere' vocabulary (see Adams 2009, 165–73).

In order to characterize Polari, Baker, following the linguist Michael Halliday, finally settled on a linguistic category called 'anti-language':

> Anti-languages can provide (multiple) lexical items for concepts considered important to a particular 'anti-society'—they allow the anti-society to remain hidden, the shared language acts as a bonding mechanism and means of identification, and, most importantly, the anti-language allows its users to construct an alternative social reality and alternative identities for themselves. (2002, 154)

Burgess' Nadsat certainly serves this purpose for Alex and his cronies in *A Clockwork Orange*, but IALs and Klingon serve similar purposes for their users. These purposes aren't exclusive—you can learn Esperanto to promote world peace, but that would be an alternative social reality, and Esperantist is an alternative identity, the shared language a means of bonding with fellow Esperantists. Inventing languages and using invented languages are all about alternatives that express, if not quite 'anti-', at least a certain dissatisfaction with language available around us.

In *Slang: The People's Poetry* I argue that slang self-consciously tests the parameters of language, what is possible, what you can get away with, and so is always, in a very strong sense, an anti-language. An invented language, the creation or use of it, similarly tests language, but with a much higher level of commitment. I also argue that slang is poetic, and in a review of the book, Marcel Danesi suggests that I am pointing to an 'originating force of poeticism, revealing the presence of a creative impulse in humans in the ways they create and use language', a 'poetic competence' (2010, 507–8) parallel and allied to linguistic competence (the innate ability to learn language) and communicative competence (the innate ability to use language in human affairs).

Poetry, or the poetic impulse, is thus inseparable from language, and, like slang, an invented language is an expression—a sustained, detailed, ambitious expression—of that impulse. While many think inventing languages is odd from a linguistic point of view (it might otherwise be justified by goals like constructing the alternative world of a fiction, or promoting world peace, or making money), it isn't really. It's perfectly natural to test 'the limits and systems of discourse' (Fraser 1977) by means of the 'originating force of poeticism'; indeed, such testing may be essential to full ownership of language. Perhaps taking the trouble of inventing a whole language is overdoing it, but Okrent is right that invented languages are actually always about natural ones and about the linguistic and communicative competencies underlying our language behaviour, whatever else they may also be about.

Because self-consciously inventive language, like slang, and full-blown invented languages, like Esperanto and Tolkien's Elvish, share so many characteristics and yet are generally distinguishable from one another, it is best to see them on a spectrum of linguistic invention. The caveat 'generally' is necessary because it is hard to tell whether Polari (following the colour spectrum) is red, like slang, or orange, or on the verge of orange; or whether Klingon, which isn't yet fully developed or codified, belongs in the same colour as Elvish or Volapük, for which the rules are more fully elaborated. This book attempts to illustrate various points along the spectrum, so includes chapters on vocabularies like Newspeak and Nadsat, as well as languages with complete grammars, like IALs and reconstructed languages. It includes a chapter on linguistic invention in literary style, not just 'inventive' language (which we expect from James Joyce, Samuel Beckett, and Paul Muldoon, the subjects of the chapter in question) but 'self-conscious invention' of idiosyncratic authorial anti-language (writers are always dissatisfied with the language they are given), invention more as a matter of practice than of principle, it might be said. Of course, the full-blown invented languages come into this account as well.

The spectrum of motives

Invention of a whole language, or of language on a smaller scale, then, can be driven by any number of motives. There is no reason to assume that each invention depends on one and only one motive, or even on one and only one type of motive. Though we accept the 'negative' motive that dissatisfaction with available natural languages drives invention of alternative languages, positive motives are also plausible. This book illustrates as many motives for inventing languages as the language or languages investigated in the various chapters support.

Certainly, there are linguistic motives for inventing a language. For instance, one might fill a 'language gap', that is, supply a language for a group, fictional or real, otherwise without an adequate language—Klingon was invented partially from this motive, as are reconstructed languages, like Modern Hebrew and Hawaiian (see Chapters 5 and 8, as well as Appendix 8). One might invent a language like Loglan (discussed briefly in Appendix 1) in order to explore what is linguistically possible, to probe linguistic limits, truths, assumptions, etc., or like any number of IALs in order to fulfil linguistic possibilities (simplicity, for instance) left unrealized in natural languages (see Chapter 2 and Appendix 2). One might also invent a language to practise linguistic or philological technique (to some extent) for its own sake and to accomplish difficult linguistic or philological things gracefully, without apparent effort (what Baldassare Castiglione, in *The Book of the Courtier* (1528), calls *sprezzatura*, a word he invented to fill what he saw as a lexical gap in Italian, with which, on this point, he was dissatisfied). Tolkien's languages are motivated thus (see Chapter 4), and so is Klingon in its later stages of development (see Chapter 5 and Appendix 5).

Though it captures a mode of conduct, *sprezzatura* is also an aesthetic term: *sprezzatura* is evident in equestrian exercises, Rembrandt's brushstrokes, Mozart's talent for composition, Oscar Wilde's eminently quotable wit. As already suggested, linguistic motives easily cooperate with aesthetic ones. In inventing a language, one may aspire to make a thing of beauty, as Tolkien did with Elvish (see Chapter 4). Of course, beauty is in the eye of the inventor, and some speakers find Klingon more attractive than Elvish; Loglan's attempt to make symbolic logic 'speakable' (see Appendix 1) suggests not only an interest in a useful language, but one whose structure reflects mathematical elegance. The inventor may also find aesthetic value in the very act of invention (whatever the outcome): in his lecture about inventing languages, 'A Secret Vice', Tolkien frequently mentions and sometimes discusses the *pleasure* of doing so. Of course, one may invent language to promote plot, theme, or character in a literary work, as in *A Clockwork Orange* (see Chapter 3), *The Lord of the Rings* (see Chapter 4), *Star Trek* (see Chapter 5), or various gaming worlds (see Chapter 6); to develop a distinctive voice, as in *Finnegans Wake* (see Chapter 7); or to promote the interactivity essential to a satisfying multiplayer online role-playing game experience (see Chapter 6).

Inventing a language may also be a political act: reconstructed and renewed languages (Néo-breton or Māori, for instance) identify cultural space and celebrate cultural heritage (see Chapter 8), while IALs attempt to erase linguistic borders in the interest of universal understanding and the world peace to which it supposedly would give birth (see Chapter 2). Inventing a language may promote intersections of culture and ideology, or provide political or cultural voice to those silenced or inhibited by natural language (or the lack of it), for instance by Irish or Scottish writers dissatisfied with British English (for both motives, see Chapter 7 and Appendix 7), or Hawaiians recovering from the imperial domination of American English, or Jews establishing Israel with a language, Hebrew, that hadn't been spoken in nearly two millennia (see Chapter 8).

Many of the aforementioned converge with personal and biographical motives. An inventor may be dissatisfied with natural language on linguistic terms but also feel a profound sense of alienation with surrounding circumstances prompting spiritual renewal in the imagination, as in Tolkien's recourse to inventing languages in the trenches during the First World War (see Chapter 4). Or, invention may reflect the inventors' sense of affiliation with a social group, as with the slang of online gamers (see Appendix 6). Or it may respond to an inventor's sense that being 'inside' a language has a spiritual dimension or that making one up is spiritual exercise. In 'A Secret Vice', another of Tolkien's favourite words is *personal*.

Two other powerful personal motives are fame and money, sometimes operating simultaneously, at others mutually exclusive. Certainly, inventors of game languages or Klingon, working for profit-making firms, have a financial stake in the languages they invent, whether in the form of a salary or a proprietary interest. Uncovering the 'secret' of language, recovering the language of Adam, like alchemy, could be done for its own sake or for the motives outlined above. But it could also be a means of making gold from base elements and thereafter being rich as Croesus. Edward Rulloff, a nineteenth-century American thief and murderer who was also a dedicated linguist, was, at the time of his execution, writing what he supposed was the ultimate philological work. He hoped to sell his book to a government or private buyer for $500,000, sure that someone would buy it because knowledge, even philological knowledge, is power. Theft was merely a stopgap, a series of advances he couldn't wrangle from a publisher. You can read the whole, unbelievable story in Richard W. Bailey's linguistic true-crime account, *Rogue Scholar: The Sinister Life and Celebrated Death of Edward H. Rulloff* (2003). Inventing a language or owning one can be quite lucrative, and practical motives predominated in invention of Klingon and the several gaming languages discussed in Chapter 6, though the terms on which one can own language, even *a* language, are complicated (see Appendix 1).

Still other motives for inventing a language are not only possible, but amply illustrated in the ensuing chapters. Those outlined here are, frankly, obvious, but human motivation is often subtle. The following passage from Tolkien's 'A Secret Vice' shows just how subtle:

> Some of you may have heard that there was, a year or more ago, a Congress in Oxford, an Esperanto Congress; or you may not have heard. Personally I am a believer in an 'artificial' language, at any rate for Europe—a believer, that is, in its desirability, as the one thing antecedently necessary for uniting Europe, before it is swallowed by non-Europe; as well as for many other good reasons—a believer in its possibility because the history of the world seems to exhibit, as far as I know it, both an increase in human control of (or influence upon) the uncontrollable, and a progressive widening of the range of more or less uniform languages. Also I particularly like Esperanto, not least because

it is the creation ultimately of one man, not a philologist, and is therefore something like a 'human language bereft of the inconveniences
due to too many successive cooks'—which is as good a description of
the ideal artificial language (in a particular sense) as I can give.

No doubt the Esperantist propaganda touched on all these points.
I cannot say. But it is not important, because my concern is not with
that kind of artificial language at all. You must tolerate the stealthy
approach. It is habitual. But in any case my real subject tonight is a
stealthy subject. Indeed nothing less embarrassing than the *unveiling* in
public of a secret vice. Had I boldly and brazenly begun right on my
theme I might have called my paper a plea for a New Art, or a New
Game, if occasional and painful confidences had not given me grave
cause to suspect that the vice, though secret, is common; and the art (or
game), if new at all, has at least been discovered by a good many other
people independently. (Tolkien 1983, 198)

Tolkien's motive, private pleasure in linguistic invention, is
approached obliquely, by contrasting the type of language he invents
with what it is not (that is, an IAL). Is inventing languages a New Art
or a New Game? In raising the possibility of 'game', Tolkien has anti-
cipated one of the subtler motives identified by James Portnow in his
chapter on gaming languages, below.

The plan of this book

Including this introduction, this book comprises eight chapters.
Chapter 2, by Arden Smith, who has a Ph.D. in Linguistics from
the University of California at Berkeley and is a noted scholar of
Tolkien's languages, is about International Auxiliary Languages from
seventeenth-century interest in a 'real character' into the twentieth
century—it is an impeccably informed and breathtaking survey, with
an unusual emphasis on Volapük, a predecessor of the more famous
Esperanto, which is also discussed in some detail. Chapter 3, by Howard
Jackson, now retired from a career as a professor of linguistics, writes

informatively and insightfully about Orwell's Newspeak and Burgess' Nadsat, two invented vocabularies prominent in the popular imagination, but not always understood, at least in terms of the motives for their invention. Chapter 4, on the languages of Middle-earth, is written by E. S. C. Weiner and Jeremy Marshall of the *Oxford English Dictionary*, co-authors with Peter Gilliver of a splendid book about Tolkien and the *OED*, *The Ring of Words* (2006). Klingon is the subject of Chapter 5, written partly by Marc Okrand, who invented the language, and partly by Judith Hendriks-Hermans and Sjaak Kroon, who have considered it sociolinguistically—I have stitched their contributions into a chapter, adding a fair amount of material in the process, and acknowledge myself (unexpectedly) as a co-author. James Portnow, game designer and game design journalist, has contributed Chapter 6 which, I believe, is the first serious account of languages invented for online role-playing games. My colleague Stephen Watt, of Indiana University, has supplied a sophisticated and wide-ranging chapter on linguistic invention in the work of major modern Irish writers (Joyce, Beckett, and Muldoon, with some Shaw added for perspective). Finally, Suzanne Romaine, one of the world's pre-eminent linguists, has contributed Chapter 8, on reconstructed and renewed languages.

The several chapters discuss the origin and development of the relevant languages, describe their structures and vocabularies, their fictional purposes (when they are languages of fiction), their social purposes (when they operate in the real world or some hybrid of real and imagined worlds, as in games), and the motives behind their making. The book assumes that people invent languages for good reasons, and that it's our business as authors and editor to expose and clarify them—we hope readers will read about them critically, but with sympathy.

For each chapter there is a complementary appendix, written by me, the editor. In some cases, appendices particularize topics raised in their chapters; in others, they introduce new but related topics; in all cases, they attempt to bring chapters into contact with one another, to make something whole out of several chapters by even severaller hands. I suppose that I have tried to invent a book from what I was given, but not from dissatisfaction. Rather, on reading the chapters, I realized how rich the book's argument is and wondered whether, perhaps, we could, well, not recover the language of Adam, but nevertheless understand something about the relations between language and human nature, not by means of what human nature gives, but by what we can make of it.

References

Adams, Michael. 2009. *Slang: The People's Poetry*. New York: Oxford University Press.

Bailey, Richard W. 2003. *Rogue Scholar: The Sinister Life and Celebrated Death of Edward H. Rulloff*. Ann Arbor: University of Michigan Press.

Baker, Paul. 2002. *Polari—The Lost Language of Gay Men*. London and New York: Routledge.

Blake, Barry J. 2010. *Secret Language: Codes, Tricks, Spies, Thieves, and Symbols*. Oxford: Oxford University Press.

Danesi, Marcel. 2010. 'The forms and functions of slang'. *Semiotica* 182: 507–17.

Fraser, Russell. 1977. *The Language of Adam: On the Limits and Systems of Discourse*. New York: Columbia University Press.

Gilliver, Peter, Jeremy Marshall, and Edmund Weiner. 2006. *The Ring of Words: Tolkien and the Oxford English Dictionary*. Oxford: Oxford University Press.

May, Herbert G., and Bruce M. Metzger. 1977. *The New Oxford Annotated Bible with Apocrypha*. New York: Oxford University Press.

Okrent, Arika. 2009. *In the Land of Invented Languages*. New York: Spiegel & Grau.

Sage, Adam. 2011. 'What's the Wardwesân for …? After 20 years of toil, Frédéric Werst has published a book in a language that no one understands'. *The Times* (2 February): 4–5.

Tolkien, J. R. R. 1983. 'A Secret Vice'. In *The Monsters and the Critics and Other Essays*, edited by Christopher Tolkien, 198–223. Boston: Houghton Mifflin.

Werst, Frédéric. 2011. *Ward*. Paris: Éditions du Seuil.

Confounding Babel:

International Auxiliary Languages

ARDEN R. SMITH

Et idcirco vocatum est nomen eius Babel, quia ibi confusum est labium universae terrae; et inde dispersit eos Dominus super faciem cunctarum regionum.   Genesis 11:9

In the biblical account, the people of the world originally spoke one language, the one Adam invented when he named the animals in the Garden of Eden. When Adam's descendants at Babel dared to build a tower reaching to heaven, God confounded their tongues, thus creating the diversity of languages. That diversity, and the confusion engendered by it, has led many (many more than most would imagine) to develop international languages that would overturn the curse of Babel, the problem of mutual unintelligibility among people of different nations. In attempting to advance an international language, arguably a solution to that problem, some have resorted to already existing languages and some to modifications and simplifications of those languages, while others have proposed entirely new linguistic creations.

The primary purpose of such schemes was to create a medium for international communication, but reasons for desiring such a medium varied. Easier dissemination of knowledge, facilitation of commerce, aid in the teaching of religious doctrine, international harmony through the use of a shared tongue—all of these are cited by various proponents of international languages. Such differing motivations would colour the languages accordingly. Other factors would also dictate the forms these new languages would take. Logical and rational organization was one desideratum of the language inventors, but its realization could take many shapes: the elaborate classificatory systems of the seventeenth-century philosophical languages, the regularized European-style grammars of languages such as Esperanto, or the symbolic logic on which the grammar of Loglan is based. The inventors also hoped to create a language that was easy to learn, as an alternative to the difficulties inherent in learning Latin or any number of vernaculars (see Appendix 2). A logical structure, free from irregularities, was one means to this end, but many language inventors also borrowed vocabulary and grammatical structures from widely spoken natural languages in their attempts at internationality.

International languages: from natural to artificial

Throughout history, languages of empire have served as bridges between speakers of different tongues. From the Greek *koinē* ('common dialect') spread by the conquests of Alexander to worldwide use of English today, the most successful international languages have been the languages of the powerful. After obliterating Oscan and Umbrian from the Italian peninsula, Latin spread throughout most of Europe and the Mediterranean regions of Africa and Asia, the linguistic camp follower of Julius Caesar and his legions. Legal and governmental institutions established by the Roman Empire, especially the Roman Catholic Church, ensured constant use of Latin internationally for a thousand years after the fall of Rome. Medieval education was education in Latin, the language of science, government, law, and church. If scholars or diplomats from various countries ever came together, Latin was the medium of communication.

The Renaissance, the Protestant Reformation, and the invention of the printing press all led to the decline of Latin and the increasing prestige of vernaculars. This shift was gradual, and Latin remained the language of scholarship, even while the first wave of artificial language schemes erupted in the seventeenth century. Those early projects were motivated less by a need for an international medium of communication than by a desire to reflect the orderly structure of the universe in language and to recapture the supposed perfection of the language of Adam, in which, according to the myth, words more accurately corresponded to the things they signified than in arbitrary, post-Babel languages. Not until the nineteenth century, with the rise of a middle class unschooled in Latin, would the idea of an international auxiliary language (IAL) become popular.

Eighteenth-century technological advances facilitated international communication, travel, and commerce, but linguistic differences remained a stumbling block to progress. Latin no longer reliably bridged the differences among vernaculars; those engaged in international activities had to learn a variety of vernacular languages instead. Languages of the more powerful European states, particularly French, English, and German, had some value as international languages, but none was truly universal, and the fierce nationalism of the period prevented any one of them from becoming so. Learning several languages is difficult and time-consuming, and in this context international languages were proposed as easy-to-learn, politically neutral solutions to the interlinguistic problem.

Although a few nineteenth-century languages made progress towards a solution, none came close to achieving what their inventors had hoped. Two factors are largely to blame. The first is nationalism: powerful nations have been reluctant to relinquish their privileged positions by promoting a universal second language not their own.

The second is the sheer diversity of universal language schemes. While many people found the idea of an IAL attractive, they could not agree on one, so what could have been a powerful lobby for an artificial international language split into squabbling factions—an ironic fate for a movement intended to bring the people of the world together. (The irony was not lost at the time—see Appendix 2.)

IALs proposed over the last four centuries display a wide variety of structural characteristics reflecting the variety of motives underlying them. Louis Couturat and Léopold Leau, in their monumental histories of international languages (1903 and 1907), divide them into three main classes: (1) *a priori* languages, which are not based on existing natural languages but invented from scratch; (2) *a posteriori* languages, which are based on elements and structures from natural languages, with varying degrees of simplification and modification; and (3) mixed systems, which combine the two. Since the overwhelming majority of the earliest invented international languages were *a priori* systems, we will begin our story there.

A priori languages

Despite the rise of vernaculars at the dawn of the modern era, Latin remained the *de facto* international language in Europe during the seventeenth century. Certain factors had begun to limit its usefulness, however. Technological advances and the exploration of distant lands provided Europe with a growing number of things for which there was no Latin word—or for which a Neo-Latin word would have to be invented. But these voyages of discovery brought something else to the attention of European scholars that provided an even more significant impetus for the universal language movement: Chinese writing.

Europeans were fascinated by Chinese characters, which were used by the speakers of many Far Eastern languages. As Europeans understood them, Chinese characters represented things and ideas rather than words, and speakers of various languages read them according to their own tongues. Europe already had characters of that sort, namely the Arabic numerals, as well as other mathematical and astrological symbols, and characters representing whole words in various systems of cryptography and shorthand (Knowlson 1975, 15–27). But the Chinese model was especially important in inspiring the idea of what was called a 'real character': a universal written language that could be understood by speakers of all tongues.

Such a language would of necessity have to be a written (or otherwise visual) medium, in which a symbol would represent either a word or an idea, which the reader would then interpret using the corresponding word in his or her own language. Ideas could thus be transmitted in writing across linguistic boundaries and be understood by a reader ignorant of the writer's native idiom. Many great thinkers debated the shape such a language should take, including the likes of John Amos Comenius (1592–1670), a Czech scholar often called 'the father of modern education'; the French philosopher and mathematician René Descartes (1596–1650); Athanasius Kircher (?1601–1680), a German Jesuit who, among other things, translated Egyptian hieroglyphs and wrote an encyclopedia of China; the German philosopher and mathematician Gottfried Wilhelm Leibniz (1646–1716); the Irish chemist Robert Boyle (1627–1691); and Sir Isaac Newton (1643–1727), to name a few (Knowlson 1975, 8). In England, much of the work was done under the auspices of the Royal Society.

The pattern of early attempts at a 'real character' is established in the works of Francis Lodowyck, a London merchant and self-described 'mechanick', whose assistance is noted in the later works of George Dalgarno (1626–1687) and John Wilkins (1614–1672), and who himself became a member of the Royal Society in 1681 (Slaughter 1982, 116). In *A Common Writing* (1647) Lodowyck proposes a real character, in which basic notions or 'Radixes' (from Latin *radix* 'root') are represented by individual symbols, and derivatives of them by the addition of assorted diacritical marks to the radical symbols.

So, for instance, the basic notion 'to drink' is represented by a character somewhat like a backwards 6. Six sorts of 'Nounes Substantive Appellative' are indicated by a series of hooks added to the right of the radix. When placed beside the radix 'to drink', these indicate such derivatives as 'the drinker', 'drink', 'the drinking', 'drunkard', 'drunkenness', and 'drinking-house'. Diagonal tally marks at the upper left of the radix indicate the first, second, and third person of the verb ('I drink', 'thou drinkest', 'he[/she/it] drinketh'), and if a horizontal stroke is written through these tally marks, it indicates the plural ('we drink', 'ye drink', 'they drink'). The passive is denoted by a 'prick' or dot in the body of the radix, whereas the tense of a verb is indicated by the position of a dot to the right of the radix: a dot within the body of the radix 'to drink' would therefore change its meaning to 'to be drunk'. If the dot were placed to the right and slightly above the radix, it would mean 'drank', to the top right of the radix 'have drunk', to the middle right 'had drunk', and to the bottom right 'shall/will drink'. Lodowyck provides even more derivative markers, but this should suffice to illustrate the system.

In any case, Lodowyck's scheme is a bare outline: the 'system' covers only a fraction of the wide range of derivatives necessary for the language to be fully functional, and characters for only a handful of radixes are presented. Lodowyck takes a somewhat different approach in *The Ground-work of a New Perfect Language* (1652), also built on a foundation of radixes and derivatives that bear a strong similarity to those in *A Common Writing*. The radical characters, however, are constructed from ten elements representing the digits 1–9 and zero. In other words, the radixes were numerical references to numbered entries in a lexicon, which would have made it easier to look up the meanings of the radical symbols, but was by no means an aid to memory: symbols representing the radixes were arbitrary and unsystematic, and they could only be learned by rote, which would require many years of study. Short of this, users of such a language would need the lexicon, as a sort of code-book, close to hand.

Later schemes offered different, not necessarily more plausible, solutions to the problem of memorizing the potentially huge inventory of radical characters or radical words. In these languages, the structure of a word reflected the place of the notion it represented in an elaborate classification of the world of things and ideas. These systems came to be known as 'philosophical languages'. Despite the number of scholars occupied with such schemes (and it seems that many of the great thinkers of the age were involved, at least to some degree), very few put their ideas into print, and fewer still presented anything more than theoretical sketches.

One such sketch is Sir Thomas Urquhart's *Logopandecteision, or an Introduction to the Universal Language* (1653), which described a language in which the nature of a thing or idea could be ascertained from the structure of the word referring to it, as in the Language of Adam. Since precision of expression was one of Urquhart's goals, the language was intended to have an immense vocabulary, 'all the words enunciable', numbering 'many thousands of millions', rather more than the 291,500 entries in the Second Edition of the *Oxford English Dictionary*. These were to be composed of all the sounds of all languages (only ten vowels and 25 consonants, according to Urquhart, not the International Phonetic Alphabet's 28 vowels and 78 consonants) and built upon 250 prime radixes.

Urquhart's language would also have a complex grammar boasting four numbers (singular, dual, plural, and 're-dual'), eleven genders, eleven cases, eleven tenses, seven moods, four voices, and twelve parts of speech. Urquhart's scheme presents a great deal of general information but few specifics. Is the re-dual perhaps a plurality of pairs? The names of the eleven genders, too, must forever remain a mystery. Despite all of this, 'of all the Languages in the world, it is easiest to learn; a boy of ten years old, being able to attain to the knowledge thereof, in three moneths [sic] space' (Urquhart 1653, 13–24). Not surprisingly, the promised grammar and lexicon never materialized.

The first real attempt at a philosophical language, however, was made by an Oxford schoolmaster, George Dalgarno, in whose system, the *Ars signorum* ('the art of signs') (1661), a word's letters indicate its place in a classification of the universe. The category of concrete mathematical objects is denoted by an initial *m*, concrete physical objects by *n*, concrete artefacts by *f*, sensible qualities by *g*, political concepts by *k*, and so on. These are then subcategorized: the *m* class, for example, contains simple forms in *m–m* (*mam* 'point', *mηm* 'line', *mem* 'surface', *mim* 'solid') and figures in *m–b* (*mab* 'circle', *mηb* 'sphere', *meb* 'spiral', *mib* 'cube', *mob* 'cone', etc.). Such a language would therefore provide coordinates by which one could locate things and ideas on a map of the universe, as it were. Systems such as this were likely inspired in part by medieval 'art of memory' practices, which made use of classificatory systems in which things were grouped according to their similarities, arranged from general to specific, and represented symbolically for easier memorization (Knowlson 1975, 78ff.).

John Wilkins, Bishop of Chester, a founding member of the Royal Society, contributed to Dalgarno's system, but later proposed, in *An Essay towards a Real Character, and a Philosophical Language* (1668), an even more detailed classification of the world of things and ideas, as well as a real character in which to express it. At the core of this real character is a series of forty symbols, each representing a genus in the table of integrals: God, World, Element, Stone, Metal, Ex[s]anguinous Animal, Fish, Bird, Beast, Magnitude, Space, Measure, Civil Relation, Judicial Relation, Military Relation, Naval Relation, Ecclesiastical Relation, and so forth. Modifications to a symbol indicate 'difference' and 'species' according to the tables, as well as various derivational and inflectional features. The 'differences' have consonantal values, and the 'species' have vocalic values. So in the word *coba* 'parent', for example, 'Co doth denote the Genus of *Oeconomical Relation*; the Letter (b) signifying the first difference under that Genus, which is Relation of Consanguinity; the Vowel (a) the second Species, which is *Direct ascending*; namely, *Parent*' (Wilkins 1668, 422). How all of this eases memorization may not be apparent to the casual reader. Though neither Wilkins' nor any other philosophical language ever caught on, similar classificatory systems—Linnaeus's biological classification (see Appendix 8), Roget's *Thesaurus*, and the Dewey decimal system—are quite familiar.

In the eighteenth and nineteenth centuries, French replaced Latin as the *de facto* international language. Nonetheless, *a priori* universal language schemes continued to be proposed, because some individuals still believed that neither French nor any other natural language could solve the problems of international communication. Solrésol, one of the more interesting of these new interlanguages, was first conceived by a French schoolteacher named Jean François Sudre in 1817, though its full vocabulary was not published until 1866, four years after Sudre's death. Instead of the usual phonetic units of spoken language, Solrésol is constructed from the seven notes of the musical scale, something most nineteenth-century Europeans considered truly universal. The notes can be expressed by saying or writing the already international names of these notes (*do, re, mi, fa, sol, la, si*) or their initial letters (with *s = si, so = sol*); by singing or playing the notes on a musical instrument; by writing them using musical notation; or by using other signs assigned to these specific notes—the numerals 1–7, colours, finger gestures, or special stenographic symbols, thus allowing the language an unusual flexibility of expression (Couturat and Leau 1903, 33 and 36).

Sudre's idea was not new: musical languages had been proposed centuries before, most notably in Francis Godwin's pioneering work of science fiction, *The Man in the Moone* (1638), whose lunar inhabitants use one (Knowlson 1975, 117–21). Sudre, however, brought the idea to its fullest formulation. Though Solrésol never won a substantial following, Sudre received encouragement from the likes of Victor Hugo and Alexander von Humboldt and was presented to Napoleon III, and there was still a 'Société pour la propagation de la Langue universelle Solrésol' in existence at the beginning of the twentieth century (Couturat and Leau 1903, 37).

A mixed IAL: Volapük

A steady stream of international language schemes flowed from the printing presses of Europe as the years passed between Lodowyck and Sudre, but the technological advances of the nineteenth century persuaded some that the need for one was especially acute. As Johann Martin Schleyer, a Roman Catholic priest in Litzelstetten, a village near Konstanz on the southern border of the German Empire, wrote:

> By means of locomotives, steamships, telegraphy, and telephony, the globe has shrunk, as it were, with regard to time and space. ... Humanity becomes more cosmopolitan every day, and longs for unification. By means of the magnificent universal post, a mighty step forward has been made towards this beautiful goal. Also with regard to money, measures, weights, division of time, laws, and language, the fraternity of the human race should continue to unite! (Schleyer 1880, iii; translation mine)

Towards this end, Schleyer published yet another in the long line of attempts at an artificial international language. However, whereas his predecessors' proposals rarely (if ever) lived beyond the covers of the books in which they were published, Schleyer's scheme, Volapük, came to be spoken on every inhabited continent.

Schleyer was born in 1831 in Oberlauda, a village in Baden. Ordained as a priest in 1856, he eventually became pastor to the small parish of Litzelstetten, where he found time to write poetry and study languages, of which he is reported to have learned as many as 55 (Haupenthal 1982, 24–5). Schleyer's creative energies and linguistic knowledge were soon directed towards the creation of an international language, which he saw primarily as a means towards international cooperation and harmony, asking God to bless his 'great work of peace' (Schleyer 1880, iv; translation mine). Volapük's motto well reflected its purpose: 'For one humanity, one language!'

In 1878, Schleyer published his *Weltalfabet* 'world alphabet', a first step towards a mixed language he called *Völkerdolmetsch* 'peoples' interpreter', comprising German, English, French, Italian, Spanish, and Russian elements. Although he never finished this language, a trip through multilingual Austria-Hungary in the same year convinced Schleyer of the need for a universal language, and he could not shake the idea. On a sleepless night in March 1879, an interlinguistic solution came to him. On 31 March he wrote out the grammar for his new *Weltsprache* 'world language', which appeared in the May issue of the *Sionsharfe*, the Catholic poetry journal he published. The name *Volapük* first appeared in print in the February 1880 issue, and later that spring a grammar of the language, combined with a 2,780-word vocabulary, was published as a 'plan for a universal language for all educated people in the whole world' (Schleyer 1880; Kniele 1889, 3–6).

The alphabet of Volapük ultimately contained the letters *a ä b c d e f g h i j k l m n o ö p r s t u ü v x y z*, in which *c* = English *j*, *j* = English *sh*, *v* = English *v*, *y* = English *y* as in *yes*, and *z* = English *ts* as in *cats*. The vowels *a*, *e*, *i*, *o*, *u* are all pronounced long, with their continental values, so approximately as in English *father*, *they*, *machine*, *go*, and *rude*, respectively. The umlaut vowels *ä*, *ö*, *ü* are pronounced like the long German umlauts; acceptable English substitutes would be the *a* of *care* for *ä* and the *o* of *word* for *ö*, whereas *ü* has no English approximation, being the *i* of *machine* with the lips rounded as for the *u* of *rude*. For these Schleyer originally used *ä*, *ö*, and *ü* only as typographical substitutes. He intended to print them with a rectangular diacritical mark instead of dots, and then devised whole new characters to represent the sounds, but at the Second Congress of Volapükists in August 1887 the spellings *ä*, *ö*, and *ü* became official. This congress also abolished '(rough breathing mark) in favour of *h*, which previously had the value of German *ch*, as in *Bach*. In Volapük, words are accented on the final syllable (Schleyer 1880, 1–3; Lott 1888, xv; Sprague 1888, 1–2).

The vocabulary is based on a system of roots and affixes. The roots generally begin and end with consonants, though function words such as conjunctions, prepositions, and pronouns, e.g., *ab* 'but', *al* 'to', *at* 'this', *bi* 'because', *da* 'through', are exceptions. Other exceptional root forms in the original vocabulary were later revised to conform to the usual pattern; thus original *apod* 'apple' was changed to *pod*. Both derivational and inflectional affixes attach to these roots. Prefixes generally end with a vowel; suffixes generally begin with one.

Volapük nouns have no grammatical gender; natural gender may be marked by means of affixes such as *ji-* 'she'. The plural suffix is *-s*, and for this reason *s* is avoided as the last letter of a root. Nouns are inflected for four cases, as in German: the nominative is represented by a bare root; genitive, dative, and accusative are marked by the suffixes *-a*, *-e*, and *-i*, respectively. The vocative is expressed by means of the nominative case, usually preceded by the interjection *o*.

Verbs are formed from the same basic roots as nouns, but use a different set of affixes. Person is marked by suffixes identical in form to the personal pronouns: *ob* 'I', *ol* 'you' (sing.), *om* 'he', *of* 'she', *os* 'it', *on* 'one'. The suffix *-s* is added to plurals, thus *obs* 'we', *ols* 'you' (pl.), etc. Tense is marked by the prefixes *ä-* (imperfect), *e-* (perfect), *i-* (pluperfect), *o-* (future), and *u-* (future perfect), thus *löfob* 'I love', *älöfob* 'I loved', *elöfob* 'I have loved', *ilöfob* 'I had loved', *olöfob* 'I will love', and *ulöfob* 'I will have loved'. The present tense marker *a-* is only used in conjunction with other verbal prefixes, namely the passive marker *p-* and the infix *-i-*, which marks repeated action; thus *flapom* 'he strikes', *paflapom* 'he is struck', *aiflapom* 'he strikes repeatedly', *paiflapom* 'he is struck repeatedly'. Other verbal affixes include *-öd* (imperative), *-öl* (participle), *-ön* (infinitive), *-la* (subjunctive), and *-li* (interrogative): *löfolöd!* 'love! (singular)', *löföl* 'loving', *palöföl* '(being) loved', *löfön* 'to love', *löfob-la* 'I would love', *löfob-li* 'do I love?', and so on.

Adjectives are marked by the suffix *-ik* (compare the adjectival suffixes *-ig* in German and *-ic* in English words derived from Latin), followed by *-um* in the comparative and *-ün* in the superlative. Thus *gudik* 'good', *gudikum* 'better', *gudikün* 'best'. Adverbs are marked by *-o*, which may follow adjectival endings, as in *gudiküno* 'in the best way'. Prepositions and interjections may be derived from roots by means of the suffixes -*ü* and -*ö* respectively. Overall, this system allows a large vocabulary to be derived by regular means from a relatively small stock of roots and affixes, increasing the language's usability, while keeping it comparatively easy to learn, as its inventor intended. Schleyer's derivational apparatus, however, often mimicked that of German too closely, which led to criticisms against Volapük and eventually to changes in the language itself (Caraco 1990).

A fair number of *a priori* elements can be seen in these affixes, as well as in such roots as those representing the cardinal numerals (*bal*, *tel*, *kil* ... 'one, two, three ...'), but most of the vocabulary is derived from English, the remainder from German and the Romance languages. This may not be immediately apparent, as Schleyer contorted the source forms to fit his system. In many instances, words were truncated, an extreme example of which is *plim* 'com*plim*ent'. Sounds were altered and clusters simplified, as in the two roots of *Volapük*: *vol* 'world' and *pük* 'language' (from English *speak*). While simplification of initial *sp-* to *p-* in Volapük would benefit speakers of languages lacking such an initial cluster, Schleyer also might well have used *i* instead of *ü*, the former being far more common in the languages of the world. Elsewhere, roots appear with initial clusters alien to speakers of most of the world's languages, such as *tlon* 'throne' and *dlim* 'dream'. These particular examples arose from a desire to minimize the use of *r*, for the sake of East Asian peoples, as well as children and the elderly (Schleyer 1880, 4).

Whatever its defects, Volapük attracted speakers at an astonishing rate. Kniele (1889, 69) estimated the number of speakers and students of Volapük in 1888 at between 1½ and 2 million. The actual number was almost certainly much lower (Schmidt 1963, 13–14), and many students probably made little progress, but by 1889 a thousand individuals were sufficiently proficient to have earned diplomas as teachers of Volapük, and there were 268 Volapük clubs. While most Volapükists lived in central Europe, clubs could be found in such far-flung locales as Cape Town, Melbourne, Shanghai, Buenos Aires, and Fort Walla

Walla in the Washington Territory. Some clubs boasted remarkably large memberships: the club in Konstanz, home of Schleyer's central office, had 260 members; the 'Association française pour la propagation du Volapük' in Paris had 310; and as far from the centre of Volapük studies as New Orleans, Louisiana, there was a club with 140 members (Kniele 1889, 72–119).

By this time, however, the movement already showed signs of decay. Internal struggles in the Munich and Nuremberg clubs weakened the movement in what had been the bastion of its strength. More devastating was the friction between Auguste Kerckhoffs, director of the Volapük Academy (*kadem volapüka*), who desired changes to the language, and Schleyer, who exercised his veto power. When Kerckhoffs announced the Third Congress of Volapükists in Paris in 1889, Schleyer declared the congress and all its decisions invalid (Schmidt 1963, 16–20). Such power struggles, combined with a rise in anti-Volapük literature, led to chaos in the ranks and, eventually, mass exodus.

Some defectors published their own international language schemes, each thinking that he had a better solution to the problem. Adolph Nicolas, vice president of the 'Association française pour la propagation du Volapük', created an *a priori* language called Spokil (begun 1889, published 1900). Unlike seventeenth-century philosophical languages, Spokil did not articulate an elaborate classification of the universe, but was composed instead of vowels and consonants, each of which had its own symbolic meaning. Other former Volapükists invented languages structurally very similar to Volapük. Georg Bauer, a professor of mathematics who had published a Volapük grammar in Serbo-Croatian, created Spelin in 1888. Julius Fieweger, president of the Volapük club in Breslau (Wrocław) and member of the Volapük Academy, published Dil in 1893. That same year Emile Dormoy, secretary of the 'Association française', published Balta. Further Volapük-style schemes were published by individuals who had not been noted Volapükists, including Veltparl by Wilhelm von Arnim in 1896,

Dilpok by Abbot Marchand in 1898, and Langue bleue (Bolak) by Léon Bollack in 1899 (Couturat and Leau 1903, 87–94, 170–93, and 198–233).

Volapük fell as speedily as it rose. Schmidt's (1963, 13–35) figures for 1888 show a total of 25 Volapük periodicals and 257 Volapük clubs, with a conservative estimate of around a million followers. By 1892 there were only 17 periodicals, about 90 clubs, and fewer than 100,000 Volapükists; in 1900, only four periodicals, some 27 clubs, and around 1,500 Volapükists remained. By the time Schleyer passed away in 1911, the last Volapük club had disbanded and the language was effectively dead.

In 1921, however, Arie de Jong began a revision of Volapük. A number of changes were introduced, especially in the vocabulary, designed to make some roots more recognizable (e.g., *lärnön* for *lenädön* 'to learn') and to regularize derivation where Schleyer had slavishly followed German constructions (Caraco 1990). This revision resulted in a new dictionary (de Jong 1931), grammars, and a revitalization of the Volapük movement, now centred in the Netherlands. A new periodical, *Volapükagased pro Nedänapükans*, was launched in March 1932 and ran until the end of 1963 (Schmidt 1963: 41–4).

Today, the Volapük movement still exists. The *Sirkülapenäd* ('circular letter') of the *Flenef Bevünetik Volapüka* ('International Friendship of the World Language') has been published since 1991 in de Jong's revised Volapük, which is also in use on the Internet. The number of people who still use the language is very small indeed, but Volapük continues to cross linguistic borders.

An *a posteriori* IAL: Esperanto

In the mid-nineteenth century, Poland was a striking example of the interlinguistic problem universal languages were meant to solve. Polish was only one of the many languages in use there. Lithuanian was spoken by villagers in the north, Belorussian in the south. German could be heard in the larger cities and Yiddish among the Jewish population. Finally, since Poland was a province of the Tsarist Empire, Russian was the language of the government and the military, and a required subject in the schools. Not surprisingly, strife among the speakers of these various languages was the order of the day.

This was the linguistic milieu into which Lazarus Ludwig Zamenhof was born on 15 December 1859. His father worked as a teacher of geography and modern languages, earning extra money as a censor of foreign periodicals, so it was no surprise that Zamenhof was himself a polyglot, learning French and German at an early age, followed by English, Latin, and Greek (Privat 1920, 23–35). As with Schleyer, this knowledge of several languages aided him in composing an artificial idiom, which he hoped would some day eradicate the turmoil between peoples that he saw close at hand.

Zamenhof completed work on what he called 'Lingwe uniwersala', begun while he was still in school, on 5 December 1878. The joy of this occasion was short-lived, however. His circle of supporters, faced with the mockery of their elders, abandoned the cause. Then Marcus Zamenhof, desiring his son's success in his medical studies, forbade him to spend any more time on linguistic fantasy and burned his papers to enforce the ban. Zamenhof, however, knew the material by heart and was able to reconstruct it (Privat 1920, 36–42). Zamenhof persevered because he believed that his invention would lead to harmony among the nations of the world. As he proclaimed in a hymn celebrating the completion of the 'Lingwe uniwersala': 'May the enmity of the nations fall, fall, now is the time! All humanity must unite itself into a family' (Privat 1920, 36; translation mine).

Zamenhof satisfied his father's great expectations, going into practice as an optician in 1886. But he did not give up on world unity or the language he hoped would promote it. In July of the following year, he published a small book in Russian, containing a grammar and vocabulary of his 'Lingvo internacia', under the pseudonym Doktoro

Esperanto, 'one who hopes' (Privat 1920, 49–52). The publication of this volume was a huge step for Zamenhof, as he later wrote:

> I was very excited before this [publication]; I felt that I was standing before the Rubicon and that from the day when my pamphlet would appear I would no longer have the ability to go back. I knew what kind of fate awaited a physician, who is at the mercy of the public, if that public sees in him a dreamer, a person who occupies himself with 'trivial matters'. I felt that I was gambling the entire future tranquility and continued existence of myself and my family; but I could not abandon the idea, which had entered into my body and blood, and ...
> I crossed the Rubicon. (Privat 1923, 30–31; translation mine)

The alphabet of Zamenhof's international language, which soon came to be known as Esperanto, consists of twenty-eight letters: *a b c ĉ d e f g ĝ h ĥ i j ĵ k l m n o p r s ŝ t u ŭ v z*. The vowels have their continental values (*a, e, i, o, u* approximately as in English *father, they, machine, go,* and *rude,* respectively), and most of the consonants have their usual values, but *j* = English *y* as in *yes* and *c* = English *ts* as in *cats,* a feature attacked by critics as a deviation from the 'one letter, one sound' rule. Also frequently criticized are Zamenhof's unusual superscripted letters: *ĉ* = English *ch, ĝ* = English *j, ĵ* = English *s* in *treasure, ŝ* = English *sh,* and *ŭ* = English *w*. In cases where the necessary typefaces were lacking, Zamenhof also allowed these to be spelt *ch, gh, jh, sh,* and *u,* but today it is common in electronic communication to use *x* (otherwise absent from the Esperanto alphabet) instead of *h,* thus *cx, gx, jx,* and *sx*. One can easily convert the superscripted characters by means of global find-and-replace.

Zamenhof presented Esperanto's grammar in the form of sixteen fundamental rules without exceptions (English version in Large 1985, 202–05), though a more detailed account of the grammar can run to hundreds of pages (e.g., Kalocsay and Waringhien 1980). Like Volapük, Esperanto is built on a system of roots and affixes. Nouns are formed by adding *-o* to the root, adjectives by adding *-a,* and adverbs *-e.*

Verbs take the suffix *-as* in the present tense, *-is* in the past, *-os* in the future: *mi amas* 'I love', *mi amis* 'I loved', *mi amos* 'I will love'. The same vowels characterize tenses of the infixed active participles (*-ant-/-int-/-ont-*), as well as the passive participles (*-at-/-it-/-ot-*): *amanto* 'loving one, one who loves', *amanta* 'loving', *amante* 'lovingly', *aminto* 'one who has loved', *amonto* 'one who will love', *amato* 'one who is being loved', *amito* 'one who has been loved', *amoto* 'one who will be loved', etc. The infinitive ends in *-i*, the imperative in *-u*, the conditional in *-us*, and the passive is rendered by means of the verb *est-* 'be' plus passive participle: *ami* 'to love', *amu* 'love!' *amus* 'should love', *esti amata* 'to be loved', etc. Nouns and adjectives are declined for two numbers (an unmarked singular and a plural in *-j*) and two cases (an unmarked nominative and an accusative in *-n*)—*nigra kato* 'black cat' is therefore *nigrajn katojn* in the accusative plural. All prepositions govern the nominative. The cardinal numbers are not marked for case, and the definite article *la* is likewise indeclinable. There is no indefinite article. Finally, all words of two or more syllables are accented on the penultimate syllable.

Rule 15 allows addition of 'foreign' words to the Esperanto vocabulary. Of course, they must conform to Esperanto orthography and take the appropriate grammatical suffix. Consequently, the Esperanto lexicon has increased dramatically over the years. Nonetheless, the sources of the original vocabulary remain readily apparent: predominantly Romance, with a large proportion of Germanic, and a smaller admixture of Slavic, Greek, and others. According to one study, speakers of Romance languages would immediately recognize 80% of Esperanto, speakers of Germanic languages 63%, and speakers of Slavic languages 17% (Gregor 1982, 28).

Whereas Couturat and Leau (1903) classify Volapük as a 'mixed system', they regard Esperanto as *a posteriori*. The language does however contain a number of *a priori* elements, most notably in the so-called 'correlatives'. These are a group of pronouns, adjectives, and adverbs constructed according to a logical scheme. Demonstratives begin with *t*-, relatives and interrogatives with *k*-, distributives and collectives with *ĉ*-, negatives with *nen*-, and indefinites with no initial consonant. To these initial elements are affixed others indicating quality (*-ia*), motive (*-ial*), time (*-iam*, originally *-ian*), place (*-ie*), manner (*-iel*), possession (*-ies*), thing (*-io*), quantity (*-iom*), and individuality (*-ies*), resulting in forms such as *tia* 'of that kind', *tial* 'for that reason', *tiam* 'at that time', *tie* 'in that place', *tiel* 'in that manner', *ties* 'that one's', *tio* 'that (thing)', *tiom* 'that quantity', *tiu* 'that one', *kia* 'of what/which kind', *ĉia* 'every kind of', *nenia* 'no kind of', *ia* 'some/any kind of', and so on (Millidge 1912, xiv–xv). Defenders praise this system's logical arrangement and easy learnability; opponents criticize its artificiality.

Zamenhof wanted an international auxiliary language; refreshingly, it did not have to be his own creation. As he wrote in 1889, 'But even now, as the number of friends of my cause has begun to grow rapidly, while Volapük is beginning to fall,—even now, for holy unanimity, I would with great pleasure cast away my labour and join with Volapük, if I could believe that Volapük, in its present form or in an improved form, has even the slightest chance of achieving the goal' (Zamenhof 1929, 263; translation mine). Unlike Schleyer, Zamenhof had no desire to rule his language by fiat, but believed it should be allowed to grow naturally, through popular usage. He wrote that he was not Esperanto's creator, but merely its initiator, and in his first book he relinquished all personal rights to the language, proclaiming it the property of everyone (see Appendix 1). Zamenhof also had no desire for people to waste their time on a scheme that would not achieve its goal: the earliest Esperanto publications contained promissory notes, which were to be signed and sent in to Zamenhof, stating that the undersigned 'promises to learn the international language of Dr Esperanto, if it is shown that ten million persons have signed the same promise' (Privat 1923, 32–6; translation mine).

Though the collection of promissory notes was soon abandoned and the number of adherents never reached ten million, the nascent

Esperanto movement quickly found converts, including a number of disenchanted Volapükists. The first Esperanto club was founded in Nuremberg in 1888, and the October 1889 *Adresaro* ('directory') of people who were learning the language already included a thousand names (Privat 1923, 43–4). Despite these initial successes, growth was slow during the remainder of the nineteenth century. In 1900, the literature of Esperanto consisted of a mere 150 booklets and two periodicals (Privat 1927, 15).

That same year, however, Esperanto moved into the public eye at the World's Fair in Paris. Until then, the majority of Esperantists lived in Russia, and most organization and propaganda for Esperanto had been German (Privat 1923, 70–74). Suddenly, France became the centre of the Esperanto universe (see Appendix 2). A 'Central Office' opened in Paris in 1906, and the French publishing firm of Hachette was at the forefront of the Esperanto publishing boom that disseminated interest in the language to America and Asia. By August 1912, the Central Office had registered 1,837 Esperanto books, and the 1911 catalogue of one collector's Esperanto library lists some 350 different periodicals, most of them very short-lived, but spread across 48 countries, including Japan, China, the Philippines, Australia, and Algeria. The number of Esperanto societies listed in the *Oficiala Gazeto* grew from 44 in 1902 to 1,455 ten years later (Privat 1927, 13–15, 37, and 89–90).

Also during this so-called 'French period', the first Universala Kongreso de Esperanto was held in Boulogne-sur-Mer in August 1905, with 688 attendees. The congress has been held annually since then, apart from interruptions caused by the two World Wars (Universala Esperanto-Asocio 2010). Indeed, the First World War hit France just as attendees arrived in Paris for the 1914 congress. The gathering was cancelled, many incoming Esperantists were turned back at the border, and others were imprisoned as citizens of enemy states (Privat 1927, 93). In other words, the Esperantists, however hopeful, did not find the world unity they were looking for in 1914 Paris.

Though many prominent Esperantists, including Zamenhof, had died, Esperanto prospered after the First World War, perhaps because the war had won converts to the cause of international cooperation. Schools in many countries taught Esperanto. International organizations, such as the Red Cross, recommended its adoption. The Universal Telegraphic Union allowed Esperanto as a 'clear language' for telegraphic and radio-telegraphic communications. The Soviet Union inscribed its postage stamps and postal stationery in Esperanto along with Russian and the languages of the other Soviet republics. One setback, however, was the failure of the League of Nations to support the language, due largely to fierce opposition by the French delegates (Privat 1927, 96–112, 133–59, and 171–3).

Another setback came in the form of censorship. Tsarist Russia had banned *La Esperantisto* (the first periodical in Esperanto) in 1895 for including a short piece by Tolstoy, and Esperantists were prohibited from wearing the green star, the emblem of the Esperanto movement (Privat 1923, 55 and 57). Even worse was the persecution of Esperantists in Stalinist Russia and Nazi Germany. In *Mein Kampf*, Hitler identifies Esperanto as part of the supposed Jewish plan for world domination (Lins 1988, 92).

Esperanto did not maintain its interwar success after the Second World War, due largely to the rise of English, bolstered by Anglo-American economic and political power, as the *de facto* international language. Nationalism still plays a major role in linguistic matters, and both the United Nations and the European Union make do with armies of translators and interpreters, rather than going so far as to adopt an IAL.

Nonetheless, the Esperanto movement refuses to die. There are those who continue to believe that an international language is necessary for communication and cooperation between nations, and that English is too closely associated with Anglo-American political, economic, and cultural imperialism to fill that role satisfactorily, or indeed to be accepted by the people of all nations. So even though Esperanto now has a much lower profile than in the past, it remains visible and vital. When Esperanto celebrated its centenary in 1987, postage stamps were issued by Bulgaria, China, Cuba, East Germany, Hungary, Malta, Poland, South Korea, Surinam, and the USSR to honour the occasion (Song 1987, 94–113). Not surprisingly, the centenary Universala Kongreso in Warsaw had 5,946 members, the largest attendance in the event's history, surpassing by far the previous record of 4,963 set by the Nuremberg congress in 1923 (Universala Esperanto-Asocio 2010). Estimates of current Esperanto speakers hover around a million, one study placing the number 'at least in the middle hundreds of thousands, very likely in the (low) millions' (Harlow 1994, 19). Even the lower end of this range grants to Esperanto a larger body of speakers than most natural languages can claim, and psychologist and linguist Sidney Culbert (1990) argues that Esperanto has more speakers than 6,000 of the 6,160 languages spoken in the world today.

Offspring of Esperanto

Almost as soon as Zamenhof published his 'Lingvo internacia', suggestions for its improvement started to roll in. Of course, many of these suggested reforms were mutually exclusive: what some saw as Esperanto's redeeming qualities, others saw as fatal flaws. Zamenhof did change the *-ian* of the temporal correlatives to *-iam* in 1888, but apart from additions to the vocabulary, he did not propose further revisions until 1894, when he published a series of articles in *La Esperantisto*, presenting a systematic reform of the language. The majority of Esperantists, however, voted against the changes, and especially vocal among these opponents was Louis de Beaufront (Drezen 1991: 245–6).

The Marquis de Beaufront had been involved in the Esperanto movement since 1888, when he was the private tutor to the family of a French count. One of the most active proponents of Esperanto in France, he was chosen by Zamenhof to represent Esperanto before the

Permanent Commission of the 'Délégation pour l'adoption d'une langue internationale' when it convened in October 1907. During the session, Louis Couturat, one of the joint secretaries of the Delegation, presented an anonymous project to the Commission, attributed to the pseudonymous 'Ido'. The project incorporated many of the previously proposed modifications to Esperanto, as well as principles proposed by Couturat and Léopold Leau in their *Conclusions du Rapport*; it intended to remedy supposed flaws in Esperanto, thereby creating a less artificial, more immediately comprehensible language. The Commission adopted Esperanto, modified in accordance with the secretaries' *Conclusions* and along the lines of the project of Ido. When it was revealed in May 1908 that Ido was in fact de Beaufront, the Esperantists felt betrayed, and in fact several members of the Commission were disturbed by the underhandedness of the whole affair (Jacob 1947, 43–5).

The Linguo internaciona di la Delegitaro (Beaufront 1908), also known simply as Ido, is largely identical to Esperanto. Of all its competitors, Ido was the only one to attract many followers. Whenever Esperantists promoted their language before a meeting of some international organization, Idists were almost sure to be there, too. A substantial literature was produced, and the dictionaries that were produced for Ido were 'the most complete works of their kind for any system of planned language' (Jacob 1947, 46).

Many other similar schemes followed, from the virtually unknown Hom-Idyomo to the somewhat more successful Occidental and Novial. Occidental, published by Edgar de Wahl in 1922, is characterized by an attempt to obtain natural forms identical to those found in major languages. Novial was invented in 1928 by Otto Jespersen, a noted linguist and scholar of the English language at the University of Copenhagen, as well as a former Idist. Jespersen chose the roots of Novial (*nov-* 'new' + *IAL*) according to the principle of greatest internationality, sometimes preferring Germanic forms to Romance, and adopting a very English use of auxiliary verbs. Jespersen aimed for a level of naturalness greater than that found in Ido and Esperanto, but did not go as far in that direction as de Wahl (Jacob 1947, 60–83).

Simplified natural languages

As the preceding section has shown, many inventors of IALs in the early twentieth century tended to include more *a posteriori* elements in their schemes, in order to correct what they saw as Esperanto's defects, a tendency extended in projects that merely simplified existing natural languages. Not surprisingly, a favoured source was Latin, the erstwhile international language, but simplified versions of Latin had in fact already been proposed long before.

In the seventeenth century, objections to the use of Latin as a means of international communication were for the most part directed at the difficulties inherent in its grammatical system. Comenius, the Czech educational reformer, retained Latin in his curriculum, though he proposed new methods for teaching the language that departed from the grammar-based methods popular in his day. He did, however, look forward to the creation of an 'absolutely new, absolutely easy, absolutely rational' artificial language as an alternative to Latin (Knowlson 1975, 30–32). The famed German philosopher, Gottfried Wilhelm Leibniz, worked towards the creation of a 'rational grammar' underlying all the languages of the world. Because of its comparative universality at the time, Leibniz chose Latin as the basis for a general grammar of languages, an intermediary between the rational grammar and the grammars of the various vernaculars. He then proceeded to construct a regular and thus more easily learned Latin grammar, stripped of all the irregularities and exceptions found in the Classical language (Pombo 1987, 157–65).

Other modified versions of Latin followed. The most significant was proposed in 1903 by Giuseppe Peano, a professor of mathematics at the University of Turin, under the name *Latino sine flexione* ('Latin without inflections'), later also known as Interlingua. In 1908, Peano was elected president of the 'Academia pro Interlingua', previously called the 'Akademi de Lingu Universal' and salvaged from what remained of the Volapük Academy. Called the 'most *a posteriori* of all *a posteriori* languages', Interlingua is essentially Medieval Latin (including Greco-Latin and Anglo-Latin) with the grammar stripped down to the barest minimum (Academia pro Interlingua 1931, 6–11).

Interlingua's alphabet consists of the twenty-six letters used in English and Medieval Latin, though the digraphs *æ* and *œ* are also used. The primary accent falls on the penultimate syllable. Interlingua nouns for the most part take their forms from the Latin ablative; nouns that only occur in the plural in Latin generally appear in Interlingua in their accusative forms. The forms of adjectives are likewise generally derived from the Latin ablative. Nouns and adjectives are not declined in Interlingua itself, and the plural ending *-s* is only used where plurality must be indicated and is not otherwise implied (e.g., by the use of cardinal numbers). The verbal stem is similarly simplified, formed by dropping *-re* from the end of the infinitive. This stem serves as both the present tense and the imperative for all persons and numbers. The past and future tenses are generally not marked; where past and future time are not otherwise indicated by adverbial constructions, they may be expressed by placing *e* and *i* respectively before the verb, thus *me e ama* 'I loved' and *me i ama* 'I shall (or will) love'. The infinitive is formed by adding *-re* to the stem, the past participle by adding *-to*, and the present participle by adding *-nte*: *amare* 'to love', *amato* 'loved', *amante* 'loving'. The passive is formed by means of a periphrastic construction: *es* 'be' + PAST PARTICIPLE, as in *filio es amato ab matre* 'the son is loved by the mother' (Academia pro Interlingua 1931, 9–10, 16, and 21–38).

A later version of Interlingua, promulgated by the International Auxiliary Language Association (IALA), though superficially similar to Peano's Interlingua, was actually constructed on a different basis. The IALA, founded in 1924, adopted E. Clark Stillman's position that words common to most of the Romance languages and English had a right to exist in the international language (Esterhill 2000, 1–4 and 11–12). The vocabulary entered in the *Interlingua-English Dictionary* (1951), produced under the direction of Alexander Gode, meets a similar criterion of internationality: to be entered, a word had to be attested, in corresponding forms with corresponding meanings, in at least three languages from among Italian, Spanish, French, English, and Spanish and Portuguese combined, with German and Russian as possible substitutes. The prototypical form chosen for entry would be the most international, devoid of characteristics peculiar to the individual languages—in most instances the etymological Latin form, though this is not always the case (Gode 1951, xxvi–xlii).

While some inventors of IALs saw Latin as the logical starting-point, others looked towards the most international language in current use: English (Drezen 1991, 222–6). The most notable of these was C.K. Ogden, who in 1932 published the first of many works on Basic English. Ogden's idea was to simplify English by reducing the size of its vocabulary to a mere 850 words: 100 'operations' (including pronouns, prepositions, basic adverbs, and basic verbs), 600 'things' (400 'general' and 200 'picturable'), and 150 'qualities' (i.e., adjectives, 100 general and 50 opposites). Definitions of these words would be taught in a systematic way, beginning with their most fundamental meanings. Supplementary word lists were compiled for specialized areas, such as science, economics, and the Bible. All words are spelt and pronounced as in standard English. If a word in Basic has any grammatical irregularities associated with it in standard English, it has them in Basic, too, so Basic is less easily learned than one might hope of an international language. Difficulties also abound in verbs, which in Basic English are largely periphrastic, with many belonging to the very idiomatic VERB + PREPOSITION/ADVERBIAL type (e.g., *go in* rather than *enter*). On the other hand, by learning standard orthographic and grammatical forms in the first place, a student moving on to the study of standard English does not need to unlearn Basic (Richards 1943, 23ff.). Of course, Basic English is not a neutral language: communities that balk at the idea of having English as an international language (for whatever linguistic, political, or economic reasons) will hardly be any more receptive to a simplified version of it.

Other major languages have also been proposed as the bases for IALs, for instance, Télfy's simplification of Ancient Greek and the Spanish-based systems of Puchner, Gavidia, and Starrenburg (Drezen 1991, 217–18 and 226–7), as well as a *Weltdeutsch*, or IAL based on German: by Lichtenstein in 1853, Baumann in 1915, and Ostwald in 1926 (Drezen 1991, 147 and 229–30). Baumann's German-based IAL, called Wede, is particularly interesting. In a time of intense German patriotism, the First World War, Adalbert Baumann, a professor of the German language, invented a version of German with modified orthography and simplified grammar, containing a considerable number of words also modified in pronunciation. All of this was done to serve speakers of foreign tongues attempting to learn Wede, as was abolition of the umlaut vowels and certain consonants and consonant clusters, though the replacement forms in Wede often have their basis in the Low German dialects (e.g., *ik* for *ich* 'I', *wat* for *was* 'what') or in earlier stages of the language (e.g., *flistern* for *flüstern* 'to whisper'). Grammatical gender was also eliminated, with the definite article reduced to *t* in the singular and *ti* in the plural. Verbal endings for different persons and numbers disappeared, and tenses were reduced to two, present and past, the latter formed by means of the auxiliary verb *hawen* and a weak past participle, thus *ik hawen geslaget* instead of *ich habe geschlagen* 'I have struck'.

Yet Wede contains an abundance of irregularities and grammatical exceptions. German *ä*, for example, can become either *a* or *e* in Wede (e.g., *woltater* 'benefactor (Ger. *Wohltäter*)', *medel* 'girl (Ger. *Mädel*)'). The consonant *ch* is replaced by either *k* or *g*: *durk* 'through (Ger. *durch*)', but *nagt* 'night (Ger. *Nacht*)', to distinguish it from *nakt* 'naked (Ger. *nackt*)'. The present tense form of the verb ends in *-en*, but this ending is usually dropped, except where necessary for clarity or euphony. Comparison of adjectives is usually marked by the addition of the regular suffixes, but in some cases the irregular German forms are also allowed, as *gute/gutere/guteste* beside *gute/besere/beste* 'good/better/best' (standard German *gute/bessere/beste*) (Baumann 1915, 79, 89, and 91). The modifications in Wede are in fact so extensive that a speaker of German would have difficulty learning all its deviations from the standard language, and someone who learned Wede (assuming such an animal ever existed) would have to unlearn a great deal of it when confronted with actual German.

Languages for part of the world

For some creators of IALs, *international* did not necessarily mean 'universal'. Wede, discussed in the previous section, may fall into this category. Even though Baumann's title page calls Wede 'the new world auxiliary language (*Welt-Hilfs-Sprache*)', it also describes it as 'the communication language of the Central Powers and their friends'. Baumann, however, also optimistically envisions a postwar world in which Germany plays a leading role:

> Through the victorious World War of 1914/15 Germany's political weight and standing have grown to an unparalleled extent. The whole world will seek the friendship of the mighty, like flowers toward the sun, all significant peoples will in the coming decades lean more and more toward Germany, to receive from it cultural light and social warmth. (Baumann 1915, 63; translation mine)

As it happened, Wede emerged from the war as no one's language, not the language of an international folk, and certainly not a universal one.

A better example of an international language for a select group can be found in the various Germanic-based projects of Elias Molee, an American of Scandinavian and German descent. In such works as *Plea for an American Language, or Germanic-English* (1888), *Germanik English* (1889), and *Pure Saxon English; or, Americans to the Front*

(1890), Molee attempts to rid English of Latin and Greek elements: He describes his project as:

> A Scheme for Uniting the English and German languages on Saxon and English bases in such a way as to obtain a language understood by the whole Germanic Race almost at first sight and one that can most easily be learned by Russians, Indians, Chinese, Japanese and the African tribes for commercial and missionary purposes on account of being built on a concentrated homogeneous base, and on account of furnishing a key to all the higher derived and compounded words. (Molee 1889, cover)

Molee recommends that *dentist* should be replaced by *toothhealer*, *mutton* by *sheepflesh*, *zoology* by *deerlore*. Some of his recommendations have already been in common use for centuries, such as *breastbone* for *sternum*. But 'Saxon English' goes even further, introducing a new orthography and a modified grammar. The reformed spelling includes such features as the use of *q* to represent the vowel of *arm* and an inverted *i* for the vowel of *eel*. In the grammar of Saxon English, plural nouns add *a* after consonants, *s* after vowels; the possessive case adds *o* after consonants, *no* after vowels; the past tense adds *o* after consonants, *do* after vowels; the present participle adds *qnd*, the past participle *en*, and so on. Among specimens of the language, Molee provides the following sentence (*!* here represents inverted *i*): 'Alexander, and Cæsar, and Napoleon wer grait mqkta in thair dai; but thai l!vo beheind sich the ferwüstung (desolation) ov kr!g (war), and thair mqkt (power) has pasen awai' (Molee 1890, 9–10, 19–20, and 32).

Molee followed Saxon English with similar projects: tutonish in 1902, niu teutonish in 1906, alteutonish in 1912, alteutonik in 1915, and toito spike in 1923. These schemes differ in points of grammar and orthography, but they all derive their vocabularies from the various Germanic languages, being intended specifically for use by Germanic peoples. Strictly speaking, these are not IALs: Molee did not invent them to serve merely as auxiliaries but rather gradually to replace all Germanic languages with a Teutonic 'union tongue'. He writes in his uncapitalized and abbreviated version of English: 'after 50 years, when all teutons then living, will h learned e common reunited language from childhood, teutonish then t b used for all national purposes in all teutonic countries z their lawful common mother tongue' (Molee 1906, 12).

Molee argued that other 'union tongues' should be created, reducing the world's languages to five: 'teutonic, romanic, slavonic, semitic n mongolic'—but 'if other races are not intelligent, active, moral n patriotic enough t form union tongues for their own language protection, e teutons ougth [*sic*] not t b held back on their account' (Molee 1906, 14). It is encouraging, actually, that Molee's schemes did not enjoy a life beyond the covers of the books in which they were published.

Conclusion

Viewing the situation realistically, it is difficult to be optimistic about the future of artificial IALs. English dominates international communication, and this seems unlikely to change anytime soon. The one million speakers of Esperanto can hardly measure up to the hundreds of millions who speak English as either a first or second language. Yet it is also unlikely that English will ever manage to become a *universal* second language. Putting aside the difficulties of learning English, far too many people around the world see it as a vehicle for Anglo-American political and cultural imperialism to accept it willingly as an official international language.

Nevertheless, invented languages such as Esperanto, Loglan, and even Volapük still find converts and enter into practical use. The Internet connects members of these small linguistic communities, wherever they may live, enabling the solidarity of speech communities by means of which their inventors could only have dreamed and which sociolinguistics has yet to confront. IALs thus continue to serve their purpose, joining people of different lands and cultures, though not as the whole humanity for which their inventors so fervently worked.

References

Academia pro Interlingua. 1931. *Key to and Primer of Interlingua*. London: Kegan Paul.

Baumann, Adalbert. 1915. *Wede: Die Verständigungssprache der Zentralmächte und ihrer Freunde, die neue Welt-Hilfs-Sprache*. Diessen: Huber.

Beaufront, Louis de. 1908. *Linguo Internaciona di la Delegitaro. Vollständige Grammatik der Internationalen Sprache*. German ed. by Robert Thomann. Stuttgart: Franckh.

Caraco, J. C. 1990. 'La evoluo de la lingvo Volapük'. *Volapük-Studoj* 1: 2–4.

Couturat, Louis, and Léopold Leau. 1903. *Histoire de la langue universelle*. Paris: Hachette. Repr. Hildesheim: Olms, 1979.

Couturat, Louis, and Léopold Leau. 1907. *Les nouvelles langues internationales*. Paris: Hachette. Repr. Hildesheim: Olms, 1979 [bound with Couturat and Leau 1903].

Culbert, Sidney. 1990. Letter. *Esperanto/USA* 26.4: 7.

Dalgarno, George. 1661. *Ars Signorum, vulgo character universalis et lingua philosophica*. London: J. Hayes. Repr. Menston: Scolar, 1968.

de Jong, Arie. 1931. *Wörterbuch der Weltsprache. Vödabuk Volapüka pro Deutänapükans*. 6th ed. Leiden: Brill.

Drezen, E. 1991. *Historio de la mondolingvo. Tri jarcentoj da serĉado*. 4th Esperanto ed. by S. Kuznecov. Moscow: Progreso.

Esterhill, Frank. 2000. *Interlingua Institute: A History*. New York: Interlingua Institute.

Gode, Alexander, ed. 1951. *Interlingua-English: A Dictionary of the International Language Prepared by the Research Staff of the International Auxiliary Language Association*. New York: Storm.

Harlow, Don. 1994. 'Editorial: How Many of Us Are There?' *Esperanto/USA* 30.3–4: 2, 18–19.

Haupenthal, Reinhard. 1982. 'Johann Martin Schleyer (1831–1912), Autor der Plansprache Volapük. Festvortrag anläßlich seines 150. Geburtstages gehalten am Martin-Schleyer-Gymnasium zu Lauda-Königshofen am 17. Oktober 1981'. In *Martin-Schleyer-Gymnasium Jahresbericht 1981/82*, ed. M. Salomon and G. Walter, pp. 23–32. Lauda-Königshofen: Martin-Schleyer-Gymnasium.

Jacob, H. 1947. *A Planned Auxiliary Language*. London: Dobson.

Kalocsay, K., and G. Waringhien. 1980. *Plena analiza gramatiko de Esperanto*. 4th ed. Rotterdam: Universala Esperanto-Asocio.

Kniele, Rupert. 1889. *Das erste Jahrzehnt der Weltsprache Volapük. Yebalsüp balid volapüka*. Überlingen: Schoy. Repr. Saarbrücken: Iltis, 1989.

Knowlson, James. 1975. *Universal Language Schemes in England and France 1600–1800*. Toronto: University of Toronto Press.

Large, Andrew. 1985. *The Artificial Language Movement*. Oxford: Blackwell.

Lins, Ulrich. 1988. *Die gefährliche Sprache: Die Verfolgung der Esperantisten unter Hitler und Stalin*. Gerlingen: Bleicher.

Lodowyck, Francis. 1647. *A Common Writing: Whereby two, although not understanding one the others Language, yet by the helpe thereof, may communicate their minds one to another*. N.p. Repr. Menston: Scolar, 1969.

Lodowyck, Francis. 1652. *The Ground-Work, or Foundation Laid, (or so intended) For the Framing of a New Perfect Language: And an Universall or Common Writing*. N.p. Repr. Menston: Scolar, 1968.

Lott, Julius. 1888. *Die Kunst, die internationale Verkehrssprache „Volapük" schnell zu erlernen*. Vienna: Hartleben.

Millidge, Edward A. 1912. *The Esperanto-English Dictionary*. Washington: American Esperantist Company.

Molee, Elias. 1889. *Germanik English*. Bristol, South Dakota: Bristol News.

Molee, Elias. 1890. *Pure Saxon English; or, Americans to the Front*. Chicago: Rand McNally.

Molee, Elias. 1906. *niu teutonish, an international union language*. Tacoma: Elias Molee.

Pombo, Olga. 1987. *Leibniz and the Problem of a Universal Language*. Münster: Nodus.

Privat, Edmond. 1920. *Vivo de Zamenhof*. 5th ed. Orelia: Esperanto Publishing Company, 1977.

Privat, Edmund. 1923. *Historio de la lingvo Esperanto. Unua parto: Deveno kaj komenco 1887–1900*. 2nd ed. Repr. The Hague: Internacia Esperanto-Instituto, 1982.

Privat, Edmund. 1927. *Historio de la lingvo Esperanto. Dua parto: La movado 1900–1927*. Repr. The Hague: Internacia Esperanto-Instituto, 1982 [bound with Privat 1923].

Richards, I.A. 1943. *Basic English and Its Uses*. New York: Norton.

Schleyer, Johann Martin. 1880. *Volapük. Die Weltsprache. Entwurf einer Universalsprache für alle Gebildete der ganzen Erde*. Sigmaringen: Tappen. Repr. Hildesheim: Olms, 1982.

Schmidt, Johann. 1963. *Geschichte der Universalsprache Volapük*. Saarbrücken: Iltis, 1986.

Slaughter, M. M. 1982. *Universal Languages and Scientific Taxonomy in the Seventeenth Century*. Cambridge: Cambridge University Press.

Song Shengtan. 1987. *Katalogo de Esperantaj poŝtmarkoj*. Beijing: Ĉina Esperanto-Eldonejo.

Sprague, Charles E. 1888. *Hand-Book of Volapük*. New York: The Office Company.

Universala Esperanto-Asocio. 2010. 'Kongresoj'. http://www.uea.org/kongresoj/uk-listo.html

Urquhart, Thomas. 1653. *Logopandecteision, or an Introduction to the Universal Language*. London: Calvert and Tomlins. Repr. Menston: Scolar, 1970.

Wilkins, John. 1668. *An Essay towards a Real Character, and a Philosophical Language*. London: Gellibrand and Martin. Repr. Bristol: Thoemmes, 2002.

Zamenhof, L.L. 1929. *Originala Verkaro*. Ed. Johann Dietterle. Leipzig: Hirt.

Invented Vocabularies:

The Cases of Newspeak and Nadsat

HOWARD JACKSON

Invented languages inevitably include invented vocabularies. So, while the title of this chapter could apply to any or all of the invented languages discussed elsewhere in this book, we shall be concerned here primarily with two very specific invented vocabularies from twentieth-century literature: Newspeak, in George Orwell's *Nineteen Eighty-Four* (1949), and Nadsat in Anthony Burgess's *A Clockwork Orange* (1962). Both these novels take place in an imagined future, both are dystopian in outlook; the invented vocabulary in both has a crucial role to play in the construction and message of the work.

George Orwell (whose real name was Eric Blair) reveals in a number of his writings an interest in the relationship between thought and language: what influence they have on each other; whether, on the one hand, language can be manipulated to control thought or to expand thought; and, on the other, whether a limited range of language reflects a poverty of thought and intellect. In the area of politics, Orwell has concerns about totalitarian regimes, in particular the Soviet Union under Josef Stalin, and the means that they use, including linguistic ones, for keeping political control and suppressing dissent. More generally, Orwell has important things to say about the language of politics. These preoccupations are reflected in *Nineteen Eighty-Four*, and in a significant way through the invention of Newspeak. Set in a future in which totalitarian governments are the norm, the novel explores how a society could be completely controlled by a political elite, together with the role of language in achieving that control.

Anthony Burgess (whose real name was John Wilson), born into a Catholic family in the north-west of England and educated at the Xaverian College in Rusholme, Manchester, wrestles in many of his works with the problems of free will and determinism. In particular, how does society deal with the thuggish behaviour of youth gangs? Is it legitimate to use psychological techniques of brainwashing, as was suggested by one government minister, in order to reform teenagers who had manifested violent tendencies? Or would this be a violation of an individual's freedom and an abuse of coercive powers on the part of the state? These are the issues that Burgess addresses in *A Clockwork Orange*, and Nadsat is the vocabulary he creates as the argot that characterizes Alex, the novel's protagonist, and his fellow teenagers. Burgess wanted to reproduce the slang of contemporary teenage gangs, but with a vocabulary that would not become dated, and so he invented one.

Newspeak

By contrast with Nadsat in *A Clockwork Orange*, Newspeak is not used extensively within *Nineteen Eighty-Four*. Orwell introduces the odd Newspeak word here and there, together with a couple of examples of how the Ministry of Truth, where the hero, Winston Smith, works, uses Newspeak in internal communications. There are fewer than forty different Newspeak vocabulary items used within the novel, and not many more than fifty instances of their use. However, Orwell provides an appendix, titled 'The Principles of Newspeak', in which he gives a fuller description of his invented vocabulary. *Newspeak* is a word we are all familiar with; it has an entry in modern dictionaries. But its influence on our cultural consciousness is disproportionate to its use within Orwell's novel. Indeed, most of the information about Newspeak we deduce not from the novel itself, but from Orwell's appendix, which gives the appearance of an academic treatise on the language. It is strange to append such a detailed description of Newspeak but not to illustrate its use more consistently in the novel. Is the appendix, we may wonder, intended as part of the novel? It deals with a fiction, in the sense that Newspeak is invented, but it is couched in factual terms.

Newspeak (*Newspeak* is itself a Newspeak word) is intended to be the official language of Oceania, one of the three superstates into which the world of *Nineteen Eighty-Four* is divided. By 1984, the definitive Eleventh Edition of the Newspeak Dictionary was being compiled, but no one used Newspeak as their exclusive means of communication. It was expected to take until 2050 for Newspeak to have completely replaced Oldspeak (English), at least for Party members; no doubt, the 'proles' would continue to speak their form of (Cockney) English, as in the novel.

Newspeak has a pared-down vocabulary. The words are based on English, but their number is reduced to the basic minimum, and their meanings are carefully controlled. The aim of so circumscribing the vocabulary is to prevent users of Newspeak from thinking any thoughts that could be deemed heretical to Party orthodoxy. Reducing the range of vocabulary was intended to reduce the range of possible thoughts. We shall return to Orwell's view of the relation between words and thoughts below.

The vocabulary of Newspeak is divided into three sets, A, B, and C. It is thought that C. K. Ogden's Basic English was one inspiration for Orwell's Newspeak; its 850 words were likewise grouped into three classes (Ogden 1930). However, Ogden's categories of words for 'Things', words for 'Qualities', and words for 'Operations' are not replicated in

Newspeak, where the A words relate to everyday life, the B words to politics, and the C words to science and technology. Words in Newspeak are categorized by topic, with B words and C words having a specialist character: only someone engaged in the fields of politics and science, respectively, would have occasion to use them. Ogden's categories relate primarily to parts of speech—A representing nouns, B adjectives, and C verbs—so that any user of Basic English would need words from all three categories. (For more on Ogden and Basic English, in a different context, see Chapter 2.)

The A vocabulary 'was intended only to express simple, purposive thoughts, usually involving concrete objects or physical actions' (Orwell 1954, 242). Its nouns and verbs were completely interchangeable: *think* is both noun and verb, as is *knife*; and the words *thought* and *cut* are not in the vocabulary. There is only one way to form adjectives—by adding *-ful* to a noun/verb, e.g., *speedful*—and only one way to form adverbs—by adding *-wise* to a noun/verb, e.g., *speedwise*, *goodwise* (for English *well*). The negative of any word could be formed by adding the prefix *un-* (e.g., *uncold*); and an emphatic form of any word by adding the prefix *plus-* (e.g., *pluscold*), which could be further heightened by adding *double-* (e.g., *doublepluscold*). Other useful prefixes included *ante-* (e.g., *antefiling* 'before filing'), *post-*, *up-* (e.g., *upsub* 'submit to a higher authority'), *down-*. Inflections had been completely regularized: the past tense was formed exclusively with *-ed*, e.g., *stealed*, *thinked*; plural was formed with *-s* or *-es* only, e.g., *mans, lifes*; and the comparative and superlative of adjectives was exclusively by means of the *-er* and *-est* suffixes, e.g., *gooder, goodest*—the alternative periphrastic form with *more* and *most* had been abolished.

The formation of words and their forms is, thus, completely regularized. The speakers' brains no longer have to cope with the messiness of natural language and its irregularities, accrued over a long history. Such a morphology requires less thinking, and so in language, as in demands of behaviour generally, conforms to a predetermined pattern.

The language is reduced to a consistent pattern by totalitarianism, just as morality, culture, and social relationships are.

Words in the political B vocabulary of Newspeak are all compounds, e.g., *goodthink* 'orthodoxy', *crimethink* 'thought crime'. They inflect like words in the A vocabulary (*goodthinked*, *goodthinking*) and are subject to the same derivations (*goodthinkful*, *goodthinkwise*). Orwell adds the derivation *goodthinker*, which he terms a 'verbal noun', but which is more accurately an 'agentive noun'. Indeed, Orwell lumps all the above under the heading of 'inflection', whereas linguists would distinguish between inflections (which indicate the grammatical status of a word, such as a noun's number or a verb's tense) and derivations (which make new words out of pre-existing elements). In the case of the B words some irregularity is permitted, in the interest of euphony; for example, the adjective *-ful* forms of the names of the government departments *Minitrue* 'Ministry of Truth', *Minipax* 'Ministry of Peace', and *Miniluv* 'Ministry of Love' are, respectively, *Minitruthful*, *Minipeaceful*, and *Miniloveful* (Orwell has *Minilovely*, but this is probably a mistake). The forms *Minitrueful* etc. are considered too awkward to pronounce. The word-formation processes permissible in Newspeak, i.e., limited affixation and extensive compounding, are reminiscent of those typical of the Germanic languages, e.g., Modern German and Old English.

The number of words in the political vocabulary is carefully controlled, as are their meanings. The aim was to progressively reduce the number of words in Newspeak. The fewer words and the more circumscribed their meanings, the less would be the temptation to 'take thought': 'the intention was to make speech ... as nearly as possible independent of consciousness' (Orwell 1954, 248). There should be no engagement of the brain, merely a reflex of the vocal cords. In Newspeak, this was called *duckspeak*; a good Party orator could be referred to approvingly as a *doubleplusgood duckspeaker*. Two principles contributed to the development of 'duckspeak': abbreviation, and euphony. Abbreviation, as in the names of the Ministries, leads to a speaker giving less thought to what they are saying. Orwell contrasts English terms such as *Comintern* with their full forms, in this case *Communist International*, noting that the full, phrasal form invites the speaker to linger over it. Apart from attention to meaning, in Newspeak attention to euphony was paramount. Particularly favoured were short two- or three-syllable words with an even stress pattern: *goodthink*, *sexcrime, joycamp, bellyfeel*. The consequence was to encourage 'a gabbling style of speech, at once staccato and monotonous' (Orwell 1954, 248). This further enabled the disassocation of speech from thought, and so the development of 'duckspeak'.

The C vocabulary receives very little attention, except to note that it is a set of words for use by scientific workers and technicians, with little currency in everyday or political speech. The words are similar to current English scientific and technical terms, although of course their meanings are carefully circumscribed. Interestingly, there is no word for 'science' itself, since its meaning is already encompassed by the word *Ingsoc* (i.e., English Socialism).

Orwell's appendix envisages a transition period between Oldspeak and Newspeak. As new generations acquire an ever more restricted Newspeak, the possibility of thinking, let alone uttering, heterodox thoughts will become impossible. One impediment to complete adoption of Newspeak, and the reason why the date of 2050 was set for that achievement, was the need to complete the difficult task of translating into Newspeak the works of writers considered worth preserving, as well as more everyday literature such as technical manuals.

Newspeak in the novel

One of the most commonly cited Newspeak words within the text of the novel is *doublethink*. It occurs 29 times, far more than any other, and is one of the Newspeak words adopted by English. Doublethink, the ability to hold two contradictory thoughts in one's mind and to believe both of them (Orwell 1954, 31–2), is an essential ability for Party members in the transition between Oldspeak and Newspeak.

A similar word is *blackwhite*, which occurs in the subversive Goldstein book given to Winston by O'Brien, which Winston reads to Julia (Orwell 1954, 169). When applied to a Party member, *blackwhite* denotes the loyal ability to say that black is white when the Party so demands, as well as to believe it, forgetting that one may have once believed the opposite. Applied to an enemy, it denotes the act of claiming something to be so in the face of clear evidence to the contrary.

In Oceania, nonconformity is a crime, and the most serious variety is a *thoughtcrime* or a *crimethink*. Orwell uses both words in the novel, though in his appendix 'thoughtcrime' is given as a gloss for *crimethink*, suggesting that the Newspeak word is, in fact, *crimethink*. However, *thoughtcrime*, as a compound word written solid, without space or hyphen, is scarcely an English word. *Thoughtcrime* is used five times within the novel, and *crimethink* only once and then only within an example of 'the hybrid jargon of the Ministries' (Orwell 1954, 137). *Thoughtcrime* is clearly a Party term (Orwell 1954, 19), and when Winston meets his neighbour, Parsons, in jail, the latter gives 'thoughtcrime' as the reason for his arrest (Orwell 1954, 187). Other types of crime include *facecrime*, or having an inappropriate expression on one's face, e.g., a look of incredulity when a victory is announced (Orwell 1954, 53), and *sexcrime*, mentioned in Orwell's appendix, which denoted any sexual act not undertaken without desire and purely for the purposes of procreation (Orwell 1954, 246), though the ideal is for children to be produced by *artsem* (artificial insemination) (Orwell 1954, 56). One other Newspeak word containing *crime* is given: *crimestop*, which is the ability to avoid thinking a heterodox thought. It is mentioned in Goldstein's subversive book, glossed as 'protective stupidity' (Orwell 1954, 169); and Winston practises crimestop during his re-education in jail (Orwell 1954, 224). The Party requires conformity, the opposite of which is *ownlife* 'individualism and eccentricity' (Orwell 1954, 69) in Newspeak. A person who is 'naturally orthodox' is called a *goodthinker* (Orwell 1954, 169), from *goodthink* 'orthodoxy' (Orwell 1954, 245) with its attendant adjective *goodthinkful* 'incapable of thinking a bad thought' (Orwell 154, 108). And those responsible for detecting unorthodoxy are the *thinkpol* 'Thought Police' (Orwell 1954, 245).

Twice in the novel, Newspeak is used in a communication internal to the Ministry of Truth. In the first (Orwell 1954, 34), Winston, in the course of his work, receives a number of instructions to 'rectify' past editions of the *Times* newspaper in order to bring them into line with subsequent events. They read:

> times 17.3.84 bb speech malreported africa rectify
> times 19.12.83 forecasts 3 yp 4th quarter 83 misprints verify current issue
> times 14.2.84 miniplenty malquoted chocolate rectify
> times 3.12.83 reporting bb dayorder doubleplusungood refs unpersons
>   rewrite fullwise upsub antefiling

A number of Newspeak words receive their introduction here: *malreport*, using a new prefix, *mal-*, likewise *malquote*, presumably meaning 'misreport' and 'misquote'. A different Ministry is mentioned: *Miniplenty* 'Ministry of Plenty, i.e., Economic Affairs', which had been introduced, along with the other three Ministries, near the beginning of the book (Orwell 1954, 7). We may wonder why Orwell didn't make this one *Miniplen*, consistent with *Minitrue* and *Miniluv*. He has abbreviated 'makes reference to' to *refs*. The final instruction contains a number of Newspeak words: *dayorder* (Order of the Day), *doubleplusungood* 'extremely bad', *unperson* 'undesirable person deemed never to have existed and therefore to be expunged from all records', *fullwise* 'fully, completely', *upsub* 'submit to a higher authority, i.e., for checking', and *antefiling* 'before filing in the records'. The abbreviation *bb* refers, of course, to Big Brother.

The other extensive instance of Newspeak is in a communication by O'Brien (Orwell 1954, 137): 'Items one comma five comma seven approved fullwise stop suggestion contained item six doubleplus ridiculous verging crimethink cancel stop unproceed constructionwise antegetting plusfull estimates machinery overheads stop end message.'

Here is *fullwise* again, and *crimethink*. Interestingly, *doubleplus* and the adjective it is emphasizing, *ridiculous*, are not written solid, either because *ridiculous* is not actually a Newspeak word, or because it would look too long. However, *plusfull* 'very full' is written solid. There is a further derivation with prefix *un-* in *unproceed* 'don't proceed', and with *ante-* in *antegetting* 'before getting'; and an adverb derivation with *-wise*, *constructionwise*, which here seems to mean 'in respect of the construction' rather than 'constructionly'.

O'Brien uses a machine called a *speakwrite* to record and send his message. The 'speak-write' (sic) is referred to earlier as a machine into which Winston 'dictates' (Orwell 1954, 9), while O'Brien 'rapped out' the message into his machine (Orwell 1954, 137), both presumably referring to speech then converted into written form. The corrections that Winston makes to the *Times* entries are said to be *speakwritten* (Orwell 1954, 35), not, as we might expect from the inflection rules given in the appendix, *speakwrited*. But then, *speakwrite* is not indicated explicitly to be a Newspeak word. Nor is *vaporize*, which is what happens to an 'unperson' (Orwell 1954, 37), though it is hinted at as Newspeak (Orwell 1954, 19). Neither is it clear whether *versificator* (Orwell 1954, 38) is a genuine Newspeak word; *versificator* refers to the machine that produces 'sentimental songs' for the proles in Minitrue, which also has a department called *Pornosec* 'Pornography Section'.

Predictably, the vocabulary of Newspeak would be embodied in a dictionary. In their first encounter (Orwell 1954, 128–9), Winston and O'Brien discuss Winston's use of two obsolete Newspeak words in one of his articles. Winston has to admit that the Records Department or *Recdep* (Orwell 1954, 247), where he works, has access only to the Ninth Edition of the Dictionary. O'Brien mentions that the Tenth Edition is not due for some months, but that he can let Winston see an advance copy. One 'advance' of the new edition is the 'reduction in the number of verbs' (Orwell 1954, 129), another echo, perhaps, of Ogden's Basic English. However, the account of Newspeak in Orwell's appendix is based on the Eleventh Edition (Orwell 1954, 241), and it is on this edition that the philologist Syme, 'one of an enormous team of experts' (Orwell 1954, 42), with whom Winston has a conversation about Newspeak, is working. The team of philologists' job is to destroy words, especially verbs and adjectives, so that the Dictionary will contain no word that will become obsolete before 2050 (Orwell 1954, 44). Every word will have 'its meaning rigidly defined' (Orwell 1954, 45), and all 'subsidiary meanings' will be expunged so that there is a one-to-one correspondence between a word and a concept. The Dictionary will thus contain 'every concept that can ever be needed' (Orwell 1954, 45) (see Chapter 1).

Orwell on language

Did George Orwell believe that Newspeak would work, that a whole population's thought could be controlled by limiting their range of vocabulary and tightly specifying the meanings that words were permitted to have? Orwell was certainly interested in language, especially the language of political discourse. While working on *Nineteen Eighty-Four*, he published his essay 'Politics and the English Language' (Orwell 1946a). In the same year, his review of Swift's *Gulliver's Travels* was published (Orwell 1946b), and Swift's work seems to have greatly influenced aspects of his own dystopian novel. Orwell notes that, in Part III of *Gulliver's Travels* especially, Swift creates 'a perception that one of the aims of totalitarianism is not merely to make sure that people will think the right thoughts, but actually to make them *less conscious*' (Orwell 1946b, 131). Swift's Houyhnhnms (a race of intelligent horses) have no word for 'opinion', and their conversations contain no differences of opinion: 'nothing passed but what was useful, expressed in the fewest and most significant Words' (quoted in Orwell 1946b, 136).

Earlier still, long before he had begun work on *Nineteen Eighty-Four*, Orwell had written an article titled 'New Words' that never reached publication but is dated tentatively to 1940 (Orwell (ed. Davison) 1998, 128).

In this essay, Orwell discusses the possibility of inventing a vocabulary of English words in order to talk precisely about our inner life, what goes on inside our brains, an area of our experience, according to Orwell, for which English lacks an adequate set of terms. Language is inadequate, everyone knows that; 'the lumpishness of words results in constant falsification' (Orwell 1998, 130); words are not always a 'direct channel of thought', they lack 'exactitude' and 'expressiveness'. What is needed is 'to invent new words as deliberately as we would invent new parts for a motor-car engine' (Orwell 1998, 131), so that 'one can give thought an objective existence' (Orwell 1998, 133).

In this article, Orwell comes at the thought/word problem from the perspective opposite that of *Nineteen Eighty-Four*: finding the appropriate words to express our thoughts accurately, rather than manipulating vocabulary in order to contain possible thoughts. What it shows, though, is that Orwell had been interested in the relationship between language and thought for a considerable time. And he seriously entertains the possibility of inventing 'several thousand' new words for thoughts that are currently 'nameless'. He, interestingly, proposes two requirements for new words: 'exactitude of meaning' and 'appropriateness of sound' (Orwell 1998, 135), a clear echo of the appendix to *Nineteen Eighty-Four*, where 'in Newspeak, euphony outweighed every consideration other than exactitude of meaning' (Orwell 1954, 248). Orwell seems to have considered official language planning a realistic possibility. Most often, language planners invent words for the technical register, as in Modern Hebrew and Welsh (for more on which, see Chapter 8). Words in ordinary language usually emerge from need in the course of everyday social interaction. The failure of the Académie Française to impose invented French words in place of borrowed ones, especially from English, is well known.

In his later article, 'Politics and the English Language', Orwell again addresses the relationship between thought and language: English 'becomes ugly and inaccurate because our thoughts are foolish, but the slovenliness of our language makes it easier for us to have foolish thoughts; and if thought corrupts language, language can also corrupt thought' (Orwell 1946a, 143 and 154). There is an influence both of language on thought and of thought on language. Orwell is particularly concerned in this essay with the debasement, as he sees it, of political discourse, and, in particular, of the use of ready-made and hackneyed phrases, which come crowding into the mind and 'perform the important service of partially concealing your meaning even from yourself' (Orwell 1946a, 152). Political speechmakers who use such a style seem like 'some kind of dummy', mouthing platitudes but not engaging the brain, rather like the Party orators in *Nineteen Eighty-Four*, in fact. Orwell sees political language as consisting 'largely of euphemism, question-begging and sheer cloudy vagueness' (Orwell 1946a, 153) and as 'designed to make lies sound truthful and murder respectable, and to give an appearance of solidity to pure wind' (Orwell 1946a, 157).

But he doesn't think that it is necessarily so: 'the decadence of our language is probably curable' (Orwell 1946a, 155). It behoves orators to dispense with 'silly words and expressions' and simplify their language. Now, Newspeak has a 'simplified' vocabulary, but not with the sense of *simplification* Orwell means here: he wants political speechmakers to use plain language rather than tired clichés and pompous expressions that only obscure meaning. Attention to the words used, he implies, will improve the thoughts conceived, presumably by both speakers and hearers. Orwell comes close here to the Newspeak idea that words can control thoughts, though, in this case, a careful choice of words is intended to be liberating, releasing the speaker from the tired, meaningless phraseology of current political language and returning to robust, meaningful political discourse. Just as language can 'corrupt' thought, so language can cleanse and renew it.

Perhaps a good example of this is the purpose behind much so-called 'politically correct' vocabulary. It is claimed, for example, that using words like *disabled* or *alternatively abled* inculcates in a person a different perspective and attitude than that implied by the former term *handicapped*. The new word conveys a more positive attitude; and by implication you think of the other person in a different way. Is this the manipulation of the language for positive ends? Its excesses, though, bring it into ridicule: *herstory* for *history*, *personhole* for *manhole*, and so on. What the Newspeak enterprise ignores is human beings' metalinguistic capacities: the fact that they can consciously reflect about the words they use.

Orwell and Sapir–Whorf

Where, then, does Orwell stand on the relationship between language and thought? Does, for him, language determine thought? Or does thought determine language? The relation between language and thought was articulated most famously by the linguist Edward Sapir (1884–1939) and his student Benjamin Lee Whorf (1897–1941) in what became known as the Sapir–Whorf hypothesis, expressed in Whorf's words: 'We dissect nature along lines laid down by our native language' (Crystal 1987, 15). The strong version of the Sapir–Whorf hypothesis, implied by these words, produces 'linguistic determinism', similar to the 'nominalist' position among ancient Greek philosophers: our language—its vocabulary and its grammar—determines the way in which we conceive the world, what counts as 'reality'. This is the Newspeak position, except that the vocabulary of Newspeak is deliberately manipulated so that only one conception of the world, only one reality, is possible: the one determined by the Party.

A weaker form of the Sapir–Whorf hypothesis would propose that our language encourages us to conceive of the world in a certain manner (known as 'linguistic relativity'); but it leaves open the possibility of alternative and creative ways of seeing. The alternative position in Greek philosophy to nominalism is that of the 'realists': facts and things exist independently of us and our conceptions, and we use language to name them and talk about them. Roger Fowler, in his book on George Orwell's language, argues strongly that Orwell 'held a fundamentally realist view … with a commitment to historical facts'

(Fowler 1995, 31–2). The problem for Orwell was finding the precise words to express the truth; so often, language failed to fulfil its purpose, and thus words obscured, even corrupted, thought.

The purpose of Newspeak

Where does that leave our assessment of the purpose of Newspeak? Nowhere in *Nineteen Eighty-Four* is Newspeak used as the regular means of communication. We are told that *Times* editorials are written in it, but given no example; the two extensive passages of Newspeak, analysed earlier, contain a mixture of Newspeak and regular English words; and when Winston practises 'crimestop', he does so in English, not Newspeak. The full development and exclusive use of Newspeak is envisaged as still being 64 years in the future. Newspeak is an enterprise of the Party; it is a tool of totalitarian control, like 'rectification' of historical records and expunging memories. The Party believes in linguistic determinism. That does not mean that Orwell does. Rather, he explores where such a view might lead, were a government to take control of vocabulary in order to restrict thought to conform entirely to its own purposes, especially the retention of power.

We are still left with Orwell's appendix on the principles of Newspeak. Did Orwell mean it seriously? Did he think that a totalitarian, Stalinist government could manipulate language as he describes? It is written in a matter-of-fact, objective way and deliberately placed outside of the novel proper, unlike, for example, the Goldstein book, extensive parts of which are reproduced within the novel. Roger Fowler suggests that in the appendix Orwell is imitating Swift in *Gulliver's Travels*, whose influence we have already noted. Just as Swift adopted a deadpan, serious style for his satire, so Orwell used 'a non-judgmental, matter-of-fact style to report a project which to him was not only absurd … but worse, philosophically and morally ill-grounded' (Fowler 1995, 225). It is not certain, either from *Nineteen Eighty-Four* or from his essays, that Orwell's views were so clear-cut. There is no indication that Orwell wrote the appendix tongue-in-cheek. His essays give the impression that Orwell is exploring the relation between language and thought, rather than expressing a considered view. It can be argued that the appendix examines the consequences of pushing the determinism line to its ultimate conclusion, where thought is totally controlled by a restricted language.

What Orwell does not consider is the metalinguistic point that the language manipulators must stand outside the process in order to fashion the language, just as he does when describing the structure and purpose of Newspeak. Why is the manipulator not manipulated? Perhaps Orwell points to the potential for governments to use language as a tool of control and obfuscation but does not believe that the Newspeak enterprise is feasible: we could see through the manipulation and challenge the conceptions; language can be an instrument of challenge as well as of control, as dictators always find to their cost. Orwell thus challenges his readers to consider the effect of language and its manipulation. *Nineteen Eighty-Four* is the novel counterpart of the essay on politics and the English language (Orwell 1946a).

Newspeak and now

Orwell's *Nineteen Eighty-Four* struck a chord with the English-speaking world. The term *Orwellian* refers largely to the picture of a controlled society, as depicted in this novel and in *Animal Farm*. The words *newspeak* and *doublethink* have come into the English language. Both are in the *New Oxford Dictionary of English* (1998), and both are to be found in the 100 million-word *British National Corpus*. Interestingly, a new word has been coined based on these two: *doublespeak*, which is also in *NODE* and *BNC*. The National Council of Teachers of English in the United States gives an annual 'Doublespeak Award', and has done so since 1974 (see NCTE website). The *Newspeak Dictionary* website contains both a full list of the Newspeak words in *Nineteen Eighty-Four* and examples of what might be considered newspeak in current political discourse. Stalinism is long past, yet Orwell's concerns about the nature of political language, its vacuousness and obfuscation, and attempts by those with political power to manipulate public perceptions are still relevant. Orwell rightly drew our attention to the power of words, their potential both to demand conformity and to challenge it.

Nadsat

We turn now to Nadsat, the vocabulary Anthony Burgess invented for *A Clockwork Orange* (1962). Nadsat serves a quite different purpose from that of Newspeak. The thrust of the novel is socio-political—the (mis)use of psychological conditioning to reform young criminals—but the invented vocabulary does not contribute directly to the manipulation of behaviour, as Newspeak does. The function of Nadsat is to characterize the world of and to reflect the worldview of a youth culture addicted to gratuitous violence. While *A Clockwork Orange* is well known, especially through its film version, Nadsat does not have the resonance in modern culture that Newspeak has, despite the fact that it is used more extensively in the novel than Newspeak in *Nineteen Eighty-Four*.

A Clockwork Orange had a chequered publishing history. The first, British edition, published by Heinemann, contained three parts of seven chapters each, which Burgess had deliberately intended as 'in traditional arithmology, the symbol of human maturity' (Burgess 1990). His American publisher, W. W. Norton, insisted that the final chapter, which sees the hero Alex grow up and renounce violence, be omitted, on the presumption that American readers would prefer a grittier ending. A film of the novel, directed by Stanley Kubrick, came out in 1971, based on the American version; and the British Penguin edition of the book that followed the film in 1972 also reproduced the American version, without the final chapter, and with a glossary of Nadsat terms. However, when it was republished in the Penguin Classics series in 1996, with an introduction by Blake Morrison, the final chapter was restored and the glossary omitted.

Unlike the 'Principles of Newspeak' appendix in *Nineteen Eighty-Four*, the Nadsat glossary is not part of the original work, nor was it compiled by Burgess, who explicitly repudiated it, for reasons made clear later on. The glossary in the Penguin (1972) edition reproduced one that had appeared in American editions and now is also available on a website titled *Nadsat Dictionary* (Hyman 1963). It contains 241 words and expressions, together with an English translation. The majority of the words (187) are attributed to a Russian origin. In the book itself, one of the doctors treating Alex in the clinic where he undergoes psychological conditioning remarks that Nadsat consists of 'Odd bits of old rhyming slang, a bit of gypsy talk too. But most of the roots are Slav' (Burgess 1972, 91).

Why Russian?

To understand why Burgess used Russian as the base for most of his Nadsat terms, we must review the genesis of the novel. Burgess says that he had long wanted to use 'Clockwork Orange' as the title of a novel, in fact ever since he had heard the Cockney expression *queer* (i.e., 'odd/strange') *as a clockwork orange*. During the 1950s, Burgess had been teaching in Malaya and Brunei, but he returned to Britain in 1959, following diagnosis of a suspected brain tumour, and witnessed the violence of rival gangs of young Mods and Rockers, 'knocking hell out of each other when we made a trip to Hastings' (Burgess 1990)—one of the resorts on the south coast of England where Mods (on their scooters) and Rockers (on their motorbikes) used to gather on public holidays. The main clashes between the rival gangs actually occurred in 1964, two years after publication of *A Clockwork Orange*, though the gangs had existed since the late 1950s. A government minister of the time suggested that one way of dealing with such youth violence would be to incarcerate the perpetrators in an institution and subject them to psychological conditioning (on the lines of Pavlov or B. F. Skinner) so that they would eschew all violence. Burgess, who deals with the problem of free will and determinism (in theological terms, Pelagianism and Augustinianism) in several of his works, saw this as 'a greater evil than the free choice of evil' (Burgess 1990).

The idea for *A Clockwork Orange* was born in the present, then, but Burgess wanted to locate it in the future, around 1970, and he wanted the young people of his novel to speak a form of teenage slang that would not be time-bound. So, it could not be the slang of the 1960s; it would have to be an invented slang. In 1961, Burgess and his wife decided to take a holiday involving a stay in Leningrad (now Saint Petersburg), and Burgess set about re-learning Russian in preparation for it. While in Leningrad, the Burgesses witnessed youth hooliganism similar to that of Britain; he thus conceived of basing his invented teenage slang on Russian. He called the slang 'Nadsat', from the Russian suffix equivalent to the 'teen' of English numbers from *thirteen* to *nineteen*.

Not surprisingly, perhaps, some have seen the choice of Russian as having a political motivation, as a warning of where society is heading, since 'for the Anglo-American reader the Slavic words connote Communist dictatorship' (Evans 1971, 409; see Appendix 3 for more from Evans). Evans's article predates Burgess's article in *The Listener* of 17 February 1972, in which he makes clear: 'The language … is no mere decoration, nor is it a sinister indication of the subliminal power that a Communist super-state may already be exerting … I chose Russian words because they blend better into English than those of French or even German' (Burgess 1972b, 198). One doubts whether this is precisely the case: Burgess can hardly have thought people would make no connection between his Russian-based slang and the brutal Soviet system of the time.

Burgess had an abiding interest in languages and dialects. He had a reputation for collecting odd words and phrases (Lewis 2002, 159). While serving as an education officer in the British Colonial Service in Malaya and Brunei in the 1950s, he had learned Malay, traces of which appear in his early novels. He undertook a number of translations from French, and he was familiar with Italian, his second wife's native language.

He wrote an analysis of the language of James Joyce's works (*Joysprick*, 1973), as well as two popular textbooks on language: *Language Made Plain* (1964) and *A Mouthful of Air: Language and languages, especially English* (1992). *A Clockwork Orange* has been described as 'a linguistic tour de force' (Aggeler 1979, 172; it was called this more than once— see Appendix 3 for more examples). Burgess's own view, however, is that it is 'too linguistically exhibitionist' (Burgess 1978, 91).

A Clockwork Orange is a first-person narrative, told by Alex, the hero and leader of a teenage gang. Nadsat is used only by Alex and his gang, and in their speech it is interwoven with English words. Approximately five per cent of the text comprises Nadsat words; so, around one word in twenty is a Nadsat term, with on average twenty-four per page. There is a certain amount of variation, with some pages containing in excess of thirty Nadsat terms, and some fewer than twenty. Burgess estimated that a reader would become accustomed to Nadsat within the first fifteen pages, by which time they would have encountered around 350 instances of Nadsat. The reader should not be able to look Nadsat words up in a glossary or dictionary, because part of the purpose of the book was to act as 'a brainwashing primer' (Burgess 1972b, 199) for the reader. The reader was to experience a little of what Alex is subjected to in the conditioning that is applied to him. As a result of reading the book, the reader would be 'in possession of a minimal Russian vocabulary—without effort, with surprise' (Burgess 1972b: 199). The process of reading *A Clockwork Orange* was to be an object lesson in the issues with which the book grapples, a purpose partly achieved by the invented vocabulary.

Nadsat words

At times, Burgess helps the reader by providing a gloss in the text itself:

> Dim had a real horrorshow length of oozy or chain round his waist, twice wound round, and he unwound this and began to swing it beautiful in the eyes or glazzies. (1972, 16)

So, *oozy* is a 'chain' (possibly from Russian *uzh* 'snake') and *glazzies* are 'eyes' (from Russian *glaz* 'eye'); and *horrorshow*, from Russian *khoroshó* 'well, good', is an adjective of general approval. Russian is written in the Cyrillic alphabet; so, Burgess's use of Russian words involves both transliteration (from the Cyrillic to the Roman alphabet) and adaptation to the English spelling system to make a pronounceable word in English. The transliterations here are based on Campbell (1995, 621).

The Russian noun *babushka* 'grandmother' becomes Nadsat *baboochka*; *dévochka* 'girl' becomes *devotchka*; *drug* 'friend' becomes *droog*; *gazéta* 'newspaper' becomes *gazetta*; *gólos* 'voice' becomes *goloss*; *golová* 'head' becomes *gulliver*; *mál'chik* 'boy' becomes *malchick*; *milícija* 'police' becomes *millicent*; *rabóta* 'work' becomes *rabbit*; *vesh'* 'thing' becomes *veshch*; and *yaz'ík* 'tongue' becomes *yahzick*. The degree of adaptation varies; it is more extensive in the case of *gulliver*, *millicent*, *rabbit*, and *yahzick*; but in these cases Burgess plays on associations of sounds and meanings in English. Once the Russian words become Nadsat, they are subject to the usual English inflections, in the case of nouns the plural -(*e*)*s*; so, the plural of *baboochka* is *baboochkas*, and of *veshch* is *veshches*. The Nadsat word for 'teeth' is *zoobies*, from Russian *zub* 'tooth', plural *zubi*; so here Burgess has added the English plural -*es* to the Russian plural form *zubi*.

The Russian verb *krást'* 'steal' becomes Nadsat *crast*; *gulyát'* 'stroll' becomes *gooly*; *govorít'* 'speak' becomes *govoreet*; *ubívát'* 'kill' becomes *oobivat*; *plákat'* 'weep' becomes *platch*; *skhvatít'* 'snatch' becomes *skvat*; *tolchók* 'push' becomes *tolchock*; and *vídet'* 'see' becomes *viddy*. As with nouns, the inflections, for past tense and for the participles, follow the pattern of English. The past tense/past participle of *viddy* is *viddied* and its present participle is *viddying*. The present participle of *govoreet* is *govoreeting*, and the past tense is *govoreeted*. The past tense of *skvat* is *skvatted*, following the rule in English for doubling of 't' after a short vowel.

The Russian adjective *bol'nój* 'ill' becomes Nadsat *bolnoy*; *bol'shój* 'big' becomes *bolshy*; *glúpyj* 'stupid' becomes *gloopy*; *málen'kij* 'small' becomes *malenky*; *uzhásnyj* 'awful' becomes *oozhassny*; *skóryj* 'quick' becomes *skorry*; and *stáryj* 'old' becomes *starry*. The basic form of the adjective in Russian ends in 'yj', reproduced in Nadsat by 'y', and note the doubling of the 'r' in *skorry* and *starry* to preserve the short vowel.

Of the non-Russian words, some are reduplications, possibly imitating schoolboy slang (Hyman 1963), such as *baddiwad* 'bad', *eggiweg* 'egg', *guttiwuts* 'guts', *jammiwam* 'jam', *skolliwoll* 'school', and possibly *Pee* and *Em* for 'father' and 'mother'. Some are based on rhyming slang, such as *charles/charlie* 'priest', from *Charlie Chaplin*, rhyming with *chaplain*; *luscious glory* 'hair', rhyming with *upper storey*; *pretty polly* 'money', rhyming with *lolly*, slang for 'money'. Both reduplication and rhyming slang are productive, if minor, word-formation processes in modern English. Examples of reduplication are: *nitty-gritty, shilly-shally, teeny-weeny*. Rhyming slang, associated with the street talk of East London Cockneys, is reflected in English by expressions such as: *apples and pairs* 'stairs', *have a butcher's* (hook) 'look', *titfer* (from *tit for tat*) 'hat'. A few words in *A Clockwork Orange* originated in other languages, such as *clop* 'knock', from Dutch *kloppen*; *orange* 'man', from Malay *orang*; *tashtook* 'handkerchief', from German *Taschentuch*; *tass* 'cup' from either French *tasse* or German *Tasse*; and *vaysay* 'toilet', from the French pronunciation of *WC*. Finally, some Nadsat words appear to be Burgess's own invention: *chumble*, perhaps a blend of *chatter* and *mumble* (Hyman 1963); *filly* 'play around with'; *guff* 'laugh'; *sharp* 'a female'; *shilarny* 'concern'; *sinny* 'films', based on *cinema*; *snoutie* 'tobacco' or 'snuff'; *staja* 'state jail', a blend of the initial syllables of *state* and *jail*; and *vellocet* 'a type of drug', perhaps taken from *velocity* (compare *speed* as a slang term for an amphetamine drug). Despite what the doctor at the clinic says (Burgess 1972, 91), no one has discovered any 'gypsy talk' among the Nadsat terms.

One further process for the creation of Nadsat terms should, though, be mentioned. A few of them seem to undergo normal English word-formation processes. For example, the noun *droog* is formed into an adjective by the addition of *-y*, *droogy* 'friendly' (Burgess 1972, 85), as is the noun *cal* 'shit' into adjective *cally* (Burgess 1972, 105). *Glaz(z)* forms a compound with the normal English word *ball(s)* to give *glaz-balls*, i.e. 'eyeballs' (Burgess 1972, 83), and *veck* 'person' combines with *counter* to form the compound *counter-veck* (Burgess 1972, 109). The verb *drat* 'fight' is formed into a noun by the addition of *-ing* and the insertion of a linking 's': *dratsing* (Burgess 1972, 86). An agentive noun is formed from *rabbit* by adding *-er*: *rabbiters* (Burgess 1972, 103). There is even the form *droogie* (Burgess 1972, 116), which is a form of endearment based on *droog*.

Effect of Nadsat

Anthony Burgess thinks that *A Clockwork Orange* 'has not been well understood' (Burgess 1978, 93). And it has been made the more difficult by Kubrick's film, which appeared to encourage some young viewers to go out and replicate the acts of mindless violence that they had witnessed on the screen. Burgess (1990) makes this comment: 'The writer's aim ... had been to put language, not sex and violence, into the foreground; a film, on the other hand, was not made out of words.' This raises the question of what effect Nadsat has on the experience of the reader.

In a paper given at a symposium at the Anthony Burgess Centre of the University of Angers, France, in 2001, Gareth Farmer argued that 'the reader's experience of the violence "depicted" in the novel is actually enhanced and made more affective by the dialect and linguistic techniques employed which characterise the dystopic world of the text' (Burgess Symposium 2001). This was not Burgess's intention, because, as we have seen, his choice of a teenage slang based on Russian was intended to distance the events being portrayed by locating them in an indeterminate future (or perhaps on other grounds—see Appendix 3). The aim of the invented vocabulary was to direct the focus of the reader to the philosophical and moral issues that the novel grapples with: free will and determinism. The effect of the language is rather to create a '*Verfremdungseffekt*', as Bertolt Brecht did in his plays, so that the reader is distanced from the action and can concentrate on the ideas.

The film is problematic not only because it is in the visual medium and relies for its effect on the creation of images, but also because the incidence of Nadsat in the film is much reduced. Film viewers, of course, cannot look back and recapitulate if they don't immediately understand a word or phrase; once a word is uttered, it is lost to view. Consequently, the distancing effect achieved by Nadsat is largely absent. Film, in any case, draws the viewer in more readily; it does not have the same possibilities of 'Verfremdung' or distancing that books and the stage have. Moreover, Kubrick based his film on the American version of the book; he was, apparently, unaware of the British version with its additional final chapter, even though he had made his home in England; and the ending he gave to the film, in Burgess's (1990) words, 'had become an exaltation of the urge to sin'.

For Burgess, the use of Nadsat, largely based on Russian words, had two purposes. The first was to create a language, a teenage slang, for his narrator that would not reflect the time of publication (the early 1960s) and would not, therefore, become dated. It was to reflect the fact that the novel was set in the future, a future that could become a reality if certain ideas relating to the control of human behaviour, such as Skinner's conditioning, were implemented. In this sense, Burgess's *A Clockwork Orange* has a similar purpose to Orwell's *Nineteen Eighty-Four*, showing what society would be like if particular ideas were taken to their logical conclusion. Burgess's second purpose with Nadsat was to give an experience of psychological manipulation, or brainwashing, to his readers. They would acquire, by reading his novel, the basis of a new language, in fact Russian. They would begin to view the world through the language/perceptions of Alex and his friends. *Nineteen Eighty-Four* asks readers to reflect objectively on the power of language to manipulate perceptions of the world in the service of political totalitarianism. *A Clockwork Orange* asks readers to experience subjectively themselves, through the process of reading, what it is like to be manipulated by a form of brainwashing, though readers are not subject to the operant conditioning that Alex undergoes. Both *Nineteen Eighty-Four* and *A Clockwork Orange* invite readers to reflect on the power and possible misuses of language.

References

Aggeler, G. 1979. *Anthony Burgess: The Artist as Novelist*. Tuscaloosa and London: University of Alabama Press.

Burgess, A. 1972a. *A Clockwork Orange*. Harmondsworth and New York: Penguin.

Burgess, A. 1972b. 'Clockwork Marmalade'. *The Listener* 87 (No. 2238): 197–9.

Burgess, A. 1978. *1985*. London: Hutchinson.

Burgess, A. 1990. *You've Had Your Time*. London: Heinemann. [excerpts reproduced at http://www.visual-memory.co.uk/amk/doc/burgess.html]

Burgess Symposium. 2001. University of Angers, http://bu.univ-angers.fr/EXTRANET/AnthonyBURGESS/colloque1/colloqueCR.html

British National Corpus. http://www.natcorp.ox.ac.uk/

Campbell, G. L. 1995. *Concise Compendium of the World's Languages*. London: Routledge.

Crystal, D. 1987. *The Cambridge Encyclopedia of Language*. Cambridge: Cambridge University Press.

Evans, R. O. 1971. 'Nadsat: the argot and its implications in Anthony Burgess' *A Clockwork Orange'*. *Journal of Modern Literature* 1.3: 406–10.

Fowler, R. 1995. *The Language of George Orwell*. London: Macmillan.

Hyman, S. E. 1963. *Nadsat Dictionary*. http://soomka.com/nadsat.html

Lewis, R. 2002. *Anthony Burgess*. London: Faber & Faber.

NCTE Doublespeak Award. http://www.ncte.org/volunteer/groups/publiclangcom/doublespeakaward

New Oxford Dictionary of English. 1998. Edited by Judy Pearsall and others. Oxford: Oxford University Press.

Newspeak Dictionary. http://www.newspeakdictionary.com/ns_frames.html

Ogden's Basic English website. http://ogden.basic-english.org/

Ogden, C. K. 1930. *Basic English: A General Introduction with Rules and Grammar*. London: Paul Treber & Co.

Orwell, G. 1940. 'New Words', reprinted in Orwell (ed. Davison) (1998), pp. 127–35; also available online at http://orwell.ru

Orwell, G. 1946a. 'Politics and the English Language'. *Horizon* No.76; reprinted in Orwell (1957), pp. 143–57.

Orwell, G. 1946b. 'Politics vs Literature: an examination of *Gulliver's Travels*'. *Polemic* No. 5; reprinted in Orwell (1957), pp. 121–42.

Orwell, G. 1954. *Nineteen Eighty-Four*. Harmondsworth: Penguin.

Orwell, G. 1957. *Selected Essays*. Reprinted in 1962 as *Inside the Whale and Other Essays*. Harmondsworth: Penguin.

Orwell, G. 1998. *A Patriot after All 1940–1941. The Complete Works of George Orwell, Volume Twelve*. Ed. P. Davison. London: Secker & Warburg.

~4~

Tolkien's Invented Languages

E. S. C. WEINER AND JEREMY MARSHALL

You can't be a Tolkien fan without liking the look of these fake languages, and I still find them aesthetically pleasing, even now. There is something wonderful about looking at a new language, noticing something of its structure, sensing its power to communicate and hold things. And I remember feeling the ground had opened up in front of me when I got to Appendix F.

Jenny Turner 'Reasons for liking Tolkien',
London Review of Books (15 November 2001)

Almost anyone who knows anything about J. R. R. Tolkien's *The Lord of the Rings* (1954–5) knows that Tolkien put invented languages into the mouths of his characters. Those who study the book's Appendices learn that these 'Elvish' and other languages are rarely just an atmospheric feature (as in the fragment of Entish in the *Lord of the Rings* [II. iv] or the single word in the language of the Woses [IV. v]), but rather part of a larger system, organized like real languages with their own imaginary linguistic history and relationships. How much larger and more elaborate becomes apparent from Christopher Tolkien's *History of Middle-earth* (1983–96; hereafter *HME*), which details the continually changing and expanding scheme. Beyond this, numerous notebooks survive, filled with material from six or more decades of linguistic invention. It becomes clear that Tolkien invested at least as much of his expertise, ingenuity, imagination, and time in constructing his languages as he did in devising his narratives.

Tolkien's notes are still being published, mainly in the journals *Vinyar Tengwar* and *Parma Eldalamberon*, and have been subject to much painstaking analysis in both print and online articles (an authoritative overview is Hostetter 2007). The purpose of this chapter is not to attempt to replicate such analyses, but to consider Tolkien's remarkable work of language invention both as a feature of his published works and as a creative activity in itself, and to do so partly in terms of his own exposition of language invention, 'A Secret Vice' (Tolkien 1983, 198–223; henceforth *ASV*), written in around 1931.

Tolkien's languages in their literary context

Readers of *The Lord of the Rings* (*LR*) encounter Tolkien's linguistic creativity in a copious stream of names, words, short utterances, and longer pieces of speech and verse in almost entirely unfamiliar languages. Some words and names are adapted or 'invented' English (see Gilliver, Marshall, and Weiner 2006, and Tolkien 2005), some are borrowed from real-world legends, and some are formed in Elvish or other languages of Middle-earth; non-expert readers can have little idea which are Tolkien's inventions and which are not. Few may realize that *Gandalf* is a name borrowed from Norse legend (*Gandalf* < Old Norse *Gandálfr*, from *gand* 'staff' and *álfr* 'elf'), but that the rather similar place name *Nindalf* is an Elvish compound (from Sindarin Elvish *nîn* 'wet' and *talf* 'flat field'); or that, while the flower names *elanor* and *niphredil* are Elvish, *simbelmynë* 'evermind' comprises Old English elements; or that *mathom* is a 'real' word in a way that *mithril* is not, though both are now in the *Oxford English Dictionary*.

After being presented with two Elvish languages (Quenya, or High-elven, and Sindarin, or Grey-elven) in books I and II (often referred to as a 'trilogy', *The Lord of the Rings* is a continuous novel in six 'books', with the chapters numbered separately in each, a convention followed here), readers may not be able to distinguish them reliably, or know that the language of Rohan introduced in book III is not likewise a pure invention, but an adaptation of Old English, especially as the sounds in words such as *éored* and *méaras* are (not coincidentally) reminiscent of Elvish names such as *Eärendil*.

The Elvish tongues, Tolkien wrote, are intended to be 'specially pleasant': a difficult aim, as he acknowledged, owing to wide differences in 'personal predilections, especially in the phonetic structure of languages' (*Lett.* 144). In 'A Secret Vice' he makes the point (often repeated) that the effectiveness of his invented languages is not readily evaluated against objective criteria, but is 'felt'. However, he also reveals his own subjective criteria, modestly introducing 'at least one language [actually, two] that has in the opinion of, or rather to the feeling of, its constructor reached a highish level both of *beauty in word-form considered abstractly*, and of *ingenuity in the relations of symbol and sense*, not to mention its *elaborate grammatical arrangements*, nor its *hypothetical historical background*' (*ASV* 210; the emphasis is ours).

The 'beauty in word-form considered abstractly' is found in the first non-English utterance encountered by the reader, the greeting *elen síla lúmenn' omentielvo* 'a star shines on the hour of our meeting' (*LR* I. iii). This language, Quenya, is presented mainly in poetic passages displaying its musicality: *Ai! laurië lantar lassi súrinen, Yéni únótimë ve rámar aldaron!* (*LR* II. viii). It is Middle-earth's 'archaic language of lore' ('Elven-latin'), resembling Latin not only in this role but also in its spelling and construction (with an admixture of Finnish and Greek characteristics; see *LR* Appendices E and F, and *Lett.* 144).

Sindarin, the living language of the Elves of Middle-earth, makes its impression differently. Many personal and place names are in Sindarin form, and the reader quickly becomes accustomed to its look and sound, which deliberately recall Welsh (*Lett.* 144, 165, and 347). By the end of the second chapter we have heard of *Eregion, Mordor, Gil-galad, Anduin* 'the Great River', *Ancalagon* (a dragon), and *Orodruin* 'the Fire-mountain'; and the stream of names continues as a constant trickle: *Gildor, Carn Dûm, Angmar, Amon Sûl*, and (*LR* I. xi) the name of a verse form, *ann-thennath*.

The first connected utterance, *Ai na vedui Dúnadan! Mae govannen!* (*LR* I. xi), is untranslated, but evidently includes words of greeting. Later, there are seven lines of a song ('*A Elbereth Gilthoniel*'; *LR* II. i), also untranslated, but providing a good idea of the sound of Sindarin, knottier and more solid than Quenya (... *o menel aglar elenath. Na-chaered palan-díriel* ...). Since most of the names have meanings (some explicitly glossed), the reader comes to recognize many Sindarin word-forming elements. From *Mordor, Gondor*, and *Eriador* we deduce the element *-dor* 'land'; from *Mordor, Moria, Morgul*, and *Morthond* we extrapolate *mor-* 'black'; likewise we can find *mith-* 'grey', *hith-* 'mist', *duin* 'river', *dûn* 'west', *adan* 'man', and others.

These euphonious combinations of simple roots extend the reader's experience from 'beauty of word-form' towards that of 'ingenuity in the relations of symbol and sense'; this is more fully realized in the context of his 'elaborate grammatical arrangements'. In the Quenya greeting quoted above, most readers probably notice that nine English words render four Elvish ones, implying great concentration in its grammar; later, Aragorn's triumphant exclamation *utúvienyes* 'I have found it' (*LR* VI. v) shows that one highly inflected Quenya word can express a whole English sentence. The resemblance of Quenya in this respect to Latin and ancient Greek (for those familiar with them) tends to convey a sense of formality, learnedness, elevation, and nobility.

The contextual aesthetic power of Sindarin lies rather in its terseness, perfectly suiting the scattered short texts such as the inscription on the

Moria Gate, *Ennyn Durin Aran Moria: pedo mellon a minno* ('the doors of Durin, Lord of Moria; speak/say friend and enter'), and Gandalf's spell *Annon edhellen, edro hi ammen! Fennas nogothrim, lasto beth lammen!* (This is untranslated in context, though soon afterwards *edro* is glossed as 'open!'; Christopher Tolkien translates this as 'Elvish gate open now for us; doorway of the Dwarf-folk listen to the word of my tongue' (*HME* VI.463).) Even the average reader is struck by the distinctive way in which Sindarin nouns form their plurals by means of vowel change: *orod* 'mountain', pl. *ered*; *amon* 'hill', pl. *emyn*; *annon* 'gate', pl. *ennyn*; *Dúnadan* 'man of the West', pl. *Dúnedain*. This feature ('umlaut' or 'mutation') closely resembles one of the kinds of plural formation in Welsh (e.g., *carreg* 'stone', pl. *cerrig*) and a similar one found in English (e.g., *woman*, pl. *women*) and German (e.g., *Tochter* 'daughter', pl. *Töchter*).

Tolkien proclaims that the 'hypothetical historical background' of an invented language is 'a necessary thing as a constructor finds in the end, both for the satisfactory construction of the word-form, and for the giving of an illusion of coherence and unity to the whole' (*ASV* 210). Whether all language constructors do find this necessary may be a moot point, but it was central to his own endeavour. In Appendix E of *The Lord of the Rings* (concerned mainly with Tolkien's invented scripts, the cursive *Tengwar* and the runic *Cirth*, which space does not permit us to discuss here) there is detailed discussion of sound changes in the Elvish languages, and the reader is made aware of the (invented) historical relationship between Quenya and Sindarin. Although this relationship was the main focus of Tolkien's attention, the narrative background demanded the development, at least in outline, of several other languages, notably the human language Adûnaic and its derivative Westron; Khuzdul (or Dwarvish); and the Black Speech of Mordor.

Secrecy and hiddenness

In 'A Secret Vice', Tolkien asserts that the secrecy of language invention is accidental, not essential: 'the makers [...] are artists and incomplete without an audience' (*ASV* 202). This aspiration towards an audience for his art is only partly fulfilled in *The Lord of the Rings*. True, he unveils the results of an art long practised in private, to the aesthetic satisfaction of the reader. However, the unveiling is carefully managed within the requirements of the narrative: only some words and utterances are glossed or explained, and the inner workings remain obscure. In the literary context of *The Lord of the Rings* this partial concealment or withholding of information is essential. The reader is in the position of the uninitiated hobbits, picking up the odd word and phrase here and there, and shares their bewilderment and curiosity.

What is shown hints at a great deal more that is unshown (genuinely in the case of Elvish, though only as a literary effect in the case of the less worked-out languages such as Dwarvish and the Black Speech). The piecemeal revelation preserves a sense of distance, ancientness, and mystery, just as does the gradual and partial revealing of the history of the Elder Days. Instructive comparison may be made with 'The Notion Club Papers' (*HME* IX), an unfinished draft in which the legend of the ancient downfall of Númenor is received preternaturally by 20th-century recipients. In a kind of linguistic thriller, the tale emerges as the characters gradually decipher fragments of two languages in which it is described, Elvish and Adûnaic. For the language enthusiast, the phonology and declension system are fascinating; but Tolkien's instinct in abandoning a story so wholly dependent on linguistic investigation was very sound.

Again despite Tolkien's assertion that the language inventor's art needs an audience, he published no detailed explanation, let alone a complete grammar or lexicon, during his lifetime (beyond an analysis of the two major Elvish songs in *The Road Goes Ever On* (1968)). A few correspondents and close associates glimpsed the extent of his efforts—C. S. Lewis, for instance, whose reaction is quoted by George Sayer: ' "Good heavens!" he exclaimed, "he seems to have invented not one but three languages complete with their dialects. He must be the cleverest man in Oxford"' (Pearce 1999, 15). Only more recently has it been possible for the 'audience' to assess and appreciate the breadth and depth of Tolkien's achievement.

The structure of the languages (1): the choice of sounds

The phonetic inventory of Tolkien's principal invented languages is little different from that of English and the major European languages with which he was familiar. Perhaps the most important difference is the absence of schwa (the indeterminate *uh*-sound of the first vowel in *again*), which in English is correlated with low stress and has the effect of dulling or darkening the palette of vocalism. The consonant inventory of Elvish is similar to that of English, though reduced by the exclusion of *z* and the palato-velars (*ch* as in *cheese*, *j* as in *judge*, *sh* as in *shop*, and the '*zh*' of *measure* or *rouge*) from both Quenya and Sindarin, and *th* (as in *thing*), and '*dh*' (as in *this*) from Quenya. (This analysis is based on the languages as published in 1954–5, not on their earlier forms, which are discussed below in 'Elvish before *The Lord of the Rings*').

It would have been easy to produce a distinctive effect by using a different set of phonemes (as in Klingon), but Tolkien had an aesthetic intent, and clearly preferred familiar rather than alien phonemes. What Tolkien did to give his languages a distinctive sound was to use different rules of phonotactics, that is, the position and combination in which sounds are permitted to stand. He makes this point himself: 'the absence of alien elements is not of first-class importance; a very alien word-form could be constructed out of purely English elements; since it is as much in habitual sequences and combinations as in individual 'phonemes' or sound-units that a language, or a language-maker, achieves individuality' (*ASV* 208). He illustrates the point by reversing *scratch* phonemically, forming a word *štærks* [ʃtærks] with all English phonemes but utterly alien shape.

Quenya, then, resembles Latin, with the restriction of some sound sequences and the addition of others. Its syllabic structure generally favours open syllables; closed ones mainly occur medially under stress, but otherwise long vowels and diphthongs are prominent. This is accentuated by having vowels and diphthongs occur in tandem (e.g., *oiolosseo*). The consonant inventory is slanted towards continuants (*f, v, s, h, y, w, l, r, m, n*). Voiced stops (*b, d, g*) are severely restricted to places where they close off nasals and continuants (*imbe, alda, ando*); continuants frequently occupy syllable-initial position. Voiceless stops (*p, t, c*) mainly occur in this position; their distribution tends to add lightness. Consonants with dental articulation predominate (*t, s, r, l, n*, especially the last three), and provide all word-final consonants. The semivowels *y* and *w* frequently occur after other consonants (*elye, vanwa*), *qu* being especially frequent, producing an effect of fluidity and softness; apart from these, consonant combinations do not occur initially.

Sindarin has Welsh-like sounds, but without the prevalent schwa (represented in Welsh by *y*) and with a more restricted set of consonant clusters. Closed syllables are usual and word-final consonants are frequent (notably *th, f, d*, and *s*). Voiced plosives are common in initial, medial, and final position (e.g., *gil-, aglar, -díriel, -chaered*). There is a larger set of fricatives than in Quenya (*th, dh, ch* as in *loch* not *cheese*) and the voiceless *lh* (comparable to Welsh *ll*). Consonants combine with the semivowel *w*, but rarely with the *y*-sound (spelt *i* in Sindarin). The overall effect is slightly harsher and heavier, more consonantal. However, Sindarin shares with Quenya the predominance of liquids and nasals (e.g., *Fanuilos, le linnathon*), the concatenation of vowels (*aearon*), and the dactylic shape of many words (e.g., *Elbereth*; compare, say, Quenya *Valimar*).

The Elvish tongues were intended to be 'of a European kind in style and structure' (*Lett.* 144). By contrast, Khuzdul (Dwarvish) and Adûnaic are Semitic in inspiration and Near Eastern in appearance. Tolkien acknowledged the Semitic inspiration of Dwarvish in an interview conducted by Denys Gueroult for the BBC, 20 January 1965. It might have been guessed from the apparent triliteral consonant stem KH-Z-D in *Khazâd* 'Dwarves' and *Khuzdul* 'Dwarvish' (*LR* App. E and F); this triliteral structure, typical of Semitic languages such as Hebrew and Arabic, is made explicit in *HME*. Into Khuzdul and Adûnaic, Tolkien introduced sounds more harsh to the ear of the Anglophone (though still familiar sounds in English): palatals such as *sh*, and the aspirated consonant *kh* (as in English 'ba*ckh*and'; e.g., Dwarvish *khazâd*, Adûnaic *Ar-Adûnakhôr*), and a frequent use of *z*. The 'alien' harshness is emphasized by the use of *k* in spelling, rather than the *c* typical of Latin, Welsh, and (later forms of) Elvish.

The converse to the 'specially pleasant' sounds of Elvish is displayed in the few fragments we have of the Black Speech of Mordor (e.g., *ash nazg thrakatulûk agh burzum-ishi krimpatul*, from the ring-inscription: *LR* II. ii) and of Orkish speech derived from it (e.g., *Uglúk u bagronk sha pushdug Saruman-glob búbhosh skai*: *LR* III. iii). We deduce the kinds of sound that Tolkien regarded as ugly—guttural and palatal consonants, including the un-English 'back spirant' *gh* (as in *ghâsh* 'fire')—noting also the absence of the 'clear' vowel *e*. The absence of *e* from these 'evil' tongues may be significant, since two words central to the mythos contain this vowel: *Eä*, the divine word of creation which became the name of all that is created (*Silmarillion* 20), and the legendary exclamation *ele!* 'behold' of the Elves on first waking and seeing the stars (*Silmarillion* 358).

The structure of the languages (2): grammar and accidence

The language inventor, says Tolkien, can 'consider the categories and the relations of words, and the various neat, effective, or ingenious ways in which these can be expressed. In this case you may often devise new and novel, even admirable and effective machinery' (*ASV* 212): he recounts overhearing a fellow soldier, during a tedious lecture, dreamily deciding to express the accusative case by a prefix (*ASV* 199).

The grammatical system of the Elvish languages is not so dissimilar from European models, but most connoisseurs of grammar would grant that their machinery is both admirable and effective.

Quenya, like Latin, Greek, and Finnish, is a highly inflected language. Nouns take a number of different endings to express relationships that in English require prepositions: e.g., *Endore-nna* 'to Middle-earth' (*ACO*; abbreviations in the following discussion refer to the Elvish texts, to which there is a key at the end of the chapter), with the ending expressing movement (on)to. Other inflected nouns include *súri-nen* 'wind-in', *alda-r-on* 'trees-of', *miruvóre-va* 'nectar-of', *ya-ssen* 'which-in', *líri-nen* 'voice-in', *ni-n* 'me-for', and *Oiolossë-o* 'Everwhite-from' (all from *N*). These are not unlike those of European inflected languages, except that they can be nested between other suffixes, as in *falma-li-nna-r* 'foaming-waves-many-upon (plural)': an original touch.

Suffixes can also be used to denote pronouns in various ingenious ways. A suffix expresses the pronominal subject (the 'person') of the inflected verb (corresponding to 'I, you, they', etc.), as in Latin and the Romance languages: e.g., *utúlie-n* 'I am come' (*ACO*), *hiruva-lye* 'you shall find' (*N*); separate pronouns are also used, mainly for emphasis: *nai elye hiruva* 'maybe you shall find' (*N*). In the second person singular there is a distinction between formal and intimate use (compare French *tu–vous*, German *du–Sie*). Suffixes are also often used for a third-person pronominal object, e.g., *utúvienye-s* 'I have found it', *tiruvante-s* 'they shall keep it' (*OC*), *laituvalme-t* 'we shall bless them' (*FC*); this is reminiscent of structures in Italian (e.g., *tienitelo* 'keep it for yourself').

Again, separate pronouns are also found, as in *laita te* 'bless them' (*FC*). Possessive pronouns (corresponding to 'my, your, their', etc.) are expressed as suffixes to nouns, following prepositional inflections, e.g., *atari-nya* 'father-my' (*LRS*), *hildi-nya-r* 'heir-my-(plural)' (*ACO*), *óma-ry-o* 'voice-her-of' (*N*), *tie-lya-nna* 'path-your-on' (*GFT*). This feature occurs in Finnish (where, however, the inflection precedes the possessive: *tie-llä-si* 'way-on-thy') and Semitic languages (e.g., the name *Malachi*, Hebrew *mal'āk̲-ī* 'messenger-my') but not in Latin or any major western European language. Another unusual resemblance to Finnish is the lack of gender distinction; not only do Quenya and Sindarin nouns lack the kind of arbitrary gender seen in Latin and Greek (and French and German), but the pronouns do not distinguish natural gender as English does with 'he' and 'she'.

Besides the usual distinction of singular and plural, there is a third option for speaking of two people, the dual. The dual in Elvish nouns, e.g., *má-rya-t* 'hand-her-two' (*N*), *Ald-u* 'the Two Trees' (Sindarin *Galadhad*), is paralleled in the verb system in first, second, and third persons, so that one can say 'the two of us', 'the two of you', or 'the two of them went'. Ancient Indo-European languages had a dual, which survived in ancient Greek and Gothic; Old English had vestigial dual pronouns *wit* 'we two' and *git* 'you two'. Elvish also distinguishes a 'partitive' and a general or 'collective' plural (see *Lett.* 144, where the example given is Sindarin *orch* 'orc', *yrch* 'some orcs', *orchoth* 'orcs collectively').

In Quenya there is also, in the first person plural ('we'), a distinction between 'inclusive' use, whereby the speaker includes the person addressed, and 'exclusive' use, whereby only the speaker and anyone he speaks for are included: e.g., *laituva-lme-t* 'we (exclusive) shall bless them' (*FC*), *omentielvo = omentie -lv(a) -o* 'of our (inclusive) meeting'. This is an especially original idea: no European language outside the Caucasus makes this distinction grammatically. The dual also distinguishes inclusive and exclusive use, so that there are in all four different ways of saying 'we': 'you others and I', 'they and I but not you', 'you and I', and 'he or she and I'. (In the first edition of *The Lord of the Rings*, the reading was *omentielmo*, because at the time *-lma* was the first person plural inclusive. In later editions it was changed to *omentielvo*, because the ending *-lma* was transferred to the first person plural exclusive and *-lva* became the new inclusive (see notes to *Lett.* 205). Tolkien similarly tinkered with Elvish words elsewhere: e.g., *vanimalda* > *vanimelda* (*LR* ii. vi); *vánier* > *avánier* (*LR* ii. viii; see Hammond and Scull 2005, 310 and 341).)

The ingenuity of grammatical categories is accompanied by a modesty of innovation in the sounds used to express them. On the whole, sounds (like *n*, *m*, *r*, *s*, *t*) familiar from Latin, Greek, etc. are employed, though Tolkien cleverly introduces *l* into the system, partly in second person and plural suffixes (as shown above), and also for participles, e.g., in Sindarin *-thoniel* 'kindling', *tíriel* 'having watched' (*EG*).

One of Tolkien's predominant linguistic tastes is for the use of nasal consonants as exponents of grammatical functions. In Elvish, nasal infixion is a frequent means of forming derivatives from roots. So the root LAB- gives in Quenya both *lavin* 'I lick' and *lambe* 'tongue'. It is also used in past tense formation: hence in Sindarin from the root of *dagor* 'battle' comes *dangen* 'slain'. (The reverse pattern appears in Indo-European, and survives vestigially in English: present tense *stand* beside past tense *stood.*) In this context irregularities in conjugation can arise as a result of regular sound changes, just as in real world languages: the past of Quenya *rer-* 'to sow' is *rendë*. The root was originally *red-*: postvocalic *d* regularly became *r* but remained when 'protected' by preceding *n*.

Nasal infixion is also a feature of Adûnaic, and in Lowdham's 'Report' (*HME* IX. 418) it is used as part of an entirely authentic-sounding piece of philological argument. It is posited that there was once a set of palatal consonants in Adûnaic which in the surviving language have become *s*, *z*, etc. One of the grounds for this is that nasal infixion only occurs before stop consonants and not usually before *z*, but it does occur before *z* in a few words. The argument runs that if these words had originally contained a palatal stop they would have been regular.

In Sindarin the loss of final vowels (as in Welsh and English) limits the occurrence of inflectional suffixes. Verbal endings are 'solider' than in Quenya (compare past tense *teithant* (*MGI*) with *ortane* (*N*)), and there are separate possessive pronouns rather than suffixes (*ionnath dîn* 'his sons', *KL*). Sindarin grammar relies heavily on initial consonant mutation in the grammatical relationships of words. This resembles a similar feature of Welsh, and has the same historical causation: the radical sound changes that affected consonants after vowels *inside* a word also affected them *between* closely linked words. We can only give a flavour of the system here. The definite article *i* is a regular cause of it: so *i pheriain* 'the Halflings' (*FC*) (*periain* 'Halflings'), *i-ngaurhoth* 'the werewolf host' (*WS*) (*gaur* 'werewolf'), *i thiw hin* 'these letters' (*MGI*) (*tîw* 'letters'), *Narn i-chîn Húrin* 'tale of the children of Húrin' (*hîn* 'children'), *Firn-i-Guinar* 'the dead that live' (*Silmarillion* 188) (*cuinar* 'they live'). Mutation also affects a noun which is the object of a verb, as in *lasto beth lammen* 'hear the words of my tongue' (*MGC*) (*peth* 'words'), and a postmodifying adjective, as in *Pinnath Gelin* 'Green Ridges' (*Silmarillion* 356) (*calen* 'green').

Besides the suffixes there is a well-developed system of prefixes. There are conventional prepositional ones like *un-* 'down', *et-* 'out', *en-* 'again' (compare English *re-*), *ter-* 'through' (compare *per-* in English words). There are more idiosyncratic ones, such as (in Quenya) the prefix *an-* marking the superlative (e.g., *ancalima* 'most beautiful'), the prefix *lin-* indicating 'many' (e.g., *lintyulussea* 'having many poplars', *HME* V. 369), and (in Sindarin) the privative prefix *ar-* (e.g., *arnoediad* 'without reckoning') and the collective prefix *go-* (as in *Legolas* from *laeg* 'green' + *golass* 'collection of leaves', from *lass-* 'leaf'). There are vocalic intensive prefixes which match the base vowel, so *Ithil, Isil* 'Moon' from *i-* + THIL-/SIL- 'shine silver', *Anor, Anar* 'Sun' from *a-* + NAR- 'flame'. In Quenya the perfect tense takes an 'augment', a prefix similarly matching the base vowel, the latter being lengthened, as in *avánier, utúlien*. This somewhat resembles the formation of past and perfect tenses in Greek, but is simpler and more elegant.

Tolkien's endless capacity for ingenious yet authentic-seeming grammatical categories is also seen in his arrangements for the dual number in Adûnaic nouns (*HME* IX. 428), used not only for nouns that come in regular pairs (e.g., *huznat* '(a person's) ears' from *huzun* 'ear') but also for contrasted ones (e.g., 'sun (*ūrē*) and moon (*nílō*)'): 'If the two objects are sufficiently different to have separate names, then either (a) the two stems can be compounded and the dual inflexion added at the end; or occasionally (b) one only of the stems is used, the other being understood, or added separately in the singular. Thus for "sun and moon" are found *ūriyat*, *ūriníl(uw)at*, and *ūriyat nílō*.'

Roots and the making of words

Working on the basis that his Elvish languages had a (fictional) historical development, Tolkien devised several hundred invented roots for them (there are roughly 600 in the 'Etymologies' published in *HME* V). They are mostly quite simple, the majority having the forms (C) VC, (C)VCV, or (C)VCVC (where C = consonant, V = vowel): e.g., AD-, BAD-, AWA-, LONO-, OLOS-, SALAP- (there are some more complex, such as (C)VCC(C)V in EKTE-, LINKWI-). From these relatively bland bases, he generated large numbers of derivatives and compounds, distributed unevenly (and therefore realistically) amongst the offspring languages.

Many of the roots appear repeatedly in the names and texts in *The Lord of the Rings* and *The Silmarillion*. For example, ORO- 'up, rise, high' appears in Quenya *oromardi* 'high halls', *ortane* 'lifted up' (*N*) and Sindarin *orod* 'mountain', *orn* 'tree'; NDU- 'go down, sink, set' underlies Quenya *Andúne* 'West', *nu* 'under', *unduláve* 'drowned' (literally 'down-licked'), *un-túpa* 'covers' (literally 'down-roofs') (*N*), and Quenya *númen*, Sindarin *annûn* 'west'; MBAR- 'dwell, inhabit' appears in Quenya *oromardi* 'high halls' (*N*) and *maruvan* 'I will abide', *ambarmetta* 'the world's end' (*ACO*), and *termaruva* 'will endure' (*OC*); ERE- 'be alone' gives Quenya *Eru* 'the One, the Creator', *eresse* 'solitude', whence *eressea* 'lonely', as in *Tol Eressëa* 'the Lonely Isle'; also Sindarin *ereb* 'isolated', as in *Erebor* 'the Lonely Mountain'. (Verlyn Flieger (1983, 49) notes the resemblance to Indo-European ER- 'set in motion' and Primitive Germanic AR- 'be, exist'.)

Christopher Tolkien describes the author as devising forms 'from within the historical structure, proceeding from the "bases" or primitive stems, adding suffix or prefix or forming compounds' and 'following through the regular changes of form that it would thus have undergone' (*HME* V. 348). As Tolkien himself puts it: 'you can posit certain tendencies of development and see what sort of form this will produce' (*ASV* 211). For example, given the root word for 'swan', **alkwâ* (> Quenya *alqua*), a corresponding Sindarin form *alph* is generated by the following sound changes: (1) primitive *kw* becomes *p* (**alkwâ* > **alpa*); (2) after a sonorant (e.g., *l*), *-p-* becomes *-ph-* (**alpa* > **alpha*); (3) final unstressed vowels are lost (**alpha* > *alph*). In other cases, a range of other, less regular tendencies may apply, such as metathesis (two sounds changing places, as in Quenya *alcare* 'radiance', Sindarin *aglar* 'glory'). The ingenuity consists in two things: choosing a very basic meaning for the root so as to envisage the semantic differentiations that would arise in the course of the root's development; and the deployment of a convincing range of formative affixes and combinations by which this differentiation would be carried through.

However, it is clear that Tolkien often actually worked in the opposite direction: you can 'construct a pseudo-historical background and deduce the form you have actually decided on from an antecedent and different form' (*ASV* 211); that is, choose a word-form you like, and fabricate its roots by running the 'tendencies of development' backwards. Tolkien's strong sense of 'the beauty of word-form' frequently led him to select sound-combinations for euphony (occasionally words or names in existing languages) and then provide them with an etymological rationalization. For example, the name of *Rohan* in Brittany appealed to him, and fortuitously could be etymologized as a compound of pre-existing Elvish elements, a root meaning 'horse' and a suffix meaning 'land' (*Lett.* 297). A key instance is the name *Eärendil*, which he adapted from the Old English name *Éarendel*, of uncertain meaning, subsequently reanalysing it as *Eäre + ndil* and generating the two roots **AYAR* 'sea' and **(N)DIL* 'to love'.

The pleasures of Elvish philology

Because Tolkien constructed his Elvish language family using the pattern of real-world language change, it is possible for the investigation of Elvish to create the same intellectual and aesthetic pleasure that can be found in real-world philology, delighting in the relations and histories of words. Even the non-linguist can derive a pleasurable satisfaction from deducing the relationship of similar names; but Tolkien has set up a whole world of connections hidden beneath dissimilar words and names. The apprehension of these complex relationships—discovering the relation of an obscure word to another element in the same or another language, or uncovering the transformative effect of a series of sound changes—is a source of fascination whether the context is Elvish or English etymology.

To take an example: two Middle-earth place names, *Ephel Duath* 'Outer Fence of Shadow' and *Ethir Anduin* 'Outflow of Anduin', contain a disguised prefix *et-* meaning 'forth, out, away', seen as a preposition in Quenya *et Earello* 'out of the sea' (*ACO*). *Ephel* is *et* + *pel-* 'fence' (as in *Pelennor* 'fenced land'), with *t* assimilated to the following *p*, and *pp* becoming *ph*; *ethir* is *et* + *sîr* 'river, stream' (as in *Sirannon* 'gate-stream') with *-ts-* becoming *-th-*. The second element of *Mitheithel* '(the River) Hoarwell' contains the same element, being ultimately from *et-kel* 'out-flow' with transposition of consonants (**ektel*). These comparisons demonstrate several of the characteristic sound changes of Sindarin, specifically the origin of voiceless fricatives (*ph*, *th*, *ch*) between vowels and the tendency of *-s-* to weaken to a breathing in that position.

A more original complexity is illustrated in two sets of initial consonants in Sindarin and Quenya: (1) S *Balan* 'Power', Q *Vala*; S *dú* 'night', Q *lómë*; S *galadh* 'tree', Q *alda*; (2) S *bar* 'dwelling' (in *Bar-en-Danwedh*), Q *mar* (in *Eldamar*); S *dûn* 'west', Q *númen*; S *Golodh* 'Gnome', Q *Ngoldo*. In set (1) Sindarin *b-*, *d-*, *g-* = Quenya *v-*, *l-*, zero, while in set (2) Sindarin *b-*, *d-*, *g-* = Quenya *m-*, *n-*, *ng-*. Why? Because

Tolkien arranges that in Primitive Elvish, there are two initial consonantal series, (1) /b/, /d/, /g/, and (2) /mb/, /nd/, /ng/; they produce the same outcomes in Sindarin, but quite different ones in Quenya. Series 1 is unsurprising, but series 2 has no parallel in any well-known European language, and rather resembles a feature in some African languages (compare *mbira*, *Ndebele*, *ngege*). The divergent development in each language is equally ingenious: Sindarin has 'strong' voiced initial consonants in both cases; Quenya 'softens' the first series into fricatives (and zero) and the second into nasals. (In origin, we may surmise, the causation may have run the other way: having produced Sindarin words related to Quenya cognates in either of two ways, Tolkien was obliged to exercise his ingenuity in finding an explanation after the fact.)

Since few people study classical or even modern languages in depth nowadays, very few have had the chance to discover such philological pleasure; but of those who have, many were introduced to it through Tolkien's languages.

Elvish before The Lord of the Rings

When anyone wrote to ask Tolkien a question about Middle-earth, he seemed often to have had the answer already, rather than inventing it *ad hoc*. Certainly he was able to provide one correspondent with pre-existing etymologies of *Elrond*, *Elros*, *Elrohir*, *Elladan*, and *Legolas*, alluding to both 'Primitive Elvish' and Elvish 'dialect' (*Lett.* 211). With the publication of *HME* and other material, the extent of this linguistic background became apparent, and the etymological relationship between Quenya, Sindarin, and various ancestral and related languages came fully into the light.

However, a hitherto unknown aspect of their development also emerged. Besides having made-up histories of internal change, the form of the languages and their relationships had undergone substantial alterations over the many years that Tolkien worked on them.

The earliest 'lexicons' of Qenya and Gnomish date from 1915 and 1917 respectively (*HME* I. 246–7). These language names themselves say something about the relations among Tolkien's Elvish languages and their development. Tolkien used *q* without *u* for the sequence *kw* until the late 1930s, perhaps on the model of the scholarly transcription of Gothic which similarly uses *q*. For many years he used the name *Gnome* for the second of the three great Elf kindreds, the Noldor, around whom much of the legendarium revolves. The Gnomes' own name for their language was originally *Goldogrin* (later *Noldorin*).

Quenya and Sindarin are later versions of Qenya and Gnomish. Sindarin developed from Gnomish/Noldorin, even though, by the time of *The Lord of the Rings*, Tolkien had transferred it from the Gnomes, or Noldor, to the Grey-elves, or Sindar (see Gilson (2000)). Quenya and Sindarin, as they eventually appeared in the works pre-pared for publication in the 1950s, are radically different from their earlier versions, having reached a final form sometimes only in the course of proof correction. This, of course, could not subsequently be altered (or, at least, not much altered).

An example appears in the *Oilima Markirya* 'The Last Ark', a short verse presented in 'A Secret Vice' and apparently reflecting Qenya as it was in about 1930. In the endnotes Christopher Tolkien prints a later version, dating from the last decade of his father's life. As he points out, the two have exactly the same meaning in English, but radically differ-ent vocabulary: compare (from the earlier text) *Aira móre ala tinwi lante no lanta-mindon* 'the old darkness beyond the stars falling upon fallen towers'; (from the later) *enwina lúme elenillor pella talta-taltala atalantië mindoninnar*. Over the years Tolkien altered the form of words and grammar to suit shifts in his taste, creating an additional layer of complexity in the linguistic material, to which no summary can do justice. In this regard, Qenya/Quenya notably contrasts with the Orkish curse (*LR* III. iii), in which the sounds remained fixed as Tolkien changed his mind about their meaning (Hammond and Scull 2005, 377), the phonetic effect being primary and the sense incidental.

It seems that the early complexities of the Elvish language family were greater than they became later. No notes giving a phonological and grammatical description of the languages survive from the earliest period, but their structure and relationship is already very sophisticated (*HME* I. 246–7). Later, in the 'Etymologies' (*HME* V), dating from the late 1930s, Qenya and Noldorin (successor to 'Gnomish') predominate, but forms from the cognate languages Danian, Doriathrin, Ilkorin, and Telerin are not infrequently cited as well. The sound laws, and to some extent the grammatical and lexical changes, by which each of these languages had become differentiated are worked out to the last detail. For example, in the early 'lexicons' of 1915–17 (*HME* I), for 'swan' the Qenya lexicon has *alqa*, and the Gnomish lexicon has *alcwi* (with the Qenya word given there as *alqë*); later, the Gnomish form *alcwi* was changed to *alfa*, explained as derived from an original *alchwa*. In the 'Etymologies' two decades later, 'swan' is given as Qenya *alqa*, Old Noldorin *alpha*, Noldorin *alf*, Telerin *alpa*, Ilkorin *alch*, and Danian *ealc*, all from Primitive Qendian **alkwâ*.

Both the internal phonology of the languages and the sound-laws governing their relationship changed noticeably. Gnomish seems sometimes, though not always, to show initial *b-*, *d-*, *g-* for Quenya *p-*, *t-*, *k-* (*Palurin, Belaurin; Taniquetil, Danigwethil; kópa, gobos*). Sound combinations which do not occur in later Sindarin are found in early Gnomish, such as *-bb-* (*Habbanan*), *-cth-* (*mactha*), *-vn-* (*Uduvna*), *-vw-* (*mavwin*), and notably *cw-* (as in *cwed-* 'say'), which in later Sindarin is always represented by *p-*, replicating a sound change that occurred early in the history of Welsh.

The sources of invented vocabulary

Where did all of Tolkien's words come from? Whether he invented a root and then derived a word-form, or chose a word-form and 'reverse-engineered' the root, he had to select a phonetic combination which satisfied his linguistic taste. In principle, invented words could be derived directly from those of another language or language group, according to more or less systematic rules (as in auxiliary languages based on simplified Latin, or an early invention of Tolkien's called Gautisk based on the methodical application of phonological and other rules to a Germanic base); but clearly this was not how Tolkien's later languages were formed.

At the other extreme, vocabulary could be generated quite randomly from any sound combinations that enter one's mind. Tolkien explicitly dismissed this more than once, and in 'The Notion Club Papers' Lowdham is clearly stating the author's view: 'Say you want a word for *sky*. Well, call it *jibberjabber*, or anything else that comes into your head without the exercise of any linguistic taste or art. But that's code-making, not language-building. It is quite another matter to find a relationship, sound plus sense, that satisfies' (*HME* IX. 239–40; see also *Lett.* 294). Tolkien's method lies somewhere between. Most of his primary lexis has no systematic relationship to words in existing languages, but it frequently bears some relationship of resemblance or reminiscence to them.

Tolkien knew that such oblique relationships were inevitable, and claimed to have made little or no effort to avoid them (*Lett.* 297). As he wrote, even a seemingly random 'vocal noise', with no intrinsic meaning, must arise from the inventor's own linguistic resources, and will have 'innumerable threads of connexion with other similar-sounding "words"' (*Lett.* 294; he also referred to 'a "leaf-mould" of memories': *Lett.* 324). Meaning is then given to it by the mind of the inventor, and Tolkien here invokes a subjective criterion that he calls 'phonetic fitness'. His acquaintance with European languages was extensive, so the resources he brought to word-invention were rich, and even quite strong resemblances arose (he would claim) not from deliberate intention, but simply from a strong sense of 'phonetic fitness' created by appeal of the word-form and its partly unconscious associations. This we will explore further later.

The resulting resemblances to real-world elements vary widely. At one end of the scale stand a large number of words that seem faintly or obliquely to echo words in real languages, but are certainly not direct borrowings. At the other end stand a relatively small number of items that appear to bear an intentional relationship to existing words.

In considering what Tolkien's intention might have been, we must explore Tolkien's motivation for inventing languages at all.

Why Tolkien invented languages

Tolkien was a linguist of a rare and exceptional kind, combining a great facility for learning and fluently using languages with that deep understanding of the inner historical development and relationships of languages which belongs to the philologist or comparative linguist. A Roman Catholic upbringing and classical education gave him an almost native facility in Latin, and enough proficiency in Greek for him to read Classics at Oxford (before switching to English). As a schoolboy he learnt Old English (Anglo-Saxon), which he later taught at Oxford, and taught himself Gothic, the oldest surviving Germanic language. He found in Gothic 'not only modern historical philology, which appealed to the historical and scientific side, but for the first time the study of a language out of mere love: I mean for the acute aesthetic pleasure derived for a language for its own sake, not only free from being useful but free even from being the "vehicle of a literature" ' (*Lett.* 163).

Unlike many scholars he could express himself in these languages— Humphrey Carpenter (1977, 48) recounts that as a schoolboy he was capable of speaking fluently in Latin, Greek, Anglo-Saxon, and Gothic —writing Gothic inscriptions in books (*Lett.* 272) and producing a short poem in it for *Songs of the Philologists* (1936), and composing parts of his legendarium in Old English (see *HME* IV. 281ff., 337ff.).

He had a comparable degree of facility in Old Icelandic, and at least a considerable reading ability in numerous other languages, including, but not confined to, those of the Germanic, Celtic, and Romance families.

For Tolkien, the shape of languages was a source of intense aesthetic pleasure: 'It has always been with me: the sensibility to linguistic pattern which affects me emotionally like colour or music' (*Lett.* 163). In particular, his rapturous encounters with Welsh and Finnish have often been commented on by himself (most notably in *Lett.* 163) and others. Though as a child he contributed to a cousin's code-language ('Nevbosh'), he was not interested in the utilitarian function of communication so much as 'the fitting of notion to oral symbol, and *pleasure in the new relation established*' (*ASV* 206). Enchanted by the shape of Spanish, he embarked on 'Naffarin', his first serious foray into coherent language creation (Carpenter 1977, 37; *ASV* 209). Then, frustrated by the limited surviving corpus of Gothic vocabulary, he extended it by inventing words which he inferred, according to Germanic sound-laws, from the cognate languages, and went on to devise an invented Germanic language called Gautisk (Carpenter 1977, 37; Garth 2003, 60).

It was as if his delight in learning new languages was so effusive that it required unknown ones to be called into existence. 'In these invented languages the pleasure is more keen than it can be even in learning a new language ... because more personal and fresh, more open to experiment of trial and error' (*ASV* 206). He regarded language invention as both instinctive and rational, and as an art form that engaged him very deeply, more so than either literature (it predated his juvenile writing) or drawing and painting (in which he too modestly disclaimed ability).

Invented languages and mythology

The crucial element that was to lead to the burgeoning of Tolkien's creativity, and to become a cardinal and remarkable feature of his linguistic work, was the interaction and interdependence of language and mythology (or imaginary history: *Lett*. 294). In his last years at school, Tolkien came across the legends of the Finnish *Kalevala* in English translation, and his enthusiasm was renewed at Oxford, where he found a grammar of the language.

At some point, inspired by this discovery, he abandoned Gautisk and embarked on the language which was to become Quenya. John Garth writes, 'At some point as 1915 came in, Tolkien took an exercise book, in which he had apparently been outlining aspects of Gautisk, and struck out his old notes, ready to make a fresh beginning' (Garth 2003, 60). Christopher Tolkien indeed dates the Qenya Lexicon to 1915 (*HME* I. 246), the year of Tolkien's final examinations and beginning of military training; but this material shows 'an already extremely sophisticated and phonetically intricate historical structure' (*HME* I. 247), and Humphrey Carpenter implies that this had been in development from as early as 1912–13 (Carpenter 1977, 59 and 75–6). Tolkien himself recalls that his interests in language construction and legends 'began to flow together when I was an undergraduate to the despair of my tutors and near-wrecking of my career' (*Lett*. 257).

And as the meeting of the two linguistic systems, German and Finnish, seems to have sparked off the invention of a new and original language family, the concurrence of Finnish and Germanic legends began to brew in his mind a new and original mythology. During the autumn of 1914 he was immersed in the *Kalevala*, giving a lecture on it (Garth 2003, 52) and writing a version of the legend of Kullervo in the style of William Morris's romances (Garth 2003, 26). He was also deeply engaged with Old English poetry, and in the late summer of the same year had written a poem, 'The Voyage of Éarendel', introducing a central figure of what was to become his legendarium.

Then in July 1915 he wrote 'The Shores of Faëry', and 'for the first time outside the Qenya lexicon, essential and permanent features of the legendarium are named' (Garth 2003, 83): *Taniquetil*, *Valinor*, and *Eglamar*, names containing Qenya elements. 'A name comes first and the story follows,' he wrote (*Lett.* 165); but since almost every name has a meaning, an etymology must also follow. Tolkien's myth-making and his language-making had reached the critical point of fusion: 'I made the discovery that "legends" depend on the language to which they belong; but a living language depends equally on the "legends" which it conveys by tradition' (*Lett.* 180). As languages and tales developed, they became deeply entwined, as each was extended and adapted to accommodate new elements in the other. (In the same letter, written in 1956, he quipped that Esperanto, Novial, and other artificial languages were dead because their authors invented no legends, though in an article published in *The British Esperantist* in 1932 he had been complimentary about the 'individuality, coherence and beauty' of Esperanto.)

Intentional links with real-world languages

In the original form of the legendarium, two decades or more before work on *The Lord of the Rings* began, there was a direct link between the mythical world of the Elves and the history of the real world: Tol Eressëa, the Lonely Isle, was ancient Britain, the town of Warwick stood on the site of Kortirion, the city of the Elves in exile, and an Anglo-Saxon mariner might stumble upon the shores of Faëry. Even as late as 'The Notion Club Papers' (on which Tolkien ceased work in order to complete *The Lord of the Rings*), texts relating to Númenor appear in Old English, purporting to have 'come through' to a writer in Anglo-Saxon times (*HME* V. 238–82).

Resemblances between words and roots in Elvish and in European (especially Germanic) languages can therefore have a clear mythopoeic motivation, since Europeans are supposed to have had contact with the Elves before they vanished westwards, and retained words and names in their legends which have 'real' origins in Elvish. As is made clear in *The History of Middle-earth* (and well summarized by John Garth): 'Tolkien meant Qenya to be a language that the illiterate peoples of pre-Christian Europe had heard, and had borrowed from, when they were singing their unrecorded epics' (Garth 2003, 98).

The prime example of this stratum of resemblance is the name of Eärendil the mariner, adapted from Old English *Earendel*: others include the name of his ship *Wingelot* or *Wingelóte* 'foam-flower' (in the 'Etymologies'; Noldorin *Gwingloth*), derived from—or, supposedly, giving rise to—Middle English *Guingelot*, the boat of the giant Wade; and *Atalantë* 'Downfallen', a name for Númenor, echoing *Atlantis*. It is not easy to interpret the footnote to *Lett.* 257, in which Tolkien calls it 'a curious chance' that Quenya *atalantie* ('downfall', from Elvish root TALAT 'slip, fall down') 'should so much resemble Atlantis'. Perhaps Tolkien was becoming ambivalent about the real-world links of his earliest legends. See 'Elvish after *The Lord of the Rings*' below.

Further compelling examples include *Avallon*, *Avallónë*, a haven in Tol Eressëa ('for it is of all cities the nearest to Valinor', *HME* V. 29), echoing *Avalon*; and Qenya *Íwerin* or *Íverind-* 'Ireland', comparable to Greek *I(w)erne*, Welsh *Iwerddon*. Some early names may have been dropped as having unsuitable associations: e.g., *Eglamar*, recalling Sir *Eglamour* of Middle English romance (and the poet *Eglamor* of Browning's *Sordello*)—though *Gil-Galad*: *Galahad* was perhaps apt enough to remain. A particularly striking example is the name of the city of *Kôr*, after which *Kortirion* was named by the Exiles. Tolkien's 'Notebook C' (*HME* II. 291–2) states that the actual Welsh place name *Caergwâr* and its English equivalent *Warwick* are derived from Gnomish *Gwâr*, the equivalent of Qenya *Kôr*. That this was the city of an elf-king named *Ingil* may hint at an embryonic 'alternative' etymology for *England*.

In his early notebooks, Tolkien mentions various distinct branches of the Ilkorin languages used by Elves in Britain, north-western Europe, and southern and eastern Europe. Tolkien perhaps imagined early Germanic languages being influenced by these Elvish dialects (see Helios de Rosario Martinez (2008)). For example, the word for 'man' in the Danian dialect takes the form *beorn*; not only is this identical to an Old English word (the source of the name of Beorn in *The Hobbit*), but its derivation incorporates a sound change characteristic of Old English ('breaking', by which *e* and *a* become *eo* and *ea*: as also in Primitive Elvish **alkwa* > Danian *ealc* 'swan'). This might imply that Old English phonology was 'actually' influenced by Danian. Other Elvish dialects show features similar to those of other specific Germanic languages.

Some echoes of early English forms found in the Qenya and Gnomish lexicons are described by Christopher Tolkien as 'obviously not fortuitous' (*HME* I. 248): *hôr* 'old' (Old English *hār*), HERE 'rule' (Old English *hearra* 'lord'), *rûm* 'secret (whisper)' (Old English *rūn*). Further resemblances to early English in particular and to Germanic in general might be cited, of which the following are typical: Qenya *autë* 'prosperity' (*HME* II. 336), compare the Germanic root *auð-* 'riches'; Qenya *maiwe* gull (*HME* V. 373), compare Old English *mæw* 'gull'; Qenya *mat-* 'eat' (*HME* V. 371): compare Gothic *mats* 'food'; Qenya *qalmë* 'death', *qalin* 'dead' (*HME* I. 264), compare Old English *cwealm* 'death', *cwelan* 'die'; Qenya *qet-* 'speak, talk', Gnomish *cwed-* (*HME* II. 348), compare Old English *cweþan* 'speak'.

Further parallels are irresistible: Qenya *atar* father: Gothic *atta* 'father'; Qenya *qoro-* 'choke': Middle English *querken* 'choke'; Qenya *yára* 'ancient': Old English *geara* (*g=y*) 'long ago'; Gnomish *cwiv-* 'be awake' and numerous relatives, some meaning 'life' or 'living': Old English *cwicu*, Gothic *qius*, *qiw-* 'alive'; the root DUN- 'dark' (of colour), Doriathrin *dunn* 'black': Old English *dunn*, modern English *dun*; Qenya *fir* 'mortal man', Noldorin *fîr* 'mortals': Old English *firas* 'men, mankind'; Gnomish *goth* 'war, strife': Old English *guþ* 'war, battle'; Gnomish *gwidh-* 'plait, weave': the Germanic base of *withe*, *withy*, as in *Withywindle*.

A notable instance is the Qenya word *irmin* 'regions inhabited by Men' (*HME* II. 343). This resembles Old English *eormen(grund)* 'the earth' and the related Old Saxon *irmin*, which occurs in *Irminsûl*, the name of a pillar used in pagan worship by the Saxons. John Garth says of this: 'the Qenya lexicon entries for *irmin* … and *sūlë*, "pillar, column", suggest that Tolkien was working towards a fictional explanation for *Irminsûl* (Garth 2003, 98). As he also says: 'Evidence suggests that in 1915, at least, Tolkien did create a small but significant proportion of his Qenya words specifically to show kinship with ancient recorded or reconstructed words' (Garth 2003, 97).

Phonetic fitness and unintentional resemblance

Many resemblances do not have any such apparent mythological reference, and must be supposed to arise from the coincidences of 'phonetic fitness'. For example, Tolkien acknowledged that the word *nazg* 'ring' in the Black Speech (the first element in *Nazgul*) was probably derived from Irish *nasc* 'bind', 'lodged in some corner of my linguistic memory' (*Lett*. 297). In the same letter he says that the elements *-and* (*an*), *-end* (*en*), and *-(n)dor* in geographical names 'owes something' to names such as *Broceliand(e)* (Beleriand was originally called *Broseliand*, after the forest Broceliande which appears in Arthurian and other medieval romances (*HME* IV. 77)) and *Labrador*. These are items adopted eclectically whose sound struck him as appropriate for their meaning.

Perhaps in a similar category are the half-dozen or so items in the Qenya lexicon that come directly from Finnish, among them the root KULU- 'gold' (Finnish *kulta*), *tie* 'path' (Finnish *tie* 'way'), and the root TUL- 'come, approach' (Finnish *tulla* 'to come'). These date from a period when Finnish had its greatest influence on Tolkien; they became central items, and one must conclude that for Tolkien they possessed that sense of 'fitness'. (Once part of his language system they did not behave like their Finnish doubles at all: Qenya *tielyanna* 'on thy paths' and *tulielto* 'they have come' have a different 'feel' from Finnish *tielläsi* 'on thy ways' and *tulivat* 'they came'.)

In the early lexicons and the 'Etymologies' we also find resemblances to Greek words: for example, *pelekko* 'axe' (Greek *pelekus*), the root PHAY- 'send out rays of light' (Greek *phaino* 'I give light'), and *sarko* 'flesh' (Greek *sarx*, genitive *sarkos*). Still further examples include Gnomish *drond* 'race, course, track' (Greek *dromos*), Qenya *erume* 'desert' (Greek *eremos*), Gnomish *macha* 'slaughter, battle' (Greek *machē*), Qenya *noa, nó* 'conception' (Greek *nous* 'mind, understanding'), Qenya *salma* 'lyre' (Greek *psallo* 'I play on the harp', *psalmos* 'psalm'), Qenya *telu-* 'to finish, end' (Greek *telos* 'end, goal'). Garth (2003, 98) explains *pelekko* like the Germanic resemblances, as indicating a feigned influence of Elvish on a European language; this may be so, but the other instances seem better placed with the Finnish examples, as adoptions whose sound happened to 'fit' their meaning.

Resemblances to Latin words are also generally indirect and suggestive, with just enough overlap in sound or sense to think that there are what Tolkien calls the 'threads of connexion'. Examples are Qenya *lambë* 'tongue' (Latin *lambere* 'to lick'), Qenya *má* 'hand' (Latin *manus*), Qenya *niqe* 'snow' (Latin *nix*, genitive *nivis*), the root ORO- 'rise' (Latin *orior*), the root UR- 'be hot' (Latin *uro* 'I burn'), Qenya *manë* 'good (moral)' (Latin *manes* 'the shades of the dead', literally 'the good'), the root OWO- and its derivative *oa* 'wool' (Latin *ovis* sheep), *talas* 'sole (of the foot)' (Latin *talus* 'ankle', Old French *talon* 'heel'), Qenya *tarukko* 'bull' (Latin *taurus*), Qenya *vâ* 'went', *vand-* 'way, path' (Latin *vado* 'I go'). Resemblances to Welsh seem rare; we have noted only the root LIN- 'pool' (Welsh *llyn* 'pond, lake'), and Gnomish *tôn* 'fire', *tan* 'firewood' (Welsh *tân* 'fire').

A few instances in the early lexicons display what Christopher Tolkien calls a kind of 'historical punning': e.g., the root SAHA 'be hot' gives rise to *Sahóra* 'the South' (compare *Sahara*), and the derivatives of NENE 'flow' include *nénuvar* 'pool of lilies' (compare *nenuphar* 'water-lily'; *HME* I. 248). An even cleverer example is *leminkainen* '23' in the Qenya glossary (Finnish *Lemminkäinen*, hero of the *Kalevala*), which Christopher Tolkien interprets as an allusion to Tolkien's age at the time (*HME* I. 246). It is not clear whether in such cases the form of the root suggested the 'derivative', or vice versa. Later his Elvish philologizing became too serious to admit such playfulness, though *The Lord of the Rings* does retain such *jeux d'esprit* as the translation of the Elvish names of the days of the week in such a way as to suggest the English names (see *LR* App. D). Compare such puns with the supposed origin of *golf* in *The Hobbit* and of the place names *Thame* and *Worminghall* in *Farmer Giles of Ham*: Tolkien's delight in devising 'alternative' etymologies for English words and names is further discussed in *The Ring of Words* (Gilliver, Marshall, and Weiner (2006)).

Fitness and phonaesthesis

More or less direct resemblances of sound and sense occur in a very small proportion of Tolkien's lexis. The sense of 'fitness' in the rest of the vocabulary is arguably due to much more indirect and elusive resemblances. Alluding to Finnish and Greek, Tolkien says that they give him 'phonaesthetic' pleasure (*Lett.* 144). He may here have meant only 'the aesthetic of sound', but the term 'phonaesthesis' generally denotes the notion that certain sound combinations symbolize basic concepts, or at least have 'recognizable semantic associations due to recurrent appearance in words of similar meaning' (*Oxford Dictionary of English Grammar*), and he may well have been aware that his 'sense of fitness' arose partly from pre-existing associations of phoneme with meaning.

A quite well-founded example in English is *sn-* symbolizing nose-related unpleasantness (*snarl, sneer, sneeze, snotty,* etc.). A less demonstrable one is the idea that the *i*-sound in combination with certain consonants often conveys small size, lightness, or insubstantiality (e.g., *little, slim, thin, flimsy, mini-,* etc.). In this connection it is interesting to note the Quenya word *lintë* 'swift' (*N*), which seems not to have a direct model in a known language, but has a parallel in the much earlier invented language Nevbosh: 'I can also remember the word *lint* "quick, clever, nimble", and it is interesting, because I know it was adopted because the relation between the sounds *lint* and the idea proposed for association with them gave *pleasure*' (*ASV* 205).

Most (or all) phonaesthetic associations may be derived from the languages which one knows, and therefore be culturally conditioned rather than universal. (Certainly the *sn-* phonaestheme is unlikely to arise in any language which does not permit such an initial combination, such as Latin, Greek, Finnish, or Japanese.) But for Tolkien's purpose this is immaterial. He was seeking words that had 'fitness' in the world of ancient north-western Europe; their resonances need only come from this milieu. In some cases it may be possible to speculate about existing words, any or all of which might have carried the appropriate associations in a given case. For example, Quenya *carnë* (Sindarin *caran*) 'red' might recall *carmine*, *carnation*, or Latin *carn-* 'flesh'. We might, reading *minas* 'tower', have *minaret* somewhere in the back of our mind, or something more insubstantial, such as *minatory* (suggesting something looming above one). Or *tin-* 'sparkle' and its derivatives, such as *tintilar* 'they twinkle' (*N*): do these suggest *twinkle* or *scintillate*? But it is probably fruitless to try to explain exactly why so many of Tolkien's invented words have their sense of fitness; the resonances are too elusive to identify.

Elvish after The Lord of the Rings

As we have seen, in the early years the resemblance between real-world languages and Elvish was explicable in terms of a feigned historical link between the mythos and real-world history. However, by the time *The Lord of the Rings* was written an enormous stretch of time had opened up between the period of the Elvish legends and the present day. The return of the Elves to Middle-earth was no longer close in time to the beginnings of English history, and an Anglo-Saxon traveller in the Elvish realm vanished from the narrative frame of the tales.

This shift had implications for the languages. Having reset Middle-earth at such a distance, Tolkien perhaps came to regard with mixed feelings the association between Elvish and real-world words, even stating explicitly that the name *Eärendil* was the sole example of a 'borrowed' sound-combination whose original context had any relevance in Middle-earth (see *Lett.* 297). In a late essay, while struggling with two unrelated Elvish elements spelt *-ros* (appearing in the names *Elros* and *Maed(h)ros* respectively), he comments: 'The first appears too reminiscent of Latin *rōs* or Greek *drosos* ['dew'], and the latter too close to well-known modern European 'red' words: as Latin *russus*, Italian *rosso*, English *russet*, *rust*, etc. However, the Elvish languages are inevitably full of such reminiscences' (*HME* XII. 368).

This case of *-ros* also exemplifies another problem: the languages and legends were so intertwined that, as each developed, it became increasingly difficult to alter either to accommodate changes in the other, especially after some names and forms (such as *Elros*) had been published in *The Lord of the Rings* and hence effectively fixed. His instinct that a name must have a story, and hence an etymology, was to cause him considerable difficulty, as the growing sophistication of his philological scheme made it increasingly hard to account for names invented decades earlier and now embedded in the legendarium.

Tolkien continued to produce narrative explanations of discrepancies in phonology and etymological relationship, of which the most elaborate was 'The Shibboleth of Fëanor' (*HME* XII. 331–66), written in the late 1960s. This sought to explain a potential linguistic conflict between two statements in the Appendices to *The Lord of the Rings*: (1) that sound changes affecting the Quenya spoken by the exiled High-elves in Middle-earth included *th* > *s* (hence the letter name *thúle* > *súle* in the Elvish script), despite the fact that (2) they had adopted Sindarin for daily use, and so would have remained familiar with *th* in everyday speech. The solution involved moving the sound change back in history, devising a complex narrative of personal grievance, and relying on an Elvish capacity for intentional language change, arising from their quasi-mystical relationship with their language, all of which is expounded in 'Dangweth Pengoloð' (*HME* XII. 395–402), where it helps to explain how language change can occur among an undying race with long memories. The entire exercise illustrates how the invented languages continued to generate mythology.

Language idealized

As Tom Shippey remarks, Tolkien held 'several highly personal if not heretical views about language' (2000, xiv). Among these was his dissent from the emphasis of modern linguistics on the purely communicative function of language. He felt instinctively that equal importance should be granted to the sound of language, and specifically to 'pleasure in articulate sound, and in the symbolic use of it, independent of communication though constantly in fact entangled with it' (*ASV* 208). Moreover, his exposition of language invention is pervaded by the notion of a sense of fitness between meaning and spoken symbol. Objectively, Tolkien accepted the view of modern linguistic theory that there is no such link, the form of a word being fundamentally independent of its meaning, and when discussing real-world philology (as in *Lett.* 209) he could cogently expound this.

Subjectively, however, he had a strong perception of language as inherently beautiful or ugly, and within his own mythical world he was able to embody value-judgements about the superiority of one linguistic form over another which real-world linguistics can no longer entertain. Pleasure in sound is a principal creative force in his language invention, and the aesthetic aspect of language is not incidental but essential: the Elvish tongues are designed to embody beauty in the highest degree. And if linguistic beauty is exemplified in Elvish, ugliness is shown in the language of Mordor (the Black Speech) and in the speech of the Orcs, who 'took what they could of other tongues and perverted it to their own liking, yet they made only brutal jargons' (*LR*, App. F).

Furthermore, just as the Orcs deliberately brutalize their language, the Elves cultivate theirs like a work of art: aware of the whole of their language at every moment, they will introduce a sound change throughout the language 'as a weaver might change a thread from red to blue' (*HME* XII. 399). Elsewhere Tolkien hints at the notion that even human speech can be shaped by individual art, describing the language inventor as having 'the same creative experience as that of those many unnamed geniuses who have invented the skilful bits of machinery in our traditional languages' (*ASV* 212).

In Tolkien's world, where so much appears in an idealized form, ideals of language can flourish which do not operate in real-world linguistics. The Elves are imagined to be in 'artistic' control of their languages, actively improving them. Orkish language is not just unaesthetic but actually debased. The complexities of Elvish languages hardly make them ideal in the sense that the makers of functional auxiliary languages would recognize; but since Tolkien's ideals of language focus on aesthetics rather than communicative function, they are, in his terms, ideal.

Tolkien's achievement as a language inventor

If there are two purposes for invented language—communicative function and art—Tolkien is (so far) the master of the art form. He has very few competitors in the field of language invention (or they are very secretive), and it is hard to imagine that his vast web of language and legend could be bettered. Reading Tolkien's major works is like looking at a painting in which a beautiful garden is glimpsed in the background, and then discovering that the garden actually exists, having been planted by the artist before the picture was painted. Tolkien created a self-consistent and technically convincing group of languages, documenting them in such a way that some are foregrounded and others dimly known, and set them within a fictional world which they suit perfectly, with names, words, snatches of discourse, and pieces of verse embedded authentically in a narrative that is widely regarded as a masterpiece of fantasy. Though they appear in their narrative context as perfectly contrived atmospheric devices, it is their pre-existence that ensures their success. As Tolkien put it: 'The "stories" were made rather to provide a world for the languages than the reverse' (*Lett.* 165). Though the invention of languages is an art in itself, for Tolkien 'the making of language and mythology are related functions', and a created language must inevitably '*breed* a mythology' (*ASV* 210–11). This his own languages famously did, and with supreme success.

Abbreviations for Elvish texts cited

ACO Aragorn's Coronation Oath (*LR* vi. v)
EG 'A Elbereth Gilthoniel' (*LR* ii. i)
FC Field of Cormallen praises (*LR* vi. iv)
GFT Gelmir's farewell to Tuor (*Unfinished Tales* 22)
KL The King's Letter (*HME* IX. 128–9)
LRS Lost Road speeches (*HME* V. i. iii)
MGI Moria gate inscription (*LR* ii. iv)
MGC Gandalf's Moria Gate command (*LR* ii. iv)
N 'Namarië' (*LR* ii. viii)
OC Oath of Cirion (*Unfinished Tales* 305)
WS Gandalf's werewolf spell (*LR* ii. iv)

References

WORKS BY J. R. R. TOLKIEN

Songs for the Philologists. 1936. London: for the Department of English, University College. [Written with E. V. Gordon and others]

The Hobbit. 1937. London: George Allen & Unwin.

Farmer Giles of Ham. 1949. London: George Allen & Unwin.

The Lord of the Rings. 1954–55. 3 volumes. London: George Allen & Unwin; second edition, 1966 (cited as *LR*).

The Road Goes Ever On. 1968. With music by Donald Swann. London: George Allen & Unwin.

'Nomenclature of The Lord of the Rings', in Hammond and Scull (2005); previously published as 'Guide to the Names in The Lord of the Rings' in Jared Lobdell, ed., *A Tolkien Compass* (1975).

The Silmarillion. 1977. Edited by Christopher Tolkien. London: George Allen & Unwin.

Unfinished Tales. 1980. Edited by Christopher Tolkien. London: George Allen & Unwin.

The Letters of J.R.R. Tolkien. 1981. Selected and edited by Humphrey Carpenter, with Christopher Tolkien. London: George Allen & Unwin (cited as Lett., with number of letter, not page).

'A Secret Vice', in *The Monsters and the Critics and Other Essays.* 1983. Edited by Christopher Tolkien. London: George Allen & Unwin (cited as *ASV*).

Texts in *The History of Middle-earth* (1983–96), edited by Christopher Tolkien in twelve volumes (cited as HME):

Vol. I: *The Book of Lost Tales, Part I.* 1983. London: George Allen & Unwin.

Vol. II: *The Book of Lost Tales, Part II.* 1984. London: George Allen & Unwin.

Vol. IV: *The Shaping of Middle-earth.* 1986. London: George Allen & Unwin.

Vol. V: *The Lost Road* (including 'The Etymologies'). 1987. London: Unwin Hyman.

Vol. IX: *Sauron Defeated* (including 'The Notion Club Papers'). 1992. London: Harper Collins.

Vol. XII: *The Peoples of Middle-earth* (including 'The Problem of Ros', 'Dangweth Pengoloð', and 'The Shibboleth of Fëanor'). 1996. London: Harper Collins.

OTHER WORKS

Carpenter, Humphrey. 1977. *J.R.R. Tolkien: A Biography.* London: George Allen & Unwin.

Flieger, Verlyn. 1983. *Splintered Light: Logos and Language in Tolkien's World.* Grand Rapids, Michigan: William B. Eerdmans.

Garth, John. 2003. *Tolkien and the Great War: the threshold of Middle-earth.* London: Harper Collins.

Gilliver, Peter, Jeremy Marshall & Edmund Weiner. 2006. *The Ring of Words: Tolkien and the 'Oxford English Dictionary'.* Oxford: Oxford University Press.

Gilson, Christopher. 2000. 'Gnomish is Sindarin: The Conceptual Evolution of an Elvish Language', in *Tolkien's Legendarium: essays on 'The History of Middle-earth'*, edited by Verlyn Flieger and Carl F. Hostetter. Westport, Connecticut: Greenwood Press.

Hammond, Wayne G., and Christina Scull. 2005. *The Lord of the Rings: A Reader's Companion.* London: Harper Collins.

Hostetter, Carl F. 2007. 'Languages Invented by Tolkien', in *J.R.R. Tolkien Encyclopedia: Scholarship and Critical Assessment*, edited by Michael Drout. New York: Routledge.

Martinez, Helios de Rosario. 2008. 'Early Ilkorin Phonology'. *Tengwestië* (online journal of the Elvish Linguistic Fellowship). http://www.elvish.org/Tengwestie/articles/DeRosarioMartinez/earlyilkorin.phtml.

Pearce, Joseph. 1999. *Tolkien: A Celebration.* London: Fount.

Shippey, Tom A. 2000. *J.R.R. Tolkien: Author of the Century.* London: Harper Collins; New York: Houghton Mifflin.

Smith, Ross. 2007. *Inside Language: Linguistic and Aesthetic Theory in Tolkien.* Zurich and Bern: Walking Tree Publishers.

~5~

Wild and Whirling Words:

The Invention and Use of Klingon

MARC OKRAND, MICHAEL ADAMS,
JUDITH HENDRIKS-HERMANS, AND SJAAK KROON

According to the 2006 edition of the *Guinness Book of World Records*, the world's 'largest fictional language' is Klingon. Though the book acknowledges that there is no way of knowing how many speakers the language actually has, it nonetheless asserts that 'there is little doubt' that Klingon is the 'most widely used language of its kind'. The appropriateness of the listing, of course, depends on what other languages 'of its kind' there may be and, perhaps more fundamentally, on what 'kind' of language Klingon is.

Klingon is a constructed language tied to a fictional context, rather than a constructed language like Esperanto (see Chapter 2) or a reconstructed one like Modern Hebrew (see Chapter 8) intended for use among speakers in everyday circumstances. Klingon started out as nothing more than a few lines of dialogue in a film, and, once devised, owes its current shape as much to the practicalities of moviemaking as it does to careful design, and its place in the record book—deserved or not—to the phenomenon known as *Star Trek*. Arika Okrent, in her very informative and clever book, *In the Land of Invented Languages*, asserts that 'Klingon is a solution to an artistic problem, not a linguistic one' (2009, 282), intended to enhance the fiction of *Star Trek* by more fully realizing the speech of those populating the imagined universe of the films and television shows that make up the *Star Trek* franchise. In a sense, then, in the case of Klingon, necessity was the mother of invention.

Origins

Klingon is a language devised for the Klingons, a fictional race of humanoids sometimes allied with but more often in conflict with members of the United Federation of Planets in *Star Trek* movies, television programmes, video games, and novels. Klingons first appeared in 'Errand of Mercy' (23 March 1967), an episode of the original *Star Trek* television series, in 1967. In a later episode that same year, 'The Trouble with Tribbles' (29 December 1967), the fact that Klingons spoke their own language was first noted (one character boasts that half of the inhabitants in their quadrant of the galaxy are learning to speak 'Klingonese'). Other than character names (and the word 'Klingon'), however, no 'Klingonese' was ever spoken in the original *Star Trek* television series, which stopped producing new episodes in 1969.

After a ten-year hiatus, the series re-emerged on the big screen with the premiere of *Star Trek: The Motion Picture* (1979). The first several lines of dialogue in the film are spoken by a Klingon captain in a language never heard before, translated in subtitles. Before his fleet of ships mysteriously vanishes, within the first few minutes of the film, the captain barks out half a dozen or so commands (subtitled) and also gives what is presumably a description of his fleet's circumstances (not subtitled, and difficult if not impossible to make out under the English dialogue going on at the same time).

These first words of 'Klingonese' were created by James Doohan, the actor who played the character Montgomery Scott (Scotty) in the series. His goal was to make a language that would not sound like any on Earth. According to Mark Lenard, who played the Klingon captain in the film, Doohan recorded the lines on a tape, and Lenard then listened to the tape and wrote down the recorded lines in a transcription useful to him in learning the dialogue. How closely the lines actually spoken on film resemble those spoken by Doohan is not known. It is also not known what sort of grammatical structure, if any, Doohan had in mind.

Klingons next appeared in the third *Star Trek* film, *Star Trek III: The Search for Spock* (1984). For this film, writer and executive producer Harve Bennett decided that the Klingons should speak their own language—at least when talking with one another. Bennett hired linguist Marc Okrand to devise the dialogue. This would be Okrand's second language assignment for *Star Trek*. Two years earlier, he devised four lines of Vulcan dialogue for *Star Trek II: The Wrath of Khan*, also written and produced by Bennett.

Unlike 'Klingonese', the language of the Vulcans—another humanoid race, but one allied closely with inhabitants of the Earth—had been heard in the original television series, as well as in *Star Trek: The Motion Picture*. On television, individual Vulcan words were used from time to time, most often uttered by Mr Spock, the most well-known Vulcan in the series. The words, presumably created by the writers or producers of the episodes in which the words were used, were mostly based on English phonology, that is, on sounds and sound combinations found in English. For example, some Vulcan words in the episode 'Amok Time' (15 September 1967, written by Theodore Sturgeon) are *ahn-woon* 'type of weapon', *koon-oot-kal-if-fee* 'marriage' or 'challenge', and *kroykah* 'halt!' The main exception to English phonological patterns is in names of female Vulcans, such as *T'Pau* and *T'Pring*; these forms begin with the consonant cluster /tp/, which is structurally unacceptable in English.

By comparison, *Star Trek: The Motion Picture* contains quite a bit of Vulcan dialogue in a scene in which Mr Spock undergoes a ritual known as Kolinahr. In this scene, the Vulcan 'masters' conducting the ritual speak only in Vulcan. When it was filmed, however, the actors were speaking English. The filmmakers later decided to replace the English dialogue with Vulcan, and did so, not by reshooting the scene, but by dubbing in dialogue that would match the English lip movements (lip-syncing) for parts when the speaker was on screen and would simply not sound like English for parts when the speaker could not be seen.

Using this lip-syncing technique, for example, the last word in the Vulcan salute *Live long and prosper* became *moz-ma* (first syllable rhymes with English *doze*), with the bilabial articulation of the two Vulcan /m/'s matching that of the English /p/'s, and the tongue position of Vulcan /z/ matching that of English /s/. The conversion also involved introducing sounds such as velar fricatives (similar to the /ch/ in German *Bach*) whose production does not involve parts of the speaker's mouth (lips, teeth, tongue tip) visible when the speaker is on camera.

In *Star Trek II*, Okrand used the same technique to replace four lines of English dialogue with four lines of Vulcan dialogue. The goal, again, was to have non-English sounds appear to be spoken by the characters who had actually spoken English. Some of the phonetic features of the Vulcan in *Star Trek: The Motion Picture* were incorporated (including the velar fricatives) so that the languages in the two films would sound somewhat alike, but there was no attempt to assign meaning to individual words or impose any sort of grammatical structure.

When it came time to devise dialogue for the Klingons for *Star Trek III*, however, the goal had shifted from simply non-English-sounding verbiage to creating an actual language. In discussing how the language would be used in the film, Bennett and Okrand agreed that the best way to make the language sound real was to make it real—to devise phonological and grammatical systems and to make use of a consistent vocabulary. The script indicated which lines spoken by Klingons were to be in English and which in 'Klingon', translated in subtitles. (The script referred to the language as 'Klingon', and this usage replaced the earlier 'Klingonese'.)

The plan, at this point, was not to create a 'full' language, but only what was necessary for the film—that is, just enough vocabulary and grammar for the lines marked as being in Klingon. This assignment was expanded to include Klingon versions of all the lines of English dialogue to be spoken by Klingon characters (when addressing other Klingons) so that if, during filming, someone thought a scene might be improved by having the character speak Klingon rather than English, the line would be instantly available. Even with the English lines included, however, the number of words and grammatical structures to be created was limited. Again, the motive for inventing Klingon, piecemeal as that invention has been, was artistic, but at the same time very practical. Klingon has developed lexically and grammatically as people needed it to develop for their particular artistic projects, first film and television, later translations of major works of world literature (see Appendix 5).

The language was to be the same as that heard in the original television series (even though that consisted of character names only) as well as in *Star Trek: The Motion Picture* (words and phrases), so all of the sounds and syllable types associated with the earlier 'Klingonese' were incorporated into the new Klingon. To expand the phonetic inventory, there were two potentially conflicting guiding principles, the first calling for creativity, the second for pragmatism: (1) the language was an alien (outer-space) language, so it should not sound like a human language; (2) the language was to be spoken by human actors without benefit of electronic enhancement, so the dialogue had to be possible for a human being to pronounce (and to memorize).

The linguistic structure of Klingon

The syllabic structure of the language in *Star Trek: The Motion Picture*, at least those parts that are audible, is basically CV(C), that is, a single consonant sound followed by a single vowel, as in the nouns *cha* 'torpedoes' and *po* 'morning', and perhaps followed by another single consonant, as in the verb *nep* 'lie' and the noun *veng* 'city', so this became the syllable type for Klingon, essentially without exception, even as the vocabulary of Klingon has expanded into thousands of words.

The relatively small number of vowels and consonants originally created (there were very few words in the film, so not many sounds) was expanded. To keep the phonology pronounceable by English-speaking actors, most of the additional sounds were also in English. To keep the language from sounding like English, a number of non-English sounds were added, such as /tlh/ in the verb *Sutlh* 'negotiate'. 'To produce this sound,' Okrand writes, 'the tip of the tongue touches the same part of the roof of the mouth it touches for **t**, the sides of the tongue are lowered away from the side upper teeth, and air is forced through the space on both sides between tongue and teeth' (1985, 15). There were also some velar and uvular consonants included because the script described the Klingon language as 'guttural' (even though the language had not yet been devised at the time the script was written). A glottal stop (actually quite common in spoken English, for instance, in place of /t/ in *mitten* and *kitten*) is frequently the syllable-final consonant (much less common in most English dialects), as in the exclamation *Qo'* 'I refuse' and the verb *ra'* 'order, command', giving the language its choppy quality.

To lend the phonology an alien feel, certain common patterns found in human languages were skewed. For example, the voiceless stop /t/ is made by placing the tip of the tongue on the alveolar ridge, just above the teeth, as in English; its voiced counterpart, rather than the alveolar /d/ in English, is a palatal stop (transcribed as /D/). So syllable-final consonants in the verbs *jot* 'be calm' and *joD* 'stoop' are not merely unvoiced and voiced alternants of otherwise identical sounds (as /t/ and /d/ are in *pot* and *pod*), but even more significantly distinct sounds. There are two velar fricatives—the /H/ of the verb *liH* 'introduce', which sounds like the coda in German *Bach*, and the /gh/ of *ghagh* 'gargle', which is a voiced alternant of /H/ (neither of which is available in English)—and a velar nasal (English /ŋ/ as in *song*), which can appear in a syllable coda (as it can in English), for instance, in the noun *ghong* 'abuse', but also in the syllable onset as in the verb *ngu'* 'identify' (as it cannot in English). There are, however, no velar stops (voiceless /k/ and voiced /g/ in English), which English speakers would expect, and this absence contributes to the un-English-like sound of the language. There is no sound in Klingon that does not occur in any number of natural languages, but the particular inventory of sounds is unique to Klingon.

Several arbitrary decisions were made about the sounds of Klingon. One was that the sound /k/ was avoided as being associated, at least at the beginning of words or names, with aliens or outer space: *Flash Gordon*'s *Kala* and *Klytus*, *Superman*'s *Krypton* and *kryptonite*, even *The Simpsons*' *Kang* and *Kodos*. These last two names were probably a nod to *Star Trek*, whose writers also used /k/ for this association (*Kang* and *Kodos*, along with *Kaylar*, *Kloog*, *Korob*, *Kelvans*, *Kalandans*, and others). The presence of /k/ in *Kirk*, the name of *Star Trek*'s principal human protagonist, of course, shows that the connection of /k/ to alien is not absolute.

Unfortunately, /k/ had already been established as part of the language in the name *Klingon* itself as well as in the names of all of the male Klingon characters in the original *Star Trek* series (such as *Kor*, *Koloth*, and *Kahless*). To keep to the self-imposed avoidance of /k/, Okrand posited that all of the names previously transcribed with *k* were Earthlings' mishearings of Klingon sounds unavailable in the inventory of English consonants: the first sound in the name *Kor* is really a uvular stop, made farther back in the mouth than the velar /k/;

the word *Klingon* begins with a lateral affricate, the /tlh/ of *Sutlh*, not a /kl/ cluster. Thus, the name represented in English as *Klingon* is actually *tlhIngan*.

A transcription system had to be developed so that the language could be written down for the actors in a way that would help them learn their lines. For the most part, letters in this system were given their usual English value (*b* is pronounced like the first letter in the English word *boy*, *ch* as in *church*, etc.). Most non-English sounds were indicated by capital letters (*H* is a voiceless velar fricative, *Q* is a voiceless uvular affricate) or by letter combinations (*gh* is a voiced velar fricative, *tlh* is a voiceless lateral affricate). Note that these letter combinations did not represent consonant clusters (like /sp/ in *spill* or /st/ in *cast*), but single consonant phonemes, however difficult for an English speaker to articulate. Capital *I* was to indicate the /ɪ/ sound in *bit* (not that in *machine* or *dine*), lower-case *q* represented a voiceless uvular stop, and an apostrophe indicated a glottal stop. The resulting system, while far from elegant—a system could have been devised with no upper-case letters and no need to be careful about upper- vs lower-case *q*—nonetheless served its purpose as a pedagogical tool.

The grammar of Klingon was also designed to make the language seem unusual (to a speaker of English, anyway). For example, the basic word order of Klingon is OBJECT—VERB—SUBJECT. Thus, *The officer sees the child* is *puq legh yaS* in Klingon, while *The child sees the officer* is *yaS legh puq* (Okrand 1985, 59). This pattern was chosen not because it is the English order in reverse, but because this particular order is one of the least frequently found in natural languages. As with sounds, any given grammatical feature of Klingon can probably be found in some language or other, but the collection is unique. Every attempt was made to keep Klingon from resembling any other language. That said, one cannot help but be influenced by what one knows, so phonological or grammatical features of some Native American languages or Southeast Asian languages—the languages with which Okrand was most familiar—worked their way into Klingon, but, for the most part, not by design.

Stay tuned for further developments

Lines of dialogue to be spoken by Klingon characters in *Star Trek: The Motion Picture* were composed on the basis of these phonological and grammatical principles and linguistic influences. If a particular vocabulary item or grammatical feature was not needed in any of the lines, it simply was not created. The choice of what sounds should come together (given the phonological patterns described earlier) to become a specific word was totally arbitrary (unless it happened to occur in the original motion picture). Later, in producing *The Klingon Dictionary* (1985), Okrand would regularize some features of word structure, for instance, pronoun prefixes, case suffixes for nouns, mood and aspect suffixes for verbs, a suffix for ordinal numbers, etc. (Okrand 1985, 162–8).

The dialogue was transcribed in the newly devised system, and these transcripts, along with tapes of Okrand pronouncing the lines, were sent to Paramount Pictures in Hollywood, where the movie was to be filmed, to be distributed to the actors. When filming actually began, for the most part, Okrand was on the set to coach the actors when they were to speak Klingon. The filmmakers were attentive to the language and checked with Okrand after each scene was filmed to see if the actors said their lines correctly. In the interest of saving time (and money), if an actor said a word or line incorrectly, but it still sounded enough like Klingon and did not conflict with anything filmed earlier, it was considered acceptable. Since, at this time, no one other than the filmmakers had heard the language, errors were easily tolerated and, in fact, were instantly incorporated as features—both phonological and grammatical—of the language. On the other hand, if a line were mispronounced in such a way that it did not sound like Klingon, the scene would be shot again.

Weeks later, the film went into post-production and was put into its final form. This process affected the Klingon language in two ways. First, it was decided that some of the lines filmed in English should be changed to Klingon. (None of the Klingon equivalents for English dialogue spoken by Klingon characters that had been prepared in advance was used during the filming.) The actors would dub in Klingon lines to match the English lip movements on the film, just as had been done with Vulcan for earlier features. This time, however, the new lines had to match, not only lip movements, but the phonology that had been devised for the language. Thus, for instance, English *animal* became Klingon *Ha'DIbaH*. Second, some of the subtitles had been changed, so that, for example, a line originally having the subtitle 'I told you, engine section only' (meaning 'I told you to target only the engine section of the ship you were to fire upon') now had the subtitle 'I wanted prisoners'. The phrase (and subtitle) 'engine only' remained in the film elsewhere, so homophony was introduced (the words for 'only' and 'want' came to be pronounced identically, *neH*). New words and new grammatical features were invented and incorporated into the now growing language as a result of the post-production process.

After work on the film had been completed, but before the film premiered, Okrand began writing a book that was to contain a description of the film's language, including a grammatical description and a list of all of the vocabulary in the film. It became clear that if the contents were limited to the words and phrases actually heard in the film, the book would seem incomplete, leaving out descriptions of certain basic grammatical features, for example, simply because no sentence in the film happened to make use of them. Similarly, had the vocabulary in the book been limited to what was heard in the film, it would have been a very short list. To add some heft, Okrand devised additional grammatical features and created a great deal of additional vocabulary just for the book. Nevertheless, the description of the grammar of the language was more like a sketch—many potential features were not included simply because they had not yet been invented—and there were only about 1,500 words.

The book was originally to appear at the same time the film came out, but its initial publication was delayed. This turned out to be fortunate since the book, as originally written, did not include any of the post-production additions and changes. The delay allowed time for revision, so when the book, *The Klingon Dictionary*, finally did appear at the tail end of 1984, the language it described matched what was heard in the film, a few typographical errors notwithstanding. This conformed to fan expectations, as many fans of *Star Trek* (Trekkers or Trekkies) are picky about facts and tend to take a canonical view of costume, language, technology, etc. presented in the films, television series, or products associated with them. If the motive for inventing Klingon in the first place was more or less instrumental, inventing more Klingon became important to the *Star Trek* brand, which is why Paramount Pictures, which holds the copyright to both editions of *The Klingon Dictionary*, saw publishing it as an opportunity not to be passed up. *Star Trek*®, we are reminded on the copyright pages of the dictionary and subsequent books about Klingon, is a registered trademark of Paramount Pictures (see Appendix 1).

Klingon vocab

From what they have seen of Klingons on the big and small screens, many assume that the core Klingon vocabulary reflects Klingon obsessions with war and honour, and certainly *The Klingon Dictionary* includes many terms that serve the stereotype: *bach* 'shoot', *boQDu'* 'aide-de-camp', *chun* 'innocent', *chuQun* 'nobility', *Doghjey* 'unconditional surrender', *Dup* 'strategy', *ghIm* 'exile', *ghIpDIj* 'court-martial', *Hay'* 'duel', *HIv* 'attack', *jey* 'defeat', *joS* 'rumour, gossip', *lay'* 'promise', *luj* 'fail', *may'* 'battle', *mIy* 'brag', *nawlogh* 'squadron', *nur* 'dignity', *ngIv* 'patrol', *ngor* 'cheat', *pIch* 'fault, blame', *pujwI'* 'weakling', *qeH* 'resent', *qu'* 'fierce', *Qoj* 'make war', *QuS* 'conspire', *ra* 'order, command', *ruv* 'justice', *Sun* 'discipline', *Suv* 'fight', *tIch* 'insult', *tuHmoH* 'shame', *vaQ* 'aggressive', *vuv* 'respect', *web* 'disgraced', *wIh* 'ruthless', *yay* 'victory', *yot* 'invade', *'Ip* 'vow', and *'urmang* 'treason'.

However, the dictionary also includes more general and sometimes surprisingly domestic terms: *bang* 'loved one', *butlh* 'dirt under fingernails', *chIS* 'white', *chuS* 'noisy', *DaQ* 'ponytail', *Du'* 'farm', *gogh* 'voice', *ghu* 'baby', *Hagh* 'laugh', *Hu* 'zoo', *jIl* 'neighbour', *juH* 'home', *loch* 'moustache', *lut* 'story', *megh* 'lunch', *mu'* 'word', *mu'ghom* 'dictionary', *mu'tay* 'vocabulary' *mu'tlhegh* 'sentence', *nIQ* 'breakfast', *noSvagh* 'deodorant', *ngav* 'writer's cramp', *nger* 'theory', *pab* 'grammar', *puq* 'child', *qej* 'grouchy', *qempa'* 'ancestor', *Qe'* 'restaurant', *Quj* 'play a game', *rejmorgh* 'worrywort', *rewbe'* 'citizen', *Saj* 'pet', *SoSnI'* 'grandmother', *taQ* 'weird', *tIv* 'enjoy', *tlhaQ* 'funny', *tlhogh* 'marriage', *vem* 'awaken', *vuD* 'opinion', *wIch* 'myth', *wIj* 'farm', *yob* 'harvest', *yuch* 'chocolate', *IH* 'handsome', and *u'* 'universe'.

Codifying Klingon

The Klingon Dictionary provides a very elementary grammar of the language, and it would be impossible to outline many of the word-formative or syntactic rules implied by recent work in Klingon here (see Appendix 5), but it will help explain the language to mention a few of the most basic grammatical features. Klingon resembles agglutinative languages, among which are many Native American and Southeast Asian languages familiar to Okrand. In agglutinative languages, meaning can be added to words in accumulations of affixes on a base, often allowing many more prefixes, infixes, or suffixes in a word than are allowed in English. In Klingon, a verb base can be encrusted in a prefix and as many as nine suffixes! There are nine types of verb suffix, and a word can include only one suffix of each type; and while a word need not include suffixes of all types, those it does include occur in type order.

So, a very complex Klingon verb might take the form PREFIX-VERB BASE-1-2-3-4-5-6-7-8-9. A less complex verb might take the form PREFIX-VERB BASE-1-7-9, as in *jIqIp'eghpu''a'* 'Did I hit myself?', where the prefix *jI-* is pronominal (not a pronoun but functioning like one) and *qIp* is the base, with serial suffixes *-egh* 'myself', *-pu'* (perfect aspect, indicating completed action), and *-'a'* (indicating a "yes/no" question). Again, it is impossible to form the verb **jIqIp'a'pu'egh*—the suffixes (9-7-1) are in the wrong order. This very rigid system is alleviated somewhat by verb suffixes called *lengwI'mey* 'rovers', which can occur in any suffix position except the final one and indicate various kinds of negation and emphasis.

Nouns work in much the same fashion as verbs, with five suffix types and no rovers. There are no adjectives in Klingon; adjective meanings are attached to verbs. So, in English you are **ruthless**, whereas in Klingon you **are ruthless**. Adverbs of manner occur at the beginning of a sentence, except *jay'* 'intensely', which occurs at the end of a sentence and can serve the function and carry the force of an expletive. It would be difficult to imagine Klingon language without an expletive, and it is surely no surprise to discover that 'cursing is a fine art among Klingons' (Okrand 1992, 178).

New demands for (and on) Klingon

The Klingon language remained static—that is, unchanged—for several years until Bennett hired Okrand once again to create Klingon dialogue for the fifth film in the *Star Trek* series, *The Final Frontier*, released in 1989. While in *Star Trek III* most of the Klingon dialogue was in the form of short exclamations or commands, in *Star Trek V* there were actual conversations. Rather than again starting virtually from scratch, Okrand relied on what was known about the language, that is, whatever was recorded in *The Klingon Dictionary*. To accommodate the film's dialogue, new vocabulary and new grammatical features were added. The same was done for *Star Trek VI: The Undiscovered Country*, released two years later.

In the meantime, Paramount launched the television series *Star Trek: The Next Generation* in 1987. A Klingon, Worf, was a regular character, and, as the series went along, more and more stories involved Klingons and their culture—and their language. The first bits of Klingon language heard on the series were not based on Okrand's work, but after a while, some writers made use of *The Klingon Dictionary*—at least for vocabulary—and occasionally some consulted with Okrand himself.

Discourse, dialects, and writing

In 1992, *The Klingon Dictionary* was reissued. The new edition included an addendum with additional grammatical information as well as another 180 or so words, mostly—but not entirely—material that had been created for *Star Trek V* and *Star Trek VI* or based on plot elements in *Star Trek: The Next Generation*. It also provided some unexpected information about pragmatic dimensions of Klingon, though, admittedly, very little information. For instance, until the new edition, we had not known of *-oy*, the noun suffix that expresses endearment, so that *SoS* 'mother' becomes *SoSoy* 'mummy/mommy' and *be'nI'* 'sister' becomes *be'nI'oy* 'sis'. Okrand notes that 'The suffix usually follows a noun referring to a relative … but it could also follow a noun for a pet and means that a speaker is particularly fond of whatever the noun refers to. It is strongly suggested that non-native speakers of Klingon avoid this suffix unless they know what they are getting into' (1992, 174). Klingons, though socially aggressive, do not tolerate what they see as *Doch* 'rude'.

By this time, Klingon was moving beyond its place as a language restricted to films and television programmes. Basing their studies on

The Klingon Dictionary, people interested in the language were starting to learn it, either individually or in groups coming together for that purpose. The contents of the dictionary were being analysed, discussed, committed to memory, and put to use. Language classes were organized, and a journal devoted to the language (*HolQed*, literally 'linguistics', published by a group of Klingon devotees known as the Klingon Language Institute) first appeared in 1992.

As interest in Klingon seemed to expand, and as Klingon stories and characters continued to play a role in *Star Trek: The Next Generation* and the subsequent television series *Star Trek: Deep Space Nine* and *Star Trek: Voyager*, Okrand added to the canon of recorded Klingon, principally in two other books: *The Klingon Way: A Warrior's Guide* (1996), a collection of Klingon proverbs (in English and Klingon) with commentary, and *Klingon for the Galactic Traveler* (1997), an examination of dialects, specialized vocabulary, idioms, and slang. This third book includes a vocabulary list of over 600 new words (including words that had been heard in various television episodes even though not created by Okrand).

With the creation of vocabulary beyond what was needed in the films, the choice of what sounds were used for what words sometimes became a little less arbitrary and a little more capricious than was originally the case. Some of the vocabulary in the original dictionary, and a not insignificant amount of vocabulary developed since then, is based on puns and other wordplay (for an interesting parallel, see Chapter 4, pages 102–3). For example, *Hat* (which sounds somewhat like English *hot*) means 'temperature'; *'om* means 'resist', based on the ohm, a unit of electrical resistance; *mon* is 'smile', as in Mona Lisa; *qogh* is '(outer) ear', based on Van Gogh; *Das* is 'boot' (based on the movie *Das Boot*, which influenced the design of the bridge of the Klingon ship in *Star Trek III*); and the word for 'joke' is *qID* (resembling English 'kid').

The transcription of Klingon used in *The Klingon Dictionary* and all other publications by Okrand, as well as by students of the language, is the same as the one originally devised for the actors, including the use of capital letters for certain (mostly non-English) sounds. In the motion pictures and television programmes, when written Klingon is shown, it is written in special characters. These characters, however, have never been matched up with the spoken language. That is, the written form of the language is not a syllabary, an alphabet, or any other known type of writing—it is artwork. Some efforts have been made, notably by the Klingon Language Institute, to map Okrand's transcription to characters that closely resemble those seen in the films and on television on a one-on-one basis (a specific character for 'a', another for 'b', and so on), but virtually all of written Klingon other than on-screen is in Okrand's romanized alphabetic form.

From the outset, Harve Bennett and Okrand had agreed that the best way to make Klingon sound real was to make it real. Over the years, that 'reality' expanded beyond phonology and grammar designed to serve particular fictional purposes in television and film into imagined historical and sociolinguistic aspects of the language. Noting that 'All Klingons are not alike', Okrand arrived at a natural conclusion: 'By the same token, all Klingons do not speak alike' (1997, 7). Klingon, that is, *tlhIngan Hol* 'Klingon language' in the works collectively known as *Star Trek*, developed from an earlier version, reflected in myths and rituals at the foundation of Klingon culture, known as *no' Hol* 'ancestors' language (Okrand 1997, 11–13).

Throughout its history, *tlhIngan Hol* comprises regional and social dialects. As the American linguist Walt Wolfram puts it, 'Languages are invariably manifested through their dialects, and to speak a language is to speak some dialect of that language' (1991, 2). Klingon could not be a 'real' language without observing metalinguistic principles like this one. As one might expect of a very hierarchical culture, Klingon has a standard variety, *ta' tlhIngan Hol* 'Emperor's Klingon' or *ta' Hol* 'Emperor's language' against which other varieties are judged: 'the more any given dialect differs from that of the emperor, the more inferior it is considered' (Okrand 1997, 14). A language so bound to tradition and prestige must be enriched, supplemented, and even covertly challenged by *mu'mey ghoQ* 'fresh words' or slang and, we are told, 'Except in formal situations, the speech of younger Klingons is apt to contain a fair amount of slang' (Okrand 1997, 142). The 'reality' of Klingon is in the extent of its *chab* 'invention', of the gradual filling in of its linguistic structures and sociolinguistic contexts.

As the *Guinness Book of World Records* announced, Klingon is an unusually successful invented language, but in a very restricted sense, for, as Okrent observes, 'it is possible for an invented language to succeed even if it has no useful features at all'. Klingon 'has no mission: it wasn't intended to unite mankind or improve the mind or even be spoken by people in the real world. But it suited the personal taste of a certain group of people so well that as soon as they saw it, they fell in love, clamored for more, and formed a community that brought it to life' (Okrent 2009, 263). It may not have been intended to be spoken by real people, but it could be spoken by some of the especially enthusiastic ones. 'How many speakers are there?' Okrent asks. 'It depends on your definition of "speaker"' (2009, 272), as well as on what 'kind' of language Klingon is. And while Klingon may have been 'brought to life' by a 'community', is it a 'speech community', with the emphasis on 'speech'?

Who speaks Klingon?

In 'Just a Touch' (22 April 2004), an episode of the popular American hospital serial *ER*, one of the show's main characters, Abby (played by Maura Tierney), during her internship on the psych ward, is confronted by a man who suddenly speaks what most of us would hear as guttural gibberish. Abby answers in the same guttural gibberish, after which she explains to her surprised superior that she speaks a little Klingon. Nothing more was explained about what Klingon is or who speaks it. The episode's writers apparently considered it common knowledge among *ER*'s worldwide audience. *ER* is fiction, but truth is often at least as strange as fiction. In May 2003, the real-world Multnomah County Hospital in Portland, Oregon, advertised for an interpreter fluent in Klingon. 'We have to provide information in all the languages our clients speak,' said Jerry Jelusich, a procurement specialist for the County Department of Human Services, which serves about 60,000 mental health clients (quoted from a story originally on CNN.com, but no longer available there; see http://www.606studios.com/bendisboard/showthread.php?11516-Qapla-!-Hospital-seeks-Klingon-speaker).

Klingon is an artificial language adjunct to a fiction (or several serial fictions, the television episodes and films): it was not designed for real human communication, and it has no native speakers. However, some people, especially *Star Trek* fans, began to use it for fun, mainly in written communication on the Internet. Yens Wahlgren (2004) considers the Klingonist community as a linguistic market in the sense developed by Pierre Bourdieu in *Language and Symbolic Power* (1991); in that market, knowledge of Klingon endows a *Star Trek* fan with sub-cultural linguistic capital. Wahlgren estimates that thousands of people worldwide have studied Klingon, but observes that it is hard to determine how many are fluent, for '"fluent" is hard to define in a community with no native speakers as reference. Lawrence Schoen [director of the Klingon Language Institute (see Appendix 5)] estimates that between 20 and 30 people could be considered fluent. With a more stringent definition [of fluency] it might be as few as ten' (2004, 11).

If there is a group of people—however small—who are bilingual speakers of Klingon, can it be considered a speech or language community, that is, a group that shares not only a common language but also common patterns of use and attitudes with respect to that language? According to Patrick (2004, 580) the term *speech community* has been used for entities as different as, on one hand, large geographically bounded urban communities and, on the other, the members of a court jury. Do Klingonists share linguistic characteristics such that they also fit somewhere on this speech community continuum or are they, in fact, not a sociolinguistic group at all?

What follows describes the characteristics of the average Klingon speaker on the basis of an Internet survey designed by Judith Hendriks-Hermans as the basis for her Master's thesis (1999), supervised by Sjaak Kroon at the University of Tilburg, and posted on various Klingon and *Star Trek*-related sites. The questionnaire is composed of three parts, in which respondents provided personal information, described their relationship to Klingon, and indicated their attitudes toward the language. In total, 109 people responded, 79 of whom identified as Klingon speakers. This level of response may not be enough to build a profile of the average Klingon user, but most of this survey's findings are corroborated by those of an earlier web survey conducted in Sweden, with 604 respondents (Annernäs 1996), and an interview study with nineteen advanced Klingonists by Wahlgren (2004).

The majority (77%) of the 79 Klingon speakers were male. Their average age was 31.5 years, ranging from 15 to 55. As to ethnicity, 70.9% identified as Caucasian; other ethnicities mentioned (somewhat unhelpfully) were Human, Celtic, Latin, Klingon, Jewish, and Apache. About half of the Klingon-speaking respondents were married. Although most of them lived in the United States (65.1%), they came from all over the world—for instance, from Canada (12.8%), Germany (7.3%), England, and the Netherlands (both 2.8%)—and mainly (64.6%) lived in cities of more than 100,000 inhabitants. A large majority (70.9%) had post-secondary educations, and their professions included information technology and computers (32.9%), other technical professions (10.1%), and a variety of other occupations (24%), such as civil servant, teacher, and actor, while 21.5% were students. Almost all were proficient in English, whereas between 10% and 20% had mastered German, French, or Spanish. The majority's first language was English (78.5%), which was also the main language used at home (81%) and at work (86.1%). As many as 19% used artificial languages other than Klingon, including science-fiction languages like Romulan or Fremen, but also Volapük and Esperanto (see Chapter 2), Lojban, and, in two cases, self-invented artificial languages.

The Klingon speakers discovered their language via *Star Trek* (63.3%), friends (12.7%), or the Klingon Language Institute on the Internet (6.4%). Klingon speakers learned the language via books (53.2%) and tapes (2.5%) produced by Marc Okrand, the Klingon Language Institute (20.2%), both (7.6%), or friends (13.9%). Most respondents had studied Klingon for from one to four years (51.9%); as a result, 94.9% could speak Klingon and nearly as many (84.8%) could understand it when it was spoken to them. Klingon readers amounted to 81%, whereas 73.4% could write in the language.

It might come as no surprise that use of Klingon in everyday life was rather limited: 46.8% (oral) and 43% (written) used it less than once a month; the scores for more than once a week were 22.8% (oral) and 15.2% (written) and for every day were 13.9% (oral) and 17.7% (written) respectively. In real numbers of Klingonists, then, only around 20 wrote or spoke the language daily, which matches Lawrence Schoen's estimate and Arika Okrent's, too (see Okrent 2009, 273).

Respondents reported writing Klingon mainly to practise Klingon grammar, or to read or write messages, usually on the Internet. Oral Klingon is used most at occasions where Klingon speakers, *Star Trek* fans, or both meet. Respondents said they use Klingon because it is fun to speak (96.2%) and because they are *Star Trek* fans (65.8%). Respondents judged their proficiency in oral Klingon as average (41.8%); in written Klingon, they rated themselves as average (24.1%), pretty good (19%), and very good (13.9%). The motives for using Klingon, unlike the motives for its invention, are not practical, but they are in a sense artistic: speaking or writing at least a bit of Klingon figures significantly in some fan performance of *Star Trek*, a sort of living fan fiction.

Apart from using the same language, a language community shares common patterns of language use and attitudes to that language.

The survey showed that most Klingon-speaking respondents considered their native language easier to use and a better means of communication than Klingon, yet 63.3% wanted their (future) children to learn both languages. About one third thought Klingon the more beautiful of their two languages, and a bit more than a third considered both languages equally beautiful. As many as 70% of all 109 survey respondents hoped that Klingon would flourish, gaining more speakers and becoming more popular. The number of people who really expected Klingon to flourish, however, was (well) below 50%. Furthermore 66.1% thought Klingon would survive only as a *Star Trek*-related hobby for a very limited group of people, i.e., the *Star Trek* fans that use Klingon as 'a way of becoming a super trekkie' as one respondent expressed it.

A Klingon speech community: myth or reality?

Can the group of Klingon users surveyed be considered a sociolinguistic group? On the basis of these survey results, we can conclude that, if there is a Klingon speech community, it is very small indeed. Most people who use Klingon belong to a subgroup of Trekkies, i.e., the most die-hard fans that live for *Star Trek* (as opposed to simple Trekkers who are just fans of *Star Trek*; see Gibberman 1991, 117). Since the survey was only sent to Klingon or *Star Trek*-related addresses on the Internet, all respondents were in one way or another related to Klingon or *Star Trek*, mainly as fans. On the basis of interviews with Klingonists, some of whom are also Trekkies, Wahlgren concludes that a bit of Klingon can build sub-cultural capital among the *Star Trek* fan community, but too much proficiency actually erodes that capital, since 'ordinary' *Star Trek* fans perceive Klingon speakers as weird, or at least 'a little strange'.

The survey, then, amounts to a profile of *Star Trek* fans who may also speak Klingon. Unless the *Star Trek* phenomenon persists, casual Klingon (that spoken or written less than once a month, or more than once a week but less than daily) will die out. Speaking Klingon, like wearing *Star Trek*-inspired costumes, collecting *Star Trek* paraphernalia, or visiting *Star Trek* conventions, supports fan group solidarity, but a fan group is by no means the same thing as a speech community, and members of that group certainly do not use Klingon frequently enough or well enough for the group to count as a speech community.

The story may be different with 'professional' Klingon users, who are interested in the language per se, such as members of the Klingon Language Institute and some of the respondents in Wahlgren (2004), who might continue to use and develop the language as a hobby even after the *Star Trek* phenomenon has passed. It remains to be seen whether the language is strong enough in terms of linguistic structure, degree of codification, number of speakers, and social embedding to survive. With the Klingon Language Institute's journal *HolQed* as a forum for scholarly discussion of Klingon, the Institute's online journal written wholly in Klingon, and various other Klingon language projects (see Appendix 5)—who knows what the future holds— there is certainly very sophisticated use of Klingon among a small cadre of speakers and a motive for continuing codification of Klingon grammar.

While hard-core Klingonists may not depend on interest in *Star Trek* to fuel their interest in Klingon language, they have depended on Okrand to make new, canonical words. Wahlgren notes, 'Marc Okrand has invented most words for Klingon and when the Klingonists need a new word they have to ask him' (2004, 21). As Okrent puts it, 'Klingonists are strict about language authority … No one but Okrand can introduce new vocabulary. And no dispute about grammar or usage is considered settled until Okrand has spoken' (2009, 279). This is no way to run a real language: in a real language, the speech community has authority over that language (see Appendix 1). If Klingonists succeed in maintaining Klingon, they will eventually do so without Okrand's help, and that will be the point at which viability of the putative Klingon speech community will be tested.

Okrent recalls that 'in 1999, the satirical paper the *Onion* ran a story under the headline "Klingon Speakers Now Outnumber Navajo Speakers". This is absolutely not true, but it would have been true had they picked nearly any other Native American language' (2009, 272). Klingon is an already endangered language, and it isn't yet fully developed for real-world conversational use! It could easily die on the vine. How many speakers of a language are required for it to be a going concern? Conversations among those at the Klingon Language Institute conference (or *qep'a'*) that Okrent attended were sometimes spontaneous, and 'it's amazing that spontaneous conversations happen at all', but too often those trying hard to converse resorted to PalmPilot dictionaries of Klingon.

There were, however, telling exceptions: 'I saw that later, as we walked over radiating sidewalks to a Mexican restaurant for the opening banquet, when I witnessed Captain Krankor and his girlfriend holding hands and chatting in Klingon, sans PalmPilots' (Okrent 2009, 273). You can bet that Captain Krankor, whose real name is Rich, is a Trekkie; the girlfriend, Agnieszka, has recently translated the *Tao Te Ching* into Klingon (see Appendix 5). It doesn't take many people to make a speech community, and a small speech community is at least a pure speech community. Captain Krankor and Agnieszka might be Klingon's Adam and Eve, chatting in their brand new language, walking hand in hand on the road from Eden to Babel.

References

Annernäs, Stefan. 1996. 'Klingon Questionnaire'. http://home1.swipnet.se/~w-12689/survey.htm

Bourdieu, Pierre. 1991. *Language and Symbolic Power*. Cambridge: Polity, in association with Basil Blackwell.

Gibberman, Susan R. 1991. *Star Trek: An Annotated Guide to Resources on the Development, the Phenomenon, the People, the Television Series, the Films, the Novels and the Recordings*. Jefferson, North Carolina: McFarland.

Hermans, Judith. 1999. *Klingon and its Users: A Sociolinguistic Profile*. M. A. thesis, Faculty of Arts, Tilburg University.

Okrand, Marc. 1985. *The Klingon Dictionary*. New York: Pocket Books.

Okrand, Marc. 1992. *The Klingon Dictionary*. Second edition. New York: Pocket Books.

Okrand, Marc. 1996. *The Klingon Way: A Warrior's Guide*. New York: Pocket Books.

Okrand, Marc. 1997. *Klingon for the Galactic Traveler*. New York: Pocket Books.

Okrent, Arika. 2009. *In the Land of Invented Languages*. New York: Spiegel & Grau.

Patrick, Peter L. (2004). 'The Speech Community', in *The Handbook of Language Variation and Change*, edited by J. K. Chambers, P. Trudgill, and N. Schilling-Estes, 573–97. Malden, Massachusetts: Blackwell.

Wahlgren, Yens. 2004. *Klingon as Linguistic Capital: A Sociologic Study of Nineteen Advanced Klingonists* [*Hol Sup 'oH tlhIngan Hol'e': Wa'maH Hut tlhIngan Hol po'wI'; nughQeD*]. Bachelor's Thesis, Department of Sociology, Lund University.

Wolfram, Walt. 1991. *Dialects and American English*. Englewood Cliffs, New Jersey: Prentice Hall.

~6~

Gaming Languages and Language Games

JAMES PORTNOW

In the two and a half decades that video games have been a major commercial force, they have generated a slew of strange dialects and spawned a thousand tongues. Why such a generative force from video games? The easy answer is that game design attracts the sort of mind likely to invent a language. The slightly more insightful answer is that game worlds need the richness and vibrancy invented languages provide, perhaps more than do fictional universes in other media. This is, in part, true. But if you were to ask me—which I suppose you are by reading this chapter—I would have to answer that it is because language is a form of play.

Playing with words

'I shall also call the whole, consisting of language and the actions into which it is woven, the "language-game".'
Ludwig Wittgenstein, *Philosophical Investigations*

Wittgenstein showed remarkable perspicacity in giving us the *Sprachspiel* or 'language-game'. He saw that languages and games share much. They both come with sets of formal rules which can be manipulated to express different outcomes. They both assume the Saussurean principle of arbitrary signification (that is to say, words and games have no bearing on the real world; they mean nothing unless a group of people agree that they do). And, perhaps most importantly, they are both fundamentally interactive. These similarities make crafting languages an obvious choice for game designers. Games are about interactivity and challenge: languages present inherently interesting and engaging challenges which are, moreover, grounded in something familiar from players' lives outside of games.

Language challenges range from basic word play, one of the oldest and most ubiquitous forms of play, to intricate language acquisition and translation tasks. They can be as simple as rhyming or as complicated as the deepest cipher. Designers hope to meet gamers' expectations of interactivity, and languages provide designers with a flexible mechanic to do so. Language games exercise gamers' mental dexterity: the better the gamer knows a language, the more fun can be had with it. As players better understand a game's language, they overcome linguistic challenges that deepen their insights about the game as a whole. All of this, coupled with the fact that one can never perfectly master a language, makes language itself more than a mere game component, but rather the perfect game.

Languages immerse players in a game's creative landscape. Languages express a great deal about the peoples and cultures to which they are attached—as mentioned in the preceding chapter, Klingon was purposely crafted to sound guttural and harsh, reflecting the aggressive character of Klingon society. Since massive multiplayer online games (MMOGs), for instance, are elaborate self-contained fictional worlds populated by characters of various cultures, they beg for languages corresponding to those cultures. The languages are an instrument of verisimilitude and thus help players to accept the strange and the foreign, to willingly suspend their disbelief.

Invented languages are especially suited to the medium of games. In other media invented language may be an engaging curiosity: only the most dedicated fans really come to learn such languages, which are otherwise an optional part of a narrative experience (see Appendix 5). One can easily skip passages in Elvish or watch *Star Trek* passively, absorbing the sounds but not the meaning of Klingon. In games, however, players aren't merely audient—they participate. Rather than observing conversations, players *have* conversations; they interact with the language, bringing it to life in the course of their game play.

The exigencies of play

Of course this level of interactivity comes with a price. The game designer's first commandment is that 'The game must be fun!' and while picking up Esperanto (or any other invented language) may be somebody's idea of a good time, its appeal is far from universal. Thus, language acquisition can't be a 'core game play mechanic': designers can't force players to learn invented languages in order to play their games. As a result, language creation for games is quite difficult. First, designers must justify having invented languages at all. Game creation is an expensive, labour-intensive endeavour requiring a multidisciplinary team of designers with disparate skills and interests. Every department will claim that they can think of better things to do with the available money than to put words no one can read in the game.

Having overcome that organizational hurdle, designers must create languages that reward the efforts of novice players, are learnable in the context of their games (there are no textbooks or teachers), are inessential to game play, fit the creative property, and can be learnt at unknown intervals. If a game doesn't do all of these things, it doesn't promote players' engagement or improve players' experience within the fiction of the game, both outcomes which should be a designer's constant goals. Games are a simulacrum of life, though they compress time and allow players to achieve things they cannot achieve in real life.

It should be rewarding to the novice

What is the first great moment in learning a language? The first time one uses the language fluently. Natural languages require months if not years of study before a learner achieves fluency. Obviously, gamers are unwilling to invest the time and effort such learning requires, so games devise shortcuts to fluency. A game language, and the game itself, are crafted so that even knowing a few words rewards learners with a plethora of otherwise mysterious and unintelligible information, thus engaging players and encouraging them to learn more of the invented language.

It is learnable in the context of the game

Designers can't expect players to 'study' or require them to bring knowledge from another medium to bear. These break the unwritten contract of fun. Game designers are supposed to provide players with entertainment. Players pay for this entertainment with money earned through work they may find tedious or unpleasant. They look to the game creator, and the game, for an escape. Does this mean designers can't teach, that playing a game at its best isn't learning? No, of course not. Every game requires designers to teach and players to learn the controls of the game, players' objectives in the game, and the rules of the world they've entered—teaching or learning a language is just another item on the list. In fact, games are an excellent means to teach, because the rewards for learning are so immediate and clear.

It must be inessential to game play

Nevertheless, as a condition of interactivity, designers can't control everything about their games: even if they leave tomes detailing how their languages work lying around, there is no guarantee that players will find them or, finding them, read them. Thus, all the interactions with an in-game language should prove rewarding regardless of what smattering of language or pastiche of vocabulary players have picked up, as specific knowledge of the language can't be required to continue the game. Additionally, designers can't force players to do something just because they, the designers, think it is 'neat' (as in, learning their awesome languages); designers' decisions must be motivated by what brings enjoyment to the players, which means allowing people who don't find languages interesting to find satisfaction in the game regardless of them.

It fits into the creative property

Language helps bring an imagined civilization to life. Invented language helps immerse people in the invented worlds and cultures presented to them. Designers have to be careful about how they craft their languages, which must coordinate historically and affectively with the cultures and people to whom they are assigned in their games. The point comes home if you imagine, just for a moment, Klingons speaking Sindarin or Tolkien's elves singing in Klingon.

It can be learnt at unknown intervals

Curiously, games occupy a shorter period of time than other activities (reading books, watching a television series) that include invented languages, and many games aren't serialized in the manner of traditional narratives: in many games (*Final Fantasy*, *Mario*, and *Zelda* come to mind), just because one game follows another in a numbered sequence doesn't mean it takes place in the same universe, time, or even (imaginary) dimension as the preceding game. Designers are lucky, then, if players interact with their game worlds—and thus their game languages—for forty hours over the course of a few months. This fact poses significant challenges to designers: the languages they invent not only need to be fun and functional for players playing in relatively short bursts, but players must be able to learn them at whatever pace they play through the game.

So what does all this mean? Simply put, it means that not many games warrant a full language, which leads instead to the creation of what I call 'flavour languages'. A flavour language is an incomplete language often comprising only a few sentences that operate unsystematically, that is, without following strict rules. A flavour language's sole purpose is to deliver just a taste of the culture of the group that speaks it, not to serve as a means of communication among game characters. Games have produced literally hundreds of flavour languages over the last three decades. The Protoss language in *Starcraft*, Yorda's language in *Ico*, and the language of the LocoRocos in *LocoRoco* are notable examples. Of course, while these proto-languages are interesting in their own right, they aren't our primary subject here.

Parallel evolution

When examining languages in games, it is important to remember that they are a function of game design, which is a relatively young science. As in the progress of most fledgling fields of study, advances in game design have been moving at a breakneck pace, which is reflected in the languages its practitioners generate. Game languages can be distributed among three distinct ages:

- The Mists of History—back when, as I understand it, video games were played on stone blocks, hand-chiselled as players made decisions (i.e., the late 1980s, really, anything up until about 2000);
- The Modern Era—anything after the launch of the PlayStation 2 in 2000;
- Massive Multiplayer Games and the Future— the title says it all.

Any game language should be taken in the context of its age. Interestingly, the languages found in games evolved in parallel with the evolution in games as they went from being the purview of a few fanatical enthusiasts to an industry that outsells the box office.

The Mists of History

GARGISH

Created by Herman Miller, Gargish, the language of gargoyles in *Ultima VI* (1990), was one of the first fully realized game languages. Gargish is planted deep in the Mists of History and makes an interesting case study. (The *Ultima* series originated in 1980 and is arguably the progenitor of graphical role-playing games.)

Gargish is a very difficult language for an English speaker to acquire. Word order in spoken Gargish is almost entirely flexible, with parts of speech and tenses made clear through gestures and intonation, rather than in affixes and vowel changes (as in synthetic languages like Ancient Greek, Latin, Old English, etc.), or sentence order (as in modern English). As far as I'm aware, this feature is unique to Gargish and not found in any natural language. Additionally, native speakers of Gargish (i.e., Gargoyles) drop pronouns in a fashion similar to modern Japanese.

Gargish is scribed in a fluid semi-runic script. There are thirty letters in the Gargish alphabet, some of which represent English sounds and sounds familiar from other European languages, such as /ny/, represented in Spanish by ñ. Yet there are also very un-English clusters, such as /nl/ and /hl/, represented by single characters in the Gargish alphabet. Gargish has five 'basic' vowels (*a, e, i, o,* and *u*), each represented by the most elementary figure in a group of six figurally related runes — vowels are the rune roots. The other five stand for consonants, and add distinctive lines and dots to the vowel rune. The consonants in each rune family are phonetically related: for instance, the alveolar sounds — /z/, /s/, /n/, /d/, and /t/ — so phonetic relations are rune relations and vice versa. Vowels can be either long or short, though there are no clear rules for when a vowel should be either, and the length distinction is not made in spelling, unless two words are homographs, in which case the vowel is doubled in the word with the long vowel.

In contrast, written Gargish has a series of suffixes which are used in place of the intonation and gestures to imply tense, mark parts of speech, and modify words: *-char* 'part', *-de* 'of' (denotes adjectives or adverbs formed from nouns, verbs, and other words), *-ku* 'with' (forms adjectives), *-le* 'end' (denotes past tense or perfective verbs), *-lem* '-er' suffix, *-re* 'begin' (denotes the future tense of verbs), *-sa* '-able' suffix, *-tas* 'quality' (denotes abstract nouns), *-te* 'in' (denotes present tense or imperfective verbs), and *-ve* 'like' (forms adjectives).

Gargish has at least 500 canonical words, though rumour has it that the count is now over a thousand. Given these and the suffix modifiers, quite a lot can be expressed in Gargish. For instance, let's consider a phrase that appears in *Ultima VI*, translating it literally and then idiomatically into English. Here is some necessary vocabulary: *ter* 'place', *esta* 'that', *sit* 'lie, rest', *lem* 'he, she, it, they; him, her, it, them; one; those', *an* 'negative, no', *ten* 'have', and *noms* 'names'.

Ter-esta sit lem antende noms.

> Literal translation: 'Place-that lie ones not-have-of name.'
> Idiomatic translation: 'Here lie those that have no names.'

This exercise demonstrates that Gargish is a decipherable language; of course, translation would have been somewhat more difficult had we chosen one of the numerous other valid forms of that Gargish sentence—remember, the words can occur in any order, so there are 120 possible versions of the sentence. Decipherable, however, is not the same as 'intuitive', and using or making sense of Gargish takes some work on the game player's part.

Clumsy but usable, Gargish is clearly a Mists of History language. Learning it requires monumental effort from users: first, students of Gargish must learn to transcribe the runes; then, they have to understand the vocabulary into which they've transcribed the runes. Once users decipher the rune script, they must then wrestle with a complex and counterintuitive grammatical system and the unnecessary opacity of dropped pronouns in order to decrypt the Gargish they find in the game. This sort of back-breaking, mind-shattering labour could only be thought reasonable when applied to a much smaller, more dedicated audience than games have today. Certainly, one of Gargish's attractions for gamers is the challenge it poses, the multilayered linguistic puzzle it offers players. The puzzle that game designers have to solve is how multilayered a game language can be, how challenging it can be, while not violating the maxims outlined above, especially the ones about rewarding the efforts of novice players and being learnable in the game context but at unknown intervals of play. However, a game language of some complexity may intensify interactivity for players interested in learning it.

D'ni

D'ni is the language of the Myst series of games by Cyan Worlds. Originating in 1993, this language is also rooted in The Mists of History. The D'ni language is one of the most intricate and complicated languages yet created for a game, although, oddly enough, the language was not actually first presented in a game at all: D'ni script was first used on a map insert for one of the fiction books about the world of Myst, *The Book of Ti'ana* (1996). D'ni is an intricate language, and we can consider only some of its most fascinating features here. If the following description piques your interest, there is a large and active Internet community devoted to the language; if you attempt to learn it, there are plenty of people who will give you a hand.

But, to begin, let's look at the written alphabet of D'ni:

v	b	t	s	š/sh	j	g	y	x/kh	k	a/ah	i	f
[v]	[b]	[t]	[s]	[ʃ]	[ʤ]	[g]	[j]	[x]	[k]	[ɑː]	[aɪ]	[f]

p	ih	i/ee	e/eh	é/ay	r	m	þ/th	ð/dh	d	h	o
[p]	[ɪ]	[iː]	[ɛ]	[eɪ]	[r]	[m]	[θ]	[ð]	[d]	[h]	[ɔː]

ó/oy	ç/ch	w	u	ú/oo	c/ts	l	æ/a	z	ñ	apostrophe	period
[ɔɪ]	[ʧ]	[w]	[ʊ]	[uː]	[c]	[ʟ]	[æ]	[z]	[n]		

143

Note the fluid nature of D'ni: it is a calligraphic language usually written in a flowing script, as seen below:

At first this may seem an odd choice of script for an invented language (it differs markedly from Gargish runes, for instance), as the fluid script makes individual letters harder to distinguish, thereby setting up an artificial barrier for the novices. But we must look at D'ni, as with all game languages, in the context of the game and the game world for which it was created.

The Myst series is predicated on the idea of an ancient race, the D'ni, with the ability to create worlds (or at least create portals to them) by writing about them in books. The fiction requires that the script used to write those books be intricate and inaccessible; it focuses on the last remnants of this race, who struggle to control the script and its powers. Where a brush stroke can alter reality a simple script is insufficient, even dangerous.

D'ni is an entirely phonetic language: all letters correspond to sounds—there are no 'silent letters'. While this eases most things, it leads to easy mistakes if you are trying to transliterate. Also, D'ni has only one punctuation mark: the 'begin sentence' mark. The D'ni 'apostrophe' marks syllable breaks where they would otherwise be unclear. The full stop or period functions exactly as in English except that it is viewed as a 'begin sentence mark' rather than an end sentence mark, so paragraphs begin with a.

Perhaps the most interesting feature of D'ni is not linguistic at all but numeric. The D'ni use a base 25 number system with characters as follows:

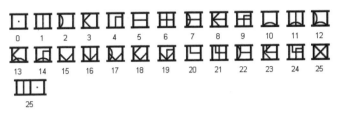

What does this mean? Well, let's take a three digit D'ni number and dissect it.

(Note that D'ni conjoins digits in order to express them as a single number.)

The smallest place value in D'ni is presented furthest to the right, in much the same way that Arabic numerals are written. Thus, the above example has 19 in the 'ones' place. That's simple enough, but the next digit over is in what we would call the 'twenty-fives' place. A 5 in the twenty-fives place, in base ten, equates to 125. Finally, we have a 3 in the 'six-hundred and twenty-fives' place. (If you are not familiar with working in non-base ten systems, each place is the next power of the system, so the first digit is the 25^0 place or 'ones' place, the second digit is the 25^1 place or 'twenty-fives' place, the third digit is the 25^2 place or the 'six-hundred and twenty-fives' place.) Three times 625 equals 1875. So, altogether, our three-digit D'ni number equals 19 + 125 + 1875, or 2019 in base ten.

This mathematical system extends into the D'ni language. By putting a 𝒵 in front of a number in a sentence that number becomes an adverb to describe degree or intensity. For example, it would be as if in English, instead of saying 'I was walking slowly,' I said 'I was walking to the five.' Thus, the whole adverbial system is predicated on a base twenty-five understanding: something done 'to the twenty-five' is extreme; something done 'to the one' is very mild. If you want to be hyperbolic about something in D'ni, you simply say it is to a number more than twenty-five.

Why such focus on the system of numeration? In order to answer, we must consider the context of the language, though, in this case, rather than looking at the fiction it was created to support, we must look at something much more practical: the game it was designed to sell. The Myst series is, fundamentally, a set of puzzles strung together by stories and images. If players are faced with a puzzle they can approach in a manner that is arguably valid but that the designer did not consider, the game ends in a frustrating and unpleasant manner—unsatisfied players don't buy sequels. Mathematical puzzles require no interpretation; there is nothing subjective about them; they are ideal for a single-player computer game like Myst. Thus Myst uses this strange numeration in order to make its unambiguous numerical puzzles more engaging and interesting and the game more compelling.

Other peculiar features of D'ni include the following:

- D'ni is a Subject -> Verb -> Object language much like English.
- D'ni requires subject-verb agreement like most Romance languages.
- D'ni employs a signal suffix to turn any noun into an adjective (*rock* to *rocky*).
- D'ni employs a signal suffix to turn any adjective into a noun (*thick* to *thickness*).
- D'ni allows for a plural indefinite article (*a dogs*).
- Due to the lack of a comma in written D'ni, lists are formed by inserting the word for 'and' between each item in the list.
- In D'ni, word order can be used to designate the importance of modifier words.

There is a striking contrast between these cumbersome, if elegant, languages of early gaming and the simple functional nature of languages of the Modern Era.

The Modern Era

Our first Modern Era language isn't a language at all; in fact, it's gibberish, but that does not prevent it from being one of the most important and widely known 'languages' ever invented for a game.

SIMLISH

Invented for *Sim Copter* (1996), Simlish has grown in popularity continuously over the last decade. In fact, Simlish was featured in more than one game release in 2008. Musical artists from Anthrax to Katy Perry, from Depeche Mode to the Black Eyed Peas, have all recorded tracks in Simlish, which isn't really a language so much as a vocabulary with a particular sound. What draws so many and various people to this 'language'? The answer is partly in its origins in the game to which it belongs: *The Sims*. *The Sims* is a game of 'virtual dolls'. In the game, one creates virtual dramas about human relationships. It is exactly what it purports to be: a light, fun simulation of everyday human experience.

Unlike other games discussed here, there is no fiction to support and no game play that requires an artistic language in *The Sims*. Why, then, would such a game have an invented language (or an invented vocabulary meant to suggest an invented language)? The answer is simple: known language limits the imagination. Will Wright, the lead designer for *The Sims*, wanted to make sure that users could tell their own stories, that they weren't limited by a small library of recorded dialogue: he needed an emotive language unfamiliar to his audience. At first he experimented with adapting Tagalog, Navajo, and Ukrainian to his purposes, but he wasn't satisfied with the results. All of those languages are too grounded in reality. He needed something hyper-expressive: a language that was, in itself, fun. At last, he hired members of a local improv troupe and told them what he was looking for: Simlish was born.

The Sims took off to become the bestselling franchise in video game history, and, to date, Simlish has been heard by millions of people worldwide. So we should return to our original question, 'What makes Simlish so compelling and so popular?'

First, to my knowledge, Simlish is the only language ever invented for the sole purpose of being enjoyed. Freed from the normal constraints of language, Simlish functions viscerally—it is not per se a language of ideas, nor is it a language embedded in a cultural history, fictional or otherwise. Second, Simlish is immediately accessible. An emotive language, it assumes an intimate relationship between its phonology and its vocabulary: the 'meaning' of the sounds is supposed to be the meaning of the words. Third, as a non-language, Simlish makes a remarkably good cross-cultural language. It is not rooted in any particular cultural/linguistic tradition, making it substantially more universal than any other game language. Additionally, its essentially improvisational quality makes Simlish an easy language to sing in. Fourth, Simlish is attached to an entertainment juggernaut: *The Sims* franchise has sold well over 30 million copies; it is published by the biggest video game publisher in the world. The resources devoted to Simlish are simply without parallel in the video game industry.

AL-BHED

The second language of interest to us from The Modern Age is also not a language in the strictest sense: it is a carefully crafted substitution cipher. Al-Bhed, the language spoken by the Al-Bhed people in *Final Fantasy 10*, can be translated using nothing more than the substitution key below:

A B C D E F G H I J K L M N O P Q R S T U V W X Y Z
Y P L T A V K R E Z G M S H U B X N C D I J F Q O W

Do you notice anything special about the above set of substitutions? It's OK—take a moment. All of the Al-Bhed vowels are identical to English vowels and substitute for them systematically. If you examine other substitutions, you'll notice phonetic similarities as well. For instance, assuming phonetic values usually represented by the letters in English, English /p/ becomes Al-Bhed /b/, and English /d/ becomes /t/; in both cases, the phonemes in question differ only in voicing, though in the former, an unvoiced bilabial stop becomes a voiced one, while in the latter, a voiced alveolar stop unvoices. Why? Because

Al-Bhed merely passes itself off as a language: it's really a sort of cipher of English, but *Final Fantasy 10* includes a considerable amount of Al-Bhed dialogue, so the cipher *must* be speakable.

As a result of these careful phonetic correspondences, almost any word in English is pronounceable after being translated into Al-Bhed, because it conforms to English phonotactic constraints, the rules that determine which sounds can appear next to other sounds and at which positions in syllables. (Sometimes, as in English, the pronunciation will rely on inserting a glide between a consonant and a vowel; for example, *cu* is often pronounced as *cue*). I have actually met someone who could translate English into Al-Bhed on the fly, much as one might do with Pig Latin.

Originally, *Final Fantasy 10* was a Japanese game. When Square, the company that created *Final Fantasy 10*, decided to bring the game to the United States, they had to invent an entirely new cipher for their language: the one you see above. Al-Bhed is clearly a more modern game language than Gargish or D'ni. It is easily accessible to players, with few rules to memorize. Its grammar is identical to English, as are its alphabet and punctuation marks. Its spelling is easily derived from English words, and its vocabulary parallels the vocabulary the user already knows.

Al-Bhed is completely integrated into the game play of *Final Fantasy 10*. As players traverse Spira (the game's world) and play through the game, they come across 'Al-Bhed Primers', each of which teaches the player how to translate a single sound from Al-Bhed to English. Moreover, the game automatically translates any sounds which the player has learnt from the primers in the game's subtitles.

What is the major difference between languages of The Modern Era and those from The Mists of History? It's not the fact that they are simpler or that they are less concerned with being a real 'language'. Rather, they are focused on spoken rather than written communication. Gone are the fancy scripts and intricate writing; Modern games are concerned with how language sounds. And this is down to a technological advance: with the popularization of the DVD as a means of data storage for games, game designers and sound engineers finally had the storage capacity they needed to include large amounts of spoken dialogue with their games, which allowed them to bring characters and languages to life intimately and personally, through the human voice.

Massive Multiplayer Online Games and the Future

In order to project the future of invented languages in games, we must consider the current state of the game industry. In this section, rather than dissecting two invented languages, we will discuss two industry trends: franchising and the online revolution. In the context of 'the online revolution', we will consider one of the most extensive symbolic languages ever crafted for a creative endeavour—and why it failed.

FRANCHISING

In the video game industry, we refer to anything with multiple sequels as a franchise. This may be confusing to those unfamiliar with video games, but it makes sense if you think of it as you would think about the 'James Bond franchise' or the 'Superman franchise'. Of course, even more than with those franchises, the original creators of a franchise in the video game business may have nothing to do with sequel games or products associated with the franchise. In the video game industry, corporations in which games are spawned, rather than the creative and technical talent that brought them to life, usually control the franchises.

This leads to some very 'interesting' sequel work. If you go to your local game retailer and peruse the shelves, you will notice a fascinating trend: finding games with the number '5' or more after the title is not that uncommon. Moreover, if you are particularly knowledgeable about the history of games, you will realize that, due to the vagaries of game numbering (which is a subject that could easily fill a chapter in some other book), the number of games that fit within a franchise with five or more titles in the series is almost mind-numbing.

Why is this? If we look to other media—film, literature, music—this sort of rabid franchising is nowhere near as common. So why is it normative in games? Because games are somewhat unique in the media world: they are equal parts software and creative endeavour, so being able to establish a franchise and reuse most of the software component gives a corporation an enormous business and creative edge. If a game becomes a franchise, the corporation that owns it can focus on polish rather than on core technology.

So what does this mean for invented languages? Well, it means that they might become worth the investment they take to create in some game franchises, as they can be developed over time and see extended use in sequels and spin-offs. At least that would be the case if what constituted a 'franchise' in the games industry wasn't literally as broad as 'anything that bears part of the same name as another title'. Overall though, the industry has come to realize how much it encourages franchising, and at least a few companies will dabble with developing invented languages in order to make their series unique. Franchising will lead to the creation of a few strong, sticky languages that may, to a limited degree, spill over into pop culture.

The online revolution

Once upon a time you built one game, shipped it off to stores, and moved on to building the next one. This is no longer the case. Over the last decade games have moved from being static products to perpetually growing entities, patched and altered long after release. Perhaps the most interesting of these entities is the MMOG or Massive Multiplayer Online Game.

MMOGs typically provide a large community of players with a living world continually updated by the developer. Successful MMOGs have a five- to ten-year life cycle, and an individual player can easily log thousands of hours during a multi-year engagement with a single game. This sounds like the perfect environment for incubating invented languages, and it will be, but to date only one group has really tried to integrate an invented language into an MMOG, and that attempt ended in commercial disaster.

LOGOS

Before we explore this language on our own, we are lucky to have a few words (written at my invitation) about its creation from its creator, Richard Garriott:

> When creating artificial languages, we are trying to create a sense of history and culture that goes beyond the normal experiences of the real player. This happens either as historical back-story or perhaps, as in the case of *Tabula Rasa*, an alien culture. You want a language to be different enough to feel strange and mysterious. But it can't be mere scribble on a wall, which I find hollow. Players can usually tell if the language is fake, because some simple line is repeated over and over, or, as is found in some cases, clearly meaningless symbols are randomly scattered about on a surface. Not only does this diminish the value of the alternative reality, but in my mind a great opportunity is lost. Why not make such a language real, with real data and clues?

> The next common error in creating a language is to make it too complex. In books and movies, Tolkien and *Star Trek* can get away with Elvish and Klingon. In an interactive world, where the player is the leading character, I believe the player needs to have success at mastering any arcane forms of communication through the normal process of play. When I see most people develop game languages, they create communication that is complex, obtuse and hard to pronounce in addition to being difficult to read, write and understand. I am a devout believer that you must work hard to find the right balance of initially unknown yet recognizable communication. Then the language must be learned casually through normal play and not require any special study. Too often I see games with names, places and characters whose names cannot be pronounced, much less provide any real meaning to the player.

To this end, when I began work on an alternative language for *Tabula Rasa*, I started with the aforementioned goals. In addition I had some specifics pertaining to the problem of *TR's* reality. For *TR* I wanted to create a language which was invented by an advanced alien race to send on probes they scattered into the cosmos for other beings to find and decipher. Thus, it was designed specifically by its fictional creators to be easy to read. So I began my work researching symbolic languages. Those who know me well understand that I am a devout believer in research for good game design. All too often designers go with their first instincts, which I find rarely to be new or compelling. I believe research will more reliably result in something truly fresh and powerful.

When I began my research into symbolic language design, I found many dead ends. Egyptian hieroglyphics, for example, are a great example of easy symbols with difficult interpretation that took scholars years to decipher. Likewise hobo writing and other colloquial systems were usually very obtuse. In fact in today's society, we now face this issue regularly with the need for international signs that can be understood without regard to language background. Also there is a lot of work with pictographic languages for use in communications with the disabled. Plus there are other ancient examples of communications like the early forms of Chinese calligraphy, which was a very complete pictographic language.

With an extensive research library of such sources I dove in to create my own language. I found that many modern creations were unnecessarily complicated and not capable of complete communication, so I built my own middle path. I started with simple pictograms of people and objects. I created batches of small slips of paper and spread them out on the floor and worked for months sorting and simplifying, often redoing many base concepts, until I arrived at a core set of symbols that I could use in combination and with modes to express fairly complete communication.

Then we began to use these symbols throughout the game, on art and architecture, to enrich the experience. And similar to Egyptian, Greek or Roman society and even modern societies, the architecture displays the history of its people. But in *Tabula Rasa*, our system could more easily be deciphered than say Latin or hieroglyphics.

After that, we built a collecting game, where players would encounter the symbols in the game, interpret them one at a time, appreciate them passively, but through gameplay understand and learn them. Finally, I think it is important that developers make sure not to press the player too hard into mastering such arcane knowledge. While there will be some hard-core players who learn to read and write such languages fluently, keep in mind that the goal is to enrich the experience, not task the player with mastering a new language to be able to advance in the game.

Before considering features of Logos itself, we should put the language in context:

- Logos was created by the same man who produced *Ultima VI* — the game that spawned Gargish.
- Logos is the only fictitious language used as a means of communication from space to earth.
- Logos is an entirely symbolic language based on languages created to communicate with the mentally disabled.
- Logos was created for a game called *Tabula Rasa*. *Tabula Rasa* was a monumental commercial failure.

Consider what Garriott says above and think back to Gargish. The evolution from the mists of history to the age of MMOGs couldn't be made clearer. Logos, the language of *Tabula Rasa*, was clearly crafted with the intention of making it easy to learn.

Practically anyone could decipher one or two Logos symbols at a glance. An upward-pointing arrow means 'up' and an hourglass-like figure means 'now'; a modified stick-person means 'self, me'. Base symbols can be modified by other, less referential (more abstract) symbols to mark grammatical (including adverbial) meaning. For instance, when the symbol marking interrogatives is placed adjacent to the hourglass base, on its left, 'now' transforms into 'when'.

The number of hash marks above a noun symbol, like the stick-person figure, signifies whether it is in first, second, or third person. Duplicating and conjoining a symbol makes it plural. So, a stick-person figure with one hash mark above its head means 'me', one with two hash marks means 'you (singular)', and one with three means 'him/her'; two hash marks above and between the two heads of two conjoined stick-persons means 'all of you', that is, 'you (plural)'. Finally, putting parentheses around a noun puts it in the genitive case: the stick-person with two hash marks 'you' thus means 'yours' when parenthetically enclosed.

After those few examples, you can probably decipher some simple statements in Logos, and the symbols are abstract enough and culturally neutral enough to be deciphered in a galaxy far, far away. Logos has all the hallmarks of a great invented language: it is simple, rewarding to the novitiate, universal (the native tongues of learners have no bearing on their ability to use Logos). And it has all the hallmarks of a great game language: it is well integrated, it is part of game play without being a requirement of game play, it has a well orchestrated learning curve, and the way it's taught is exciting and fun. So again, we must ask, 'Why did it fail?'

Tabula Rasa was one of the biggest commercial disasters in the MMOG landscape: it was in development for seven years and took over a hundred million dollars to make, yet it was shut down a year after it launched. Thus, Logos will disappear long before D'ni or Al-Bhed. This very book may end up becoming one of the principal sources for future students of invented languages to discover what Logos was.

Logos failed because too much time and money was spent creating a game that wasn't ready when delivered to the public. It is easy to talk about invented languages in isolation, but it is essential to remember that they are not isolated at all. Invented languages are intimately bound to the worlds for which they are created. Had *Tabula Rasa* been a flawless game, Logos would eventually have taken its place next to Elvish or Klingon. So, all would-be architects of language, remember: spending too much time on your language and not enough on its game context will ensure that the world learns about neither. The fate of the language depends on the fate of the game.

1337

Thus far we have discussed languages found *in* games, but no study of video game languages would be complete without looking at 1337 or Leet, the international language of gamers (see Appendix 6).

Leet has evolved to be an entirely disruptive and exclusionary language: it has no other purpose than to exclude the uninitiated (at least for those who take it seriously). Even the language's name comes from a shortening of *elite*. Originally, though, Leet was invented by hackers in the early 1980s as a diversion, a sort of game in and of itself, for it served as an unconventionally fun way to write on a computer. Since then, it has evolved to a degree both mind-boggling and ridiculous, but very effective in serving as an in-group social identifier.

It is rare for people to communicate entirely in Leet, even for the duration of a single conversation; instead, 1337 peppers conversation and accentuates statements. Today, Leet is used to communicate everything from good-natured approbation to mockery and (figurative) emasculation. By many, the language itself is seen as a joke, as the purview of twelve-year-olds who believe using it makes them 'cool'.

So, what is 1337?

L337 15 n07 4 L4n6U463 8U7 |247H3|2 4 f0|2M 0f |}16174L C4LL16|24pHy. 17 U535 45C11 CH4|24C73|25 70 |}|24w 7H3 |20M4n 4LpH4837. N w1LL 83 7|24n5f0|2M3|} 1n70 |\| 4n|} 3 1n70 3. 7H3 H16H3|2 4 p3|250n'5 5K1LL w17H L337 15 7H3 L355 7H3y w1LL H4v3 70 U53 L471n L3773|25, w17H M4573|25 0f 7H3 L4n6U463 831n6 48L3 70 7|24n5C|2183 4ny7H1n6 pH|2453 w17H0U7 |2350|271n6 70 7H3 4LpH4837. 17 15 1Mp0|274n7 70 n073 7H47 L337 3v0Lv3|} 1n 4 CUL7U|23 0f 5p33|} 7yp1n6 50

7H47 C0MM0n L3773|2 7|24n5p051710n 7H47 0CCU|2 wH1L3
7yp1n6 H4v3 83C0M3 4CC3p73|} 5p3LL1n65 (0|2 3v3n
p|23f3|2|23|} 5p3LL1n65) 0f w0|2|}5. F0|2 3x4MpL3 "7H3" H45
83C0M3 "73H" 4n|} "0wn" H45 83C0M3 "pwn".

Or, in plain English:

Leet is not a language but rather a form of digital calligraphy. It uses
ASCII characters to draw the Roman alphabet. N will be transformed
into |\| and E into 3. The higher a person's skill with Leet is, the less
they will have to use Latin letters, with masters of the language being
able to transcribe any phrase without resorting to the alphabet. It is
important to note that Leet evolved in a culture of speed typing so that
common letter transpositions that occur while typing have become
accepted spellings (or even preferred spellings) of words. For example
the has become *teh* and *own* has become *pwn*.

A more sophisticated and advanced version of Leet can be seen in
the following transcription of the above paragraph (note the complete
absence of the Roman alphabet):

|337 15 |\|07 4 |4|\|6|_|463 8|_|7 |247|-|3|2 4 |=0|2|\/| 0|= |}16174|
(4||16|24|*|-|`/. 17 |_|535 45(11 (|-|4|24(73|25 70 |}|24\X/ 7|-|3
|20|\/|4|\| 4||*|-|4837. |\| \X/1|| 83 7|24|\|5|=0|2|\/|3|} 1|\|70 |\| 4|\||} 3
1|\|70 3. 7|-|3 |-|16|-|3|2 4 |*3|250|\|'5 5|<1|| \X/17|-| |337 15 7|-|3 |355
7|-|3`/ \X/1|| |-|4\/3 70 |_|53 |471|\| |3773|25, \X/17|-| |\/|4573|25 0|=
7|-|3 |4|\|6|_|463 831|\|6 48|3 70 7|24|\|5(|2183 4|\|`/7|-|1|\|6 |*|-||2453
\X/17|-|-|0|_|7 |2350|271|\|6 70 7|-|3 4||*|-|4837. 17 15 1|\/||*0|274|\|7
70 |\|073 7|-|47 |337 3\/0|\/3|} 1|\| 4 (|_||7|_||23 0|= 5|*33|} 7`/|*1|\|6
50 7|-|47 (0|\/||\/|0|\| |3773|2 7|24|\|5|*051710|\| 7|-|47 0((|_||2 \X/|-
|1|3 7`/|*1|\|6 |-|4\/3 83(0|\/|3 4((3|*73|} 5|*3||1|\|65 (0|2 3\/3|\|
|*|23|=3|2|23|} 5|*3||1|\|65) 0|= \X/0|2|}5. |=0|2 3><4|\/||*|3 "7|-|3"
|-|45 83(0|\/|3 "73|-|" 4|\||} "0\X/|\|" |-|45 83(0|\/|3 "|*\X/|\|".

Leet includes features from other playful exclusionary strategies in
language like rhyming slang or back slang. *Woffles* can be substituted
for *ROFL* 'rolling on the floor laughing'. *Banned* can be spelled '|3&'.

Phrases like 'Roxors your Soxors' are as common as they are meaningless.

But, as Leet is mostly relegated to teh 12 year old N3wbs out to pwn, such creative and enjoyable uses of the language are rare. Everyday Leet resembles the following: 'STFU N3wb', or 'J00 Roxor', or 'We totally pwned that mob'. For an older crowd, peppering speech with Leet often conveys sarcasm. For example, a player who says 'Good job guys, you rock' is probably being serious, but one who says 'GJ guys, joo teh roxor' is probably mocking fellow players. The next line of this script of mockery is 'GG newbs'.

Which brings us to the ubiquitous use of the term *GG*: this stands for 'good game' and is often offered seriously after a quality match against a respected opponent; but it is also used to mock a person's ineptitude, in or out of a game. On one hand, it is legitimate to say *GG* if your buddy walks into a lamp post or if he buys his girlfriend football tickets for their anniversary; on the other hand, it can be used to congratulate someone who makes a small fortune on the stock market. *GG* completely encapsulates the rest of 1337: it is obscure, self-contradictory, only tangentially related to its English basis, and completely incomprehensible to an outsider. 1337 is intended to be exclusionary and is a culture as much as a language—in fact, it is several cultures—and the only way to learn Leet is to live it. Its ever-evolving idiom prevents it from being taught, so, if you aspire to learn this abominable argot, hop on an MMOG or troll the boards at 4chan. Just be warned: 'Abandon hope, all ye who enter here.'

1 4p0|061z3 70 4|| 73h |337 h4x0r5 f0r 5p3||1n6 |337 "leet" 50 m4ny 71m35

Conclusion

Games stand now where film stood at the turn of the last century, on the verge of making the transition from an entertainment to an art form. With this transition we will see a rash of new ideas and an explosion of experimentation. People will push the bounds of the medium and expand it far beyond what we can imagine today, and all of this progress is tied to language.

Games themselves form their own language, some of it visual, some of it auditory, some of it linguistic, to describe the exigencies of artificial experience. Games present an alternative reality, one invented and foreign, one that allows players to go far beyond their prosaic, everyday lives—but to enter this alternative reality requires strong communicative competence in an alternative discourse. It requires the transfer of concepts as strange and alien as the worlds they allow us to explore, and this requires the invention of new language, the language of games. Games are fertile ground for invented languages. Wittgenstein told us that language is a game; today the inverse is also true—games cannot help but be a sort of language.

~ 7 ~

'Oirish' Inventions:

James Joyce, Samuel Beckett, Paul Muldoon

STEPHEN WATT

'When I say that I am an Irishman I mean that I was born in Ireland, and that my native language is the English of Swift and not the unspeakable jargon of the mid-XIX. century London newspapers.'
Bernard Shaw, 'Preface for Politicians' (1906)

'The language in which we are speaking is [the dean's] before it is mine. How different are the words home, Christ, ale, master, on his lips and on mine! I cannot speak or write these words without unrest of spirit. His language, so familiar and so foreign, will always be for me an acquired speech ... . My soul frets in the shadow of his language.'
James Joyce, A Portrait of the Artist as a Young Man (1916)

It is a widely accepted fact, perhaps even a cliché, that much significant Irish literature of the twentieth century adopts a peculiar, even adversarial, stance towards established languages. At times, this antipathy emerges in what are finally minor rebellions against grammar, syntax, and convention. So, for example, Bernard Shaw at times eschewed apostrophes when writing contractions and invented a method for indicating verbal emphasis in which spaces were added between letters; in this way, *revolt* became r e v o l t. James Joyce avoided quotation marks when writing dialogue, perhaps the least radical of his myriad experiments with language leading inexorably to *Finnegans Wake*. Sometimes, however, the struggles between artist and convention are waged over somewhat larger stakes than marks of punctuation and, not surprisingly, the most vexed of these obtains between Irish writers and the English language an uneasy *mésalliance*.

An Irish writer might discover that English failed to express Irishness, and the Irish modernist, James Joyce, for instance, might discover that it also failed to express matters of concern to what, in another but parallel context, has been called 'the international modernist avant-garde'. Such a writer might then attempt to *find* a medium to express Irishness, by appropriating the Irish-English resulting from the Ascendancy, for instance, or by renewing use of Gaelic, at least for literary purposes—but approaches such as these do little to promote modernism; moreover, one of them carries negative associations, while the other, renewal of Gaelic, was and remains a challenging project for the Republic. So the writer, unable to find an apt medium, would have to *invent* one, to construct a something, perhaps not a 'synthetic Irish' on the model of Hugh MacDiarmid's 'synthetic Scots' (see Appendix 7), but something enough to mark Irishness in modern and postmodern literature.

The inadequacy of English to the modern Irish writer's project, then, is a strong motive for inventing language. It is often assumed that the invented languages are the ones constructed systematically on typological principles, unique in phonology, morphology, syntax, and discourse, usually with a synchronic surface of structure and a diachronic back story (strong on both counts in Tolkien, much weaker in the case of Klingon, for instance). Sometimes, however, invention can be restrained, stylistic, just enough to do the political, cultural, literary work at hand.

English as the 'Oirish' speak it

A century ago, P. W. Joyce began *English As We Speak It in Ireland* (1910) by identifying features of what is often referred to as 'Hiberno-English': the disparity between the English *t* and *d* and the Irish *t* and *d*, which leads to the eccentric pronunciation of many English words (*laddher* for 'ladder', *thrue* for 'true'); the residue of Irish expressions that have insinuated themselves into English as it is spoken in Ireland; and the influence of idioms from Gaelic—those concerning personal pronouns, for instance, that manifest themselves in such constructions as 'He interrupted me *and I writing my letters*', as opposed to 'He interrupted me while I was writing my letters' (P. W. Joyce 1988, 1–9 and 33). All of this is, of course, the stuff of stereotype, even in Joyce's description, but stereotype derived from the dialects of many Irish speakers.

In his introduction to Joyce's book, Terence Dolan traces the genealogy of English in Ireland, a narrative inflected by conquest, nationalist resistance, and, in the case of the Great Famine of the mid-nineteenth century, historical nightmares that have exerted a profound influence on the fate of the Irish language. As historian R. F. Foster describes the post-Famine period, 'The Gaelic language was increasingly abandoned: a large proportion of emigrants came from Irish-speaking areas, and those left behind were not anxious to preserve it. Its eradication was the achievement of ambitious parents as much as of English-speaking schoolteachers' (1988, 340). This devolution, however, as P. W. Joyce understood it, led not only to the enervation of Irish, but also to the wider reliance on a fascinating hybrid: Hiberno-English, or English as the 'Oirish' speak it.

As my epigraph from Shaw's preface to *John Bull's Other Island* (the 'Preface for Politicians') confirms, the matter finally proves more complicated than a writer's or reader's linguistically impoverished education, or the recrudescence of Gaelic idioms in Hiberno-English, or the occasional animation of a sentence by a *gombeen, shoneen, smithereen,* or other expression. For the principal complicating factors are politics and history. As Shaw makes abundantly clear, one strategy of the English colonial project in Ireland—a strategy conspicuous at moments of tension between the two countries such as those following the violent Fenian insurrection of the 1860s—was the construction of stereotypes of Irishness partially defined by disparaging, albeit entertaining, linguistic features. The 'Paddy' or Stage Irishman, a constant presence on the London stage from the time of Macmorris's appearance in Shakespeare's *Henry V*, brought with him an all too familiar brogue and patois—manifestations of the 'unspeakable jargon' that Shaw derides—to complement his dishevelled (at times simian) appearance, pugnacity, and predilection for strong drink.

As Shaw's retort indicates, through the cultural work of such institutions as the theatre and the press, Irishness became associated in the Victorian imagination with specific linguistic excesses and inadequacies; thus, Tim Haffigan's exploitation of these conventions in the opening scene of *John Bull's Other Island* (1904) allows him to dupe the play's protagonist Tom Broadbent with relative ease. Haffigan reproduces the familiar Irish caricature expertly, complete with inflamed nose and comic patter: 'Dhrink is the curse o me unhappy counthry. I take it meself because I've a wake heart and a poor digestion; but in principle I'm a teetoatler' (Shaw 1963, 2.506). Weary of such representations in popular melodrama, among other literary genres, Lady Gregory, in her later 1913 manifesto *Our Irish Theatre* (1972, 20), pledged to 'show that Ireland is not the home of buffoonery and of easy sentiment, as it has been represented, but the home of an ancient idealism'. Irish cultural modernism, therefore, including the founding of the Gaelic League and the Irish Literary Theatre in the 1890s, might be regarded as a reaction against language or, more specifically, against depictions of Irishness that braided nationality with an amusing torture of English.

This observation, however, amounts to little more than a prolegomenon to any assessment of linguistic invention in Irish modernist and postmodernist writing, adjectives commonly, often problematically, applied to the three writers discussed here, who manifest a literary 'Oirish': James Joyce, Samuel Beckett, and Paul Muldoon. Joyce's surrogate Stephen Dedalus, as the second epigraph from *A Portrait of the Artist as a Young Man* suggests, regards English with a wary ambivalence, as Joyce himself did in his essay 'The Home Rule Comet' (1910), published originally in an Italian periodical: '[Ireland] has abandoned her own language almost entirely and accepted the language of the conqueror without being able to assimilate the culture or adapt herself to the mentality of which this language is the vehicle' (J. Joyce 1959, 212–213). This cultural dissociation is exactly what motivates MacDiarmid and others to promote Lallans, or 'synthetic Scots', in the Scottish Renaissance of roughly the same period (see Appendix 7).

What exactly *are* the British 'mentality' and culture? The latter serves as a target of Joyce's lacerating wit in *Ulysses*, where in the 'Aeolus' episode one commentator reduces the achievement of both the Roman and British cultures to the construction of efficient sewer systems:

> The Roman, like the Englishman who follows in his footsteps, brought to every shore on which he set his foot ... only his cloacal obsession. He gazed about him in his toga and he said: *It is meet to be here. Let us construct a watercloset.* (1986, chapter 7, lines 491–5)

However irresistible British culture or its 'syphilisation', as one character quips in the later 'Cyclops' episode, proved as a source of derision or scatological humour for Joyce's Dubliners, the irony existed that while many writers associated with the Irish literary renaissance read Irish—Lady Gregory and Douglas Hyde, to name but two—many others, including Joyce, did not.

Joyce underscores this irony in the opening episode of *Ulysses* when an old woman, an image of Mother Ireland, appears in the morning to deliver a 'measureful and a tilly' of milk (1986, chapter 1, lines 398–9). When Haines, an Englishman and Hibernophile staying with Stephen Dedalus and Buck Mulligan, speaks to her in Irish, she asks, 'Is it French you are talking, sir?' (1986, chapter 1, line 425). After the woman is informed that it is Irish, she laments, 'I'm ashamed I don't speak the language myself. I'm told it's a grand language by them that knows' (1986, chapter 1, lines 433–4). This dilemma, as Joyce phrases it in 'The Home Rule Comet', of abandoning Irish and speaking English yet failing to adopt its culture or 'mentality', contributes to Stephen's estrangement in *Portrait* when listening to the words 'home, Christ, ale, master'. The experience 'casts a shadow' over his soul, producing an estrangement from—yet intense fascination with—language that influences all of Joyce's writing and that of writers in the generations that succeeded him, represented here by Beckett and Muldoon, both of whom have acknowledged their profound indebtedness to Joyce.

Etymological Joyce

Scholars and critics intrigued by Joyce's linguistic invention invariably turn to the early pages of *Stephen Hero* (1944), once a part of the manuscript of *Portrait* but revised into a separate text by its author after the book was rejected by several editors. It was sold as a manuscript by Joyce's friend Sylvia Beach in the 1930s and later published after his death. While many sentences from *Stephen Hero* survive in the final text of *Portrait*, this passage describing Stephen's fascination with etymology does not:

> He was at once captivated by the seeming eccentricities of the prose of Freeman and William Morris. He read them as one would read a thesaurus and made a garner of words. He read Skeat's *Etymological Dictionary* by the hour and his mind, which had from the first been only too submissive to the infant sense of wonder, was often hypnotised by the most commonplace conversation. People seemed to him strangely ignorant of the value of the words they used so glibly … .
> (J. Joyce 1955, 26)

In addition to his near-obsession with etymology, Stephen also insists, as Joyce did, that words possess a 'certain value in the literary tradition and a certain value in the market-place—a debased value'.

In the literary tradition, words receive 'more valuable thoughts' (1955, 27), yet by the time Joyce published *Finnegans Wake* (1939), it became apparent that both words and conventional syntaxes and structures—even when borrowed from several languages so as to expand the possibilities of verbal representation (see Appendix 7)—would finally prove inadequate for his literary art. Joyce, as Beckett and Muldoon at times do, would have to invent his own language. And, at the risk of over-simplification, their principal motives for doing so are almost contradictory or paradoxical: for, on the one hand, while they endeavour to describe material reality more accurately with the always already inadequate tool of language, all three, on the other hand, suggest that such things as Time and Being are neither univocal nor singular, but inherently more plural and complex than any known language can capture. This is the sort of complexity, an Irish writer might propose, missing from English national consciousness and beyond articulation in the English language, much like the 'Caledonian antisyzygy', though for the Irish writer, unlike many Scots contemporaries, dialect—even MacDiarmid's synthetic dialect—might not be an 'Oirish' sufficient to contain the Irish mind (see Appendix 7).

More precisely, as Gregory Downing describes, Joyce regarded words as tools 'consciously employed in the creation or capture, and conveyance, of every kind of meaning—old and new, ordinary and abstruse, plain and mannerist' (1997, 33). At the most basic level of objective representation, linguistic invention allows for a more precise recording of the sights and sounds of everyday life. So, in *Ulysses*, Leopold Bloom's hungry cat greets him in the morning with 'Mkgnao!' rather than 'meow', and moments later her passive and contented 'mewing' and 'Prr' turn into a more insistent 'Mrkgnao!' after Bloom offers, 'Milk for the pussens' (1986, chapter 4, lines 16 and 24–5). In 'Aeolus', set in the offices of a daily newspaper, the sound of paper moving through printing presses produces a 'Sllt' in the background, a demonstration that, much like the sound of a door creaking, 'Everything speaks in its own way' (1986, chapter 7, line 177). In addition, throughout Joyce's writing, separate words are often combined to convey, for either literal or parodic purposes, the duality of an otherwise single thought or entity: the irreverent nicknaming of God as 'Nobodaddy', for instance, in the 'The Oxen of the Sun' episode of *Ulysses*. In part, this neologism marks the culmination of an ongoing discourse in the novel concerning the mystery of the Holy Trinity, the consanguinity of Father and Son, and the premise of the Nicene Creed that Christ was begotten, not made. Earlier, Stephen contemplates the Trinitarian notions of a 'Formless spiritual. Father, Word, and Holy Breath' (1986, chapter 9, line 61) and of a deity 'He Who Himself begot middler the Holy Ghost and Himself sent Himself' (1986, chapter 9, lines 493–4) to be crucified as His Son. As spiritual and therefore 'formless', the Christian God literally has 'no body'; as God the Father, creator of all things, he is 'daddy'. The term 'Nobodaddy' registers both qualities.

These lines from *Ulysses,* however, only dimly illuminate what Stephen Whittaker identifies as Stephen's (and Joyce's) 'etymological sense of the world' (1987, 178). Although Whittaker correctly argues that this sense 'tended more to opportunism and the good joke than to rigorous scholarship' (1987, 181), he also discerns more serious traces of this etymological sensibility in *Ulysses*. The cancer that killed Stephen's mother before the novel begins, for example, a death from which Stephen struggles to recover in part because his growing estrangement from Catholicism prompted him to refuse to pray for her as she lay dying, informs the hallucinatory 'Circe' episode. An image of his guilt, the ghost of his mother magically appears in the chapter to remind Stephen of his mortality, to pray for his redemption, and to urge him to 'Beware God's hand' (1986, chapter 15, line 4219). As she utters this admonition, a 'green crab with malignant red eyes sticks deep its grinning claws in Stephen heart' (1986, chapter 15, lines 4220–1).

Whittaker examines four editions of Skeat's *Etymological Dictionary of the English Language*, correcting the misimpression that Joyce knew the revised fourth edition published in 1910 and maintaining that the first three editions (published in 1882, 1884, and 1898) are 'virtually identical' (1987, 182). And in the earlier editions, Skeat defines cancer as 'a crab, a corroding tumour … named from the notion of "eating" into the flesh' (qtd. in Whittaker 1987, 184), a metaphor that undergirds Whittaker's reading of yet another motif in *Ulysses*, 'Agenbite of inwit' or guilt: 'For Stephen the Agenbite of inwit has become inwit's agenbite; the cancer of conscience literally *bites* his heart' (1987, 184). An allusion to the fourteenth-century inventory of sins and virtues *Ayenbite of Inwyt* (1340), itself a translation of a thirteenth-century French text, 'Agenbite of inwit' does more than reference the prick of conscience or remorse; it *performs* the interconnected quality of Being and thought itself.

As Downing explains, much linguistic invention in Joyce originates in precisely this sense of language that he gleaned from Skeat's *Etymological Dictionary*: 'The etymologies, and resultant connotations of the words and their images, insist on the "overlaps" of … putatively distinct areas of culture … . To Joyce, things are complex in themselves, as well as interconnected with each other. This inclusive tendency would have been reinforced in Joyce by the inclusive tropism in Skeat' (1997, 54). Following this logic of interconnection, in 'Circe' Joyce metaphorically links cancer with the crab: both eat bodies, some of which are already dead; therefore, each is a 'corpsechewer'.

Inclusive tropism

Joyce's etymological sensibility and inclusive tropism manifest themselves most fully in *Finnegans Wake*, one of the most challenging, linguistically complex texts of the previous (or any) century. In his study of the book, John Bishop identifies Joyce's manipulation of some forty-one languages and dialects—from Albanian to Welsh, from Finnish to Russian, from Romani to Sanskrit (1986, xii). Forty-one languages and dialects, though, as I have suggested, finally prove insufficient for Joyce's purposes, one of which, according to Bishop, is the creation of a text of 'stupefying obscurity'. Bishop recounts the 'pains Joyce took to deepen the opacity' of his *Work in Progress*, the original title of *Finnegans Wake*, not merely to baffle the reader for his own amusement, but for the entirely different representational purpose of depicting the complexities of dreaming and perception at night. The 'action of *Ulysses*,' Joyce is reported to have said, 'was chiefly in the daytime, and the action of [*Finnegans Wake*] takes place chiefly at night. It's natural things should not be so clear at night, isn't it now?' (1986, 3–4; Joyce's comment is quoted from Ellmann 1983, 590). From this premise, Bishop crafts an elegant defence of Joyce's project:

> Had Joyce made *Finnegans Wake* less obscure than it is, he would have annihilated everything about his material that is most essential, most engaging, funniest, and most profound—rather in the same way that an intrusive sweep of 'floodlights' would destroy any nightscape (134.18). The obscurity of *Finnegans Wake* is its essence and its glory. In its own artful form of 'chiaroscuro', the book renders the dark matters we have considered eminently 'clearobscure' (247.34 [the Eng. 'chiaroscuro' derives from the It. *chiar-oscuro*, 'clear-dark']). (1986, 10)

Somewhat paradoxically, therefore, linguistic obscurity in the *Wake*, as it is commonly abbreviated, actually operates in the service of mimesis, as things often combine blurrily in our night vision and in the composite pictures that emerge in dreams: 'I wished to invade the world of dreams,' Joyce told Samuel Beckett, and 'I have put the language to sleep' (Ellmann 1983, 546). The 'nightscape' to which Bishop refers differs radically from a landscape bathed in sunlight, and Joyce's book of the dark endeavours to represent this distinction.

Finnegans Wake is constituted, literally, of thousands of linguistic inventions. Many of these, following Downing's thesis concerning Joyce's comic use of etymology, are exploited for humorous effect. One famous and oft-quoted passage points good-naturedly to his friend Beckett's struggle to understand the book, parts of which Joyce narrated aloud after his eyesight deteriorated and he required assistance in transcription that the younger man was only too pleased to provide:

> You is feeling like you was lost in the bush, boy? You says: It is a puling sample jungle of woods. You most shouts out: Bethicket me for a stump of a beech if I have the poultriest notions what the farest he all means. (J. Joyce 1939, 112, lines 3–8)

Paul Muldoon attributes the motif of trees and forests in this elaborate inside joke to Joyce's knowledge of the etymology of *Beckett* as *bec* 'may be construed as a version of the Old English *boc* 'beech', a word that lies behind *book*' (2000, 15). Joyce's 'jungle of woods'—or 'jumble of words'—has 'stumped' this son of a beech, son of a Beckett, with the result that the younger writer is lost in a dense verbal forest or thicket.

Indeed, here Beckett is the embodiment of puzzlement itself: as 'Bethicket' he is both 'thick' and ensnared in a thicket at the same time. Such neologisms abound in *Finnegans Wake*, some based in etymology, others in clever portmanteau constructions of homonymic or punning origin: *collideorscape* (*collide* plus *kaleidoscope*) and *funferal* (an Irish funeral where having fun is the order of the day), for instance; the two young girls Earwicker supposedly spied in the Phoenix Park bushes are *gigglesomes minxt the follyages* 'young minxes in the foliage'. Proper names are subjected to the same essentially comic lacerations: *Camelot prince of dinmurk*, *Marely quean of Scuts*, and many more. Writers, Joyce seems to argue, naturally employ these verbal tools; those more pornographically inclined might even produce a *sinscript* under a *sootynemm* (1939, 420, line 5).

Joycean invention, however, involves more than neologisms and puns, plays on words like *syphilisation* and *sootynemm* that combine and distort familiar English words, and can at the same time exhibit stereotyped features of Irish English (in these examples the unvoicing of /z/ and /d/). As Bishop's and other studies explain, Joyce also deploys

European languages—and syntactical constructions—to similar effect. Roland McHugh, who bravely spent some three years reading the *Wake* before consulting glosses or scholarly studies to assist him, offers a persuasive reading of one of these:

> The older sisars (Tyrants, regicide is too good for you!) become unbeurrable from age (the compositor of the farce of dustiny however makes a thunpledrum mistake by letting off this pienofarte effect as his furst act as that is where the juke comes in) having been sort of nineknived and chewly removed (this soldier-author-batman for all his commontory-ism is just another of those souftsiezed bubbles who never quite got the sandhurst out of his eyes so that the champaign he draws for us is as flop as a plankrieg) the twinfreer types are billed to make their reupprearance as the knew kneck and knife knickknots on the deserted *champ de bouteilles*. (1939, 162, lines 1–11)

The passage appears in a longer comparison of *twinfreer types* (twins and brothers, i.e., twin *frères*) like Shem and Shaun, Earwicker's two sons in the *Wake*. In this chapter, historical periods are conflated in the extended comparison of Caseous and Burrus (Cassius and Brutus), one of whom is also a *caviller* 'Cavalier' and the other a *roundered head* 'Roundhead'. In the passage rendered above, McHugh identifies other pairs like *Caesars* (*sisars*) and extracts from the phrase *unbeurrable from age* a tandem of French words for butter and cheese, *beurre* and *fromage*. The *farce of dustiny* refers to Verdi's opera *La Forza del Destino*, but 'is distinguished by its composer's mistake: his first act is to let off a musically unsound triple trumpet kettledrum effect on the pianoforte, a thunder-drum sound like a full (Italian, *pieno*) fart' (McHugh 1981, 3–4). By the end of the passage, the rivals are prepared to meet each other not on the battlefield, but the 'bottle field', or *champ de bouteilles*. And, of course, this summary barely scratches the surface of puns and allusions in the passage, which, again, are bundled with dialectal allusions, as in the vowels of *farce of dustiny* and the almost incredibly indirect *bottle* behind *bouteilles*.

The motives for this continuous but unsystematic invention are thus complex: they are certainly political, performing a distinctive Irish voice aware of language difference, language history, language attitudes, and more than a little willing to play on them. But also and simultaneously, they are philosophical and symptomatic of modernism. Whether based in a convenient cleaving of homonyms or expressions from another language, or a creative and purposeful distortion of idiom or syntax, Joycean invention frequently contributes to what is finally an epistemological claim about the interconnection of two or more phenomena. That is to say, what Downing regards as Skeat's 'inclusive tropism', his illumination of the 'overlaps' of putatively distinct cultural discourses or realities, also describes linguistic invention in Joyce. Much the same might also be said about invented language in the writing of Samuel Beckett and Paul Muldoon.

Beckett is Joyce is Beckett

With his tongue firmly planted in his cheek, Friedhelm Rathjen, editor of an anthology of scholarly essays provocatively titled *In Principle, Beckett Is Joyce*, mused, 'The title of this volume declares that in principle, Beckett is Joyce—but the question remains as to what this principle may be' (1994, viii). Indeed. One answer, given the brevity of his later prose pieces and the minimalist aesthetic of his plays, is that Beckett represents the 'less' to Joyce's 'more'. But surely another principle would complement the argument about linguistic invention adumbrated above: namely, that like Joyce, Beckett (1906–1989) assumed an often antipathetic stance to language, to words and idioms as most people—or the 'market' to which Stephen Dedalus refers—employ them.

As a result, at times he needed to invent his own vocabulary and syntax. The titles of some of Beckett's last, some believe greatest, works intimate his criticism of language: *Ill Seen Ill Said* (1981) and *Worstward Ho*

(1983), for instance. The latter title, an allusion to Charles Kingsley's popular adventure yarn *Westward Ho!* (1855), reverses Victorian notions of Progress to signal Beckett's opposite sense of life's inevitable decline, while the former title succinctly captures his view of the inevitable failures of perception *and* the language used to communicate it. In *Ill Seen Ill Said*, an old woman, 'for want of better', gazes out of her window with a 'widowed eye', an eye that 'digests its pittance' in the dim light (1982, 22 and 24). The language Beckett affords his narrator is no more accurate or capacious than the 'vile jelly' with which his aged protagonist surveys her surroundings (1982, 52). What 'is the word? What the wrong word?' (1982, 17), Beckett's narrator wonders early in the narrative when endeavouring to describe the woman's resumption of movement, and throughout he labours at the tasks of verbal representation: 'Real and—how ill say its contrary?' (1982, 40); 'With what one word convey its change? Careful' (1982, 52), and so on.

The narrator's guarded utterances are, of course, less the result of his own failings than those of language itself and, more particularly, of words. In the short prose sketch *Stirrings Still* (1988), words like *thought*, *time*, *grief*, and *self* are often preceded, hence undercut, by the modifier *so-called*. In fact, *Stirrings Still* concludes with the sentiment 'Time and grief and self so-called. Oh all to end' (1988, n.p.). Perhaps the most concise, if also enigmatic, articulation of language's deficiencies appears in *Worstward Ho* (and, because of the obsessive scrutiny of language in Beckett's later fiction, it is difficult not to regard the title as a pun both on 'Westward Ho' and 'Worst-word Ho'). The passage appears near the book's conclusion: 'Whenever said said said missaid' (1983, 37).

As is often the case in Beckett's writing, particularly at its sparsest moments, the reader or audience must supplement lacunae in the text. Beckett's invention is in compression and elision; the reader's invention is in supplementing or etymologically 'intervening' in what Beckett wrote. In this instance, the reader invents syntax to render the sentence more intelligible and intervenes with mental punctuation:

for example, the line 'Whenever said said said missaid' becomes 'Whenever said [is] said [,] said [should be read as] missaid.' The motive for Beckett's ad hoc invention is thus to implicate the reader in a way of thinking, drawing not only on the repertoires of Irish speech and world languages, as Joyce had done, but on the reader's resources as well, no less political or epistemological than Joyce, but distinct in technique and effect nevertheless.

Human perception, thought, and language—words, idioms, and syntactical constructions—are invariably suspect in Beckett, which is precisely why such terms as *hubbub, farrago,* and other intimations of confusing mixtures or multiple internal voices appear repeatedly in his later prose works. Such a thesis seems consistent with the 'inclusive tropism' Joyce learned and appropriated from Skeat's etymologies, in part because for Beckett, nothing is 'pure' or, to borrow phrasing from *Ill Seen Ill Said,* 'unalloyed': 'If only she could be pure figment. Unalloyed' (1982, 20). Not surprisingly, then, Skeat appears allusively in Beckett's 'A Wet Night' from the early short-story collection *More Pricks Than Kicks* (1934) when the university student Belacqua Shuah, walking down a Dublin street, is 'run plump into by one Chas, a highbrow bromide of French nationality with a diabolical countenance compound of Skeat's and Paganini's and a mind like a tattered concordance' (1972, 49). Borrowing from George Berkeley's philosophy, in Beckett's writing 'To be is to be perceived' (the script of Beckett's film entitled *Film* (1964) is preceded by the epigraph '*Esse est percipi*') and perception is always already alloyed— tempered, mixed, and in decline like knowledge itself: 'Know nothing no. Too much to hope. At most mere minimum. Meremost minimum' (Beckett 1983, 9). Linguistic invention in Beckett seems thus both a necessary product of language's failing and an epistemological claim about the overlap or multiple nature of otherwise unitary things.

As in Joyce, neologisms abound in Beckett, many for comic or sharply ironic effect: the titles of his early volume of poetry *Whoroscope* (1930), for instance, and of his landmark play *Waiting for Godot*

(1953), in which two 'knockabouts' (Irish term for comic types) stand by a roadside waiting for a man or a little 'god' (*God* plus the French diminutive suffix *-ot*) who famously never arrives. To take another example, later in his life, as Beckett reached his seventies, he grew increasingly depressed about the ill health and death of old friends and associates. His aesthetic response to these losses was to scrawl very short poems—what he called 'mirlitonnades'—on any scrap of paper he could salvage: an envelope, beer mat, even a label from a bottle of Johnnie Walker Black Label whisky (Knowlson 1996, 568–9). Biographer James Knowlson notes that Beckett initially named these verses 'rimailles' or 'versicules' before settling on 'mirlitonnades', which some editors have translated as 'bird calls'; but, given the definition of *mirliton* in the *Oxford English Dictionary*, the name also recalls the buzzing or nasal quality of the sound produced by a musical instrument that resembles a kazoo. Even in the darkest of circumstances, Beckett sought unlikely sources of ironic humour and invented words to supply what he felt were lexical gaps.

More frequently, however, linguistic invention in Beckett, as in Joyce, originates in an epistemology of inclusivism that, much like the etymological relationship between *cancer* and *crab* in *Ulysses*, emphasizes the failings of the body and man's eventual mortality. So, for example, in many of Beckett's writings, bodily functions and products serve as either titles or analogies to the outpouring of words. In his early volume *Echo's Bones and Other Precipitates* (1935), originally titled *Poems*, 'Sanies I' and 'Sanies II' take their titles from a thin or fetid pus secreted by a wound or ulcer. In 'Cascando' (1936), 'the churn of stale words in the heart again/love love love thud of the old plunger/ pestling the unalterable/whey of words', conveying a similar figure of language's thinness or wateriness (Beckett 2002). In *Ill Seen Ill Said*, the metaphorization of language as fluid takes on a more specifically excretory quality: 'See now how words too. A few drops mishaphazard. Then strangury' (1982, 52). A sign of the body's decline as it reaches an advanced age, urination often becomes slow and painful;

strangury—etymologically deriving from two Greek words meaning 'twisted' and 'urine'—names this diminished capacity, one comparable to a similar and painful reduction in linguistic capacity. *Worstward Ho* contains numerous instances of a similar trope: 'Enough still not to know . . . Not to know what it is the words it says say. Says? Secretes' (1983, 30). Like pus or other bodily fluids, words in Beckett are secreted, not merely uttered.

More important, there are few absolutes, few static or permanent states, in Beckett; rather, things proceed entropically or devolve from 'bad to worsen' (1983, 23), raising the question 'What words for what then?' Then, words 'ooze'—'How all but uninane' (1983, 34). By the end of *Ill Seen Ill Said*, Beckett succeeds in depicting this constantly changing universe both outside his protagonist's eye and behind it:

> Far behind the eye the quest begins. What time the event recedes. When suddenly to the rescue it comes again. Forthwith the uncommon common noun collapsion. Reinforced a little later if not enfeebled by the infrequent slumberous. A slumberous collapsion. (1982, 55)

The suddenness of the event's return does not equate to the drowsy, even slow process of decline; thus, 'collapse' would hardly serve the narrator's purpose—a 'collapsion' better fits the temporal scheme he endeavours to describe. Further, as the Director from Beckett's short play *Catastrophe* (1982) might phrase it, in pressing for further justification for this invention one might also be exhibiting an objectionable 'craze for explicitation ... every i dotted to death!' (1984, 299). Beckett not only invents to denominate phenomena as the modern world must understand them, but also provides a meta-commentary on linguistic invention, a bargain for the price of admission.

The ungetroundable

Paul Muldoon (born 1951), Pulitzer Prize winner and one of the twenty-first century's most acclaimed poets, follows in this tradition of linguistic invention, often for the very reasons of inclusivism that motivated Joyce and Beckett before him. A Northern Irish writer who moved to the United States in 1987, Muldoon, like his predecessors, possesses a marked facility with a number of languages, including Irish, and a broad knowledge of literature, music, and the other arts. At times, his displays of erudition irritate readers, who voice their 'exasperation at the many private references' in his poems and complain, as Helen Vendler did in regard to Muldoon's volume *The Annals of Chile* (1994), that he engages too often in a 'Joycean game of baffle-the-reader' (Vendler 1996, 58 and 59). A decade later, Vendler levied a similar charge against Muldoon's *Horse Latitudes* (2006), initiating her review with the question, 'How allusive should a poem be?' (2006, 26).

As in Joyce's later fiction and in Beckett—the eye as a 'vile jelly' in *Ill Seen Ill Said* refers to the particularly grisly spectacle in *King Lear* of Gloucester's eyes being plucked out—allusions in Muldoon's poems encompass the widest imaginable range of possibilities: from classical and Shakespearean literature, mythology, painting, and world history to virtually every conceivable form of contemporary mass culture, including rock music, television, music videos, and every manner of schlock. Such intertextual eclecticism, not surprisingly, has motivated some commentators to describe Muldoon's art as postmodernist, and perhaps in this sense it is.

But language is equally responsible for this description, as Richard Tillinghast explained in connection to *The Annals of Chile*: 'Paul Muldoon ... has long been celebrated for a witty, oblique poetry that in the best post-modernist fashion focuses on the slippery equivocations of language itself' (1994, 25–6). More than equivocation is at stake, however, both in Muldoon's poetry and in his critical writing on the craft of poetry, whether one wishes to invoke the context of modernist or postmodernist aesthetics. And, as in the cases of Joyce and Beckett, on occasion no extant language or orthodox syntax will serve Muldoon's poetic or epistemological purposes; then, he invents his own.

Such is also the case when Muldoon meditates upon the nature of poetry itself. In *The End of the Poem* (2006), based on lectures he delivered at Oxford, Muldoon cultivates the notion that virtually all poetry is haunted by traces of prior historical events, literary texts, and other phenomena. Emily Dickinson's 'I tried to think a lonelier thing' is 'ghosted by the fate of Sir John Franklin ... who set sail from England on the 19th of May, 1845, in search of a northwest passage'. Similarly, the aspect of 'recollection' in Stevie Smith's 'I Remember' is 'faintly ghosted' by William Wordsworth's famous phrase in the preface to *Lyrical Ballads* about poetry being 'the spontaneous overflow of powerful feelings ... *recollected* in tranquility' (2006, 116 and 144; Muldoon's emphasis). Both instances serve as examples of an assimilative process Muldoon recognizes in William Butler Yeats' poem 'All Souls' Night':

> As I've tried to suggest, the text or texts to which 'All Souls' Night' might stand as an epilogue is not so much *A Vision* but a selection of poems by Keats ... from whom [Yeats] *conglomewrites* key words and images. (2006, 27; my emphasis)

It is arguable that, for Muldoon, *all* great writing is 'conglomewriting': Seamus Heaney's poem 'Widgeon' echoes the name *Widgery*, after the Lord Chief Justice who reported on the tragic events on 'Bloody Sunday' in Derry in 1972; the historical 'nightmare' from which Stephen Dedalus in *Ulysses* attempts to awaken contains the nightmare in which Macbeth feels 'helpless and desperate', and so on (2006, 392–3).

A similar concept underlies Muldoon's formulation of the 'ungetroundable', the thesis of a lecture he delivered at Oxford in the late 1990s. Muldoon began his lecture with an enumeration of five images that took residence in his consciousness at about this time, or slightly before; they include a white horse standing on a hillside, a hole in an eighteenth-century plaster wall, and an old Irishman, 'one of the thousands who died in the early nineteenth century digging what would become the Delaware and Raritan Canal, which lies across the road' from the house with the ancient plaster walls (1998, 107). The 'ungetroundable' connotes not only the pressure of such images on Muldoon's consciousness, but also the connection between two or more of them:

> The image of the horse standing with its back to the wind and rain. The image of the hole in the plaster showing the strands of horsehair [once used to bind the plaster]. I immediately see a connection. Put more graphically, a connection sees me. The horse and the house are one. One has the other under its skin. (1998, 109)

Muldoon's poetry reflects, or rather, embodies this trope of inclusivism. In 'The Loaf' from *Moy Sand and Gravel* (2002), for example, Muldoon's speaker hears the sounds of the Canal being dug every time he puts his ear to a hole in the wall of his eighteenth-century house:

> When I put my ear to the hole I'm suddenly aware
> of spades and shovels turning up the gain
> all the way from Raritan to the Delaware. (2002, 51)

In these ways, the hole 'in a wall of plaster stiffened with horsehair' binds all three images together. A similar phenomenon appears in the volume's closing—and longest—poem, 'At the Sign of the Black Horse, September 1999'. Here, Muldoon (or his persona) watches the Canal overflow its banks while his infant son Asher—part Irish, part Jewish after his mother—sleeps peacefully in his pram. The ethnic hybridity of his son gradually informs the historical vision that emerges in the poem; by its end, one old navvy who built the canal becomes an 'Irish schlemiel'; the group of nineteenth-century construction workers become so many 'Irish schmucks who still loll/still loll and lollygag,/ between the preposterous towpath and the preposterous berm' (2002, 104–5).

As Fran Brearton has observed, in volumes like *The Annals of Chile* Muldoon, like Robert Graves before him—and like Joyce and Beckett as well—also transforms 'etymological quests into literary interpretive strategies' (2004, 46). This strategy is evident in the two longest poems of the collection, both of which are elegies, 'Incantata' and 'Yarrow'. The title of the former poem, which concerns the battle of Muldoon's former lover, the artist Mary Farl Powers, with the cancer to which she eventually succumbed, combines *incantation* and *cantata*, conferring on the poem qualities both of magical chanting and music, but also suggesting—as in the term *canto*—that this long, elegiac song might be understood as divided into discrete sections. In several of these, Beckett or his characters appear, often to provide companionship. And, while working in the kitchen, Muldoon recalls a print of Power's engraving *Emblements*, which now appears to him as a blighted potato being slowly devoured by a legion of army worms:

> I crouch with Belacqua
> And Luck and Pozzo in the Acacacac-
> ademy of Anthropopopometry, trying to make sense of the
>   '*quaquaqua*'
> of that potato-mouth. (1994, 20)

The 'whatness' or 'as if-ness'—the 'qua'—of the image are, for Muldoon, as mystifying and impenetrable as the notions of God and Being in Lucky's monologue from *Waiting for Godot*, from which much of the linguistic invention in this stanza is taken. As in *Godot,* the academy that purports to understand such mysteries amount to so much 'caca' or 'popo' and, of course, like the cancerous crab in *Ulysses*, the cankered potato serves as an emblem of Powers' body suffering the devastations of cancer. How are we to understand this process? What does the glyph etched into the potato signify?

The duality of phenomena, perhaps, or the inherent multiplicity of seemingly singular things might provide one answer. In this way, Paul Muldoon and Samuel Beckett share the project of linguistic invention with James Joyce, a writer both revere. In the end, all three suggest that the myriad languages they know fail to communicate the connectedness or inclusivism of which they so frequently write—or the pain and mystery they endure. Yet, while linguistic invention allows them to poke fun at 'syphilisation' or to describe man's inevitable 'collapsion', while words at times ooze, gush, chant, or painfully leak in their writing, often to hilarious or naughty effect, invented language in all three writers' work also serves the greater purpose of making profound, at times moving statements about life, love, and our common mortality.

References

Beckett, Samuel. 1972. *More Pricks than Kicks*. New York: Grove Press. FP 1934.

Beckett, Samuel. 1982. *Ill Seen Ill Said*. London: John Calder.

Beckett, Samuel. 1983. *Worstward Ho*. New York: Grove Press.

Beckett, Samuel, 1984. *Collected Shorter Plays*. New York: Grove Press.

Beckett, Samuel. 1988. *Stirrings Still*. New York: North Star Line.

Beckett, Samuel. 2002. *Poems 1930–1989*. London: Calder.

Bishop, John. 1986. *Joyce's Book of the Dark: Finnegans Wake*. Madison, Wisconsin: University of Wisconsin Press.

Brearton, Fran. 2004. 'For Father Read Mother: Muldoon's Antecedents', in *Paul Muldoon: Critical Essays*, edited by Tim Kendall and Peter McDonald, 45–61. Liverpool: Liverpool University Press.

Downing, Gregory M. 1997. 'Skeat and Joyce: A Garner of Words'. *Dictionaries: Journal of the Dictionary Society of North America*, 18: 33–65.

Ellmann, Richard. 1982. *James Joyce* 2/e. New York: Oxford University Press.

Gregory, Augusta. 1972. *Our Irish Theatre*. Gerrards Cross: Colin Smythe. FP 1913.

Joyce, James. 1939. *Finnegans Wake*. New York: Viking.

Joyce, James. 1955. *Stephen Hero*. New York: New Directions. FP 1944.

Joyce, James. 1959. *The Critical Writings of James Joyce*. Ed. Ellsworth Mason and Richard Ellmann. Ithaca, New York: Cornell University Press.

Joyce, James. 1964. *A Portrait of the Artist as a Young Man*. Ed. Richard Ellmann. New York: Viking. FP 1914–15.

Joyce, James. 1986. *Ulysses: The Corrected Text*. Ed. Hans Walter Gabler. New York: Vintage. FP 1922.

Joyce, P. W. 1988. *English as We Speak It in Ireland*. Ed. Terence Dolan. Dublin: Wolfhound Press. FP 1910.

Knowlson, James. 1996. *Damned to Fame: The Life of Samuel Beckett*. New York: Grove Press.

McHugh, Ronald. 1981. *The Finnegans Wake Experience*. Dublin: Irish Academic Press.

Muldoon, Paul. 1994. *The Annals of Chile*. New York: Farrar, Straus and Giroux.

Muldoon, Paul. 1998. 'Getting Round: Notes towards an *Ars Poetica*'. *Essays in Criticism*, 48: 107–28.

Muldoon, Paul. 2000. *To Ireland, I*. Oxford: Oxford University Press.

Muldoon, Paul. 2002. *Moy Sand and Gravel*. New York: Farrar, Straus and Giroux.

Muldoon, Paul. 2006. *Horse Latitudes*. New York: Farrar, Straus and Giroux.

Muldoon, Paul. 2006. *The End of the Poem*. Oxford: Oxford University Press.

Rathjen, Friedhelm. 1994. 'Preliminary Notes', in *In Principle, Beckett is Joyce*, edited by Friedhelm Rathjen, vii–xi. Edinburgh: Split Pea Press.

Tillinghast, Richard. 1994. 'Poets Are Born, Then Made'. *New York Times Book Review*, 11 December: 25–6.

Vendler, Helen. 1996. 'Anglo-Celtic Attitudes'. *The New York Review of Books*, 6 November: 57–60.

Vendler, Helen. 2006. 'Fanciness and Fatality'. *The New Republic*, 6 November: 26–33.

Whittaker, Stephen. 1987. 'Joyce and Skeat'. *James Joyce Quarterly*, 24: 177–92.

FP: First Published.

~8~

Revitalized Languages as Invented Languages

SUZANNE ROMAINE

At first glance, the link between revitalized languages and other invented languages discussed in this volume may not seem obvious. After all, one can trace an actual historical linguistic lineage for revived languages such as Hebrew, Irish, Cornish, Hawaiian, and numerous other revitalized languages. By contrast, Klingon, Esperanto, Láadan (discussed later in this chapter), Elvish, and their ilk spring abruptly ex nihilo from the minds of their creators without etymological ancestors or native speakers.

Nevertheless, the connection becomes evident from a brief consideration of the historical circumstances surrounding Modern Hebrew, a case which is often cited as proof that a 'dead' language can be revived. Hebrew was dead, of course, only as a spoken vernacular after Jews adopted Aramaic during the second century CE. Although it was no one's mother tongue between the second and nineteenth centuries, it remained in active use as a written literary and religious language. However, to be used as a modern spoken language in everyday life, Hebrew needed to be 'revernacularized' and modernized, a process begun by Eliezer Ben-Yehuda (1858–1922) and today carried out primarily by the Hebrew Language Academy, established in 1953. Modernization required, among other things, the creation of thousands of new words. Ben-Yehuda's son, Itamar Ben-Avi (1882–1943), is symbolically considered to have been the first native speaker of Modern Hebrew and with him comes the beginning of a new and distinct linguistic lineage.

Modern Hebrew did not evolve naturally over generations in a continuous chain of native speakers, but is the product of deliberate efforts undertaken by individuals and groups. Its revival can be considered a kind of language planning. Although language planning directed at changing aspects of language form and use is rather old as a practice, it is a relatively modern discipline comprising four stages: selection of norms, codification, elaboration, and implementation (Haugen 1966, Cooper 1989). Once we acknowledge deliberate normative planning as part and parcel of revival and revitalization, it is but a short slip of the tongue from intervention to invention. The so-called revival of Hebrew did not, however, resuscitate what was dead. Time's proverbial arrow points only forward and cannot be reversed. Hence, the enterprise of revitalization might be more appropriately thought of as a transformation rather than revival of past norms (Bentahila and Davies 1993, 376).

Although Modern Hebrew's planners attempted to use mainly internal sources of lexical elaboration, ancient Hebrew lacked sufficient native roots. According to Ghil'ad Zuckermann, there are 8,198 attested words in Biblical Hebrew and fewer than 20,000 in Rabbinic Hebrew. Over 100,000 new words have come into Hebrew from a variety of sources, including foreign borrowings and words coined from native Hebrew/Semitic roots. He contends that the Modern Hebrew spoken as a mother tongue by more than 5 million Jews in the state of Israel is really 'a "reinvented language" in which purists had to work hard to coin new words' (Zuckermann 2003, 63–94). Indeed, in his view the revitalized form is sufficiently different from earlier forms of

Hebrew to be considered a separate, only partly related language. This manifests itself not only lexically but grammatically. While Biblical Hebrew is genetically clearly a Semitic language (related to Arabic), Modern Hebrew (which Zuckermann prefers to call Israeli) is a hybrid of inherited Semitic traits and influences from Yiddish and other European languages spoken by its creators.

In similar fashion, Glanville Price (1984, 134) argued that the gap between historic and revived Cornish was sufficiently large to warrant calling the modern form 'pseudo-Cornish' or 'Cornic'. The linguistic continuity of other revitalized languages has also been cast into doubt, even in cases without a break in transmission. Leonora Timm (2003, 41), for example, views the so-called Néo-breton arising from the movement to revive Breton in Brittany as 'a quite distinct form of the language, or even a different language'. Because it is a second language for both teachers and students in the new Breton immersion schools called Diwan established in 1977, it is 'no one's native language variety'. Néo-breton is a 'xenolect', that is, a slightly foreignized and largely synthetic, consciously normalized variety (Jones 1998, 323).

Learning revitalized varieties of their language is alien to many traditional speakers. Revived Cornish may not be 'real' Cornish, but this begs the question of what 'real' Cornish is or was. Nancy Dorian (1994, 488) describes how different approaches to locating 'true' Cornish created rival revivalist factions, each promoting its own version of the language. The rivalry was both acute and unfriendly, with each faction competing vigorously for the loyalties of prospective learners. In 2004, the installation of a welcome mat in Cornish at the Camborne county offices in southwest Cornwall sparked a heated dispute over how to spell 'welcome'. Although the county government tried to defuse the tension by installing signs using all the different spellings (e.g., *dynnargh* on the welcome mat outside the county offices, but *dynargh* on another sign inside the building), this approach did not bring the community to consensus.

These brief examples suggest various senses in which revitalized languages are invented. *Oxford English Dictionary* definitions for *invention* fall out along two lines. One suggests a forceful act of bringing something into being, e.g., to introduce, to bring into use formally or by authority, to establish, institute, appoint; the other includes notions like to plot, plan, devise, or contrive— something rather more sinister and manipulative. Indeed, the establishment of Modern Hebrew involved no less an ideological than a linguistic struggle. For the sake of Hebrew, nearly all political forces were mobilized against Yiddish and other diasporic languages spoken by early Israeli settlers. In the 1920s and 1930s the *gdud meginéy hasafá* 'the language defendants regiment', whose motto was *ivrí, dabér ivrít* 'Hebrew, speak Hebrew!', boycotted and disrupted Yiddish theatre performances and publications, and tore down signs in foreign languages (Shohamy 2008).

Similarly, Néo-breton activists have pasted the newly created word *pellgomz* 'speak from afar' on telephone booths in Brittany in an attempt to displace the French borrowing *téléphone* preferred by native Breton speakers. The almost predictable eruption of sign wars in Israel, Cornwall, Brittany, and other places reveals how battles for control over the linguistic landscape can be read as a minefield of language ideologies serving as powerful tools of symbolic domination. Claims premised on the supposed correctness of one spelling or word over another articulate hegemonic ideologies about authenticity and purity.

Nevertheless, the point 'is not to declare ethnicity invented and stop there, but to show in historical perspective how it was invented and with what consequences' (Rosaldo 1990, 27). Considering revitalized languages as invented languages requires that we examine the contexts of revitalization and the factors motivating it in detail. In doing so, we confront the fact that revitalization or revival does not produce a class of languages distinct from other so-called 'natural' languages that have undergone conscious normative planning. The origins of the languages called English, Italian, French, and even more recently Serbian, Bosnian, and Croatian are not found ready-made in antiquity: nineteenth-century Romantic and later cultural and political nationalists deliberately fashioned them into languages to unite populations—standardization and restandardization of language norms articulate ideological preferences. Like standardization of coinage, weights, and measures, language standardization aims to eliminate variation and establish a uniform language for all within the group of its users. Modern standard varieties of French, English, etc., like Modern Cornish, also have no native speakers: they are artificial varieties codified in dictionaries and grammars and learned in school, but not spoken in everyday, face-to-face interactions.

The context of language revitalization

Revitalization arises as a consequence of language shift. Language shift involves loss of speakers and domains of use, both of which are critical for survival of a language. The possibility of impending shift appears when a language once used throughout a community for everything is restricted as another language intrudes on its territory. Typically, the imposing language prevails in all areas of official life—government, school, media—requiring bilingualism of the subordinate group. Usage declines in domains where the language was once secure—churches, the workplace, schools, and most critically, the home, as growing numbers of parents no longer transmit their language to their children. Fluency in the language depends on age: younger generations prefer to speak the dominant language for socio-economic advancement. The link between dominant language and social mobility, along with the dominant language's pre-eminence in public institutions, leads the community to devalue its own language, culture, and identity.

Consider what happened to Hawaiian after the arrival of Captain James Cook in 1778. Within 200 years of contact with English, Hawaiian went from being everyone's everyday language, as well as the language of government, education, and religion, to being the home language of only a few hundred Hawaiians, most of whom live on the privately owned, isolated island of Ni'ihau, the westernmost island in the chain. Outside Ni'ihau, there are perhaps another hundred or so Hawaiian speakers on neighbouring Kaua'i, plus a few elderly speakers scattered across the other islands, but they do not live in Hawaiian-speaking communities and are surrounded by English in their everyday lives. Due to American political and economic domination, Hawaiians are now a minority in what was once their homeland, only a quarter of the state's multi-ethnic population of 1.2 million. Hawaiian is at present a severely endangered language.

Similar historical and political factors—population loss, loss of political autonomy, and cultural and physical dislocation—led to a decline in the use of Irish. Before the seventeenth century, the majority of Irish overwhelmingly spoke Irish, and English was dominant only in a small eastern region around Dublin. By 1851, however, Irish was almost absent from the eastern half of the country and losing ground among young people everywhere except in the far western margins. Before the great famine lasting from 1845 to 1849, Irish ranked comfortably within the top 100 of the world's 7,000 or so languages in terms of number of speakers (Romaine 2008). The famine killed around one million and led to mass emigration of another 1.5 million. By 1900 these losses reduced the population by more than half, and Irish no longer ranked as high. (See Chapter 7 for some possible literary consequences of this shift.)

Some factors responsible for the decline of Hawaiian and Irish now affect other languages on an unanticipated scale. Indeed, what happened to the Celtic languages is but an early example of a process now playing out globally, with English, French, Spanish, and Chinese spreading at the expense of the world's many hundreds of small, largely rural, vernaculars. Some linguists predict that between 50 and 90% of the world's some 6,900 languages will disappear over the next century (Nettle and Romaine 2000). Not coincidentally, the vast majority of today's threatened languages are found among socially and politically marginalized and/or subordinated national and ethnic minority groups within nation-states.

Disappearance of a minority language almost always forms part of a wider process of social, cultural, and political displacement as languages of colonial conquest and dominant languages of nation-states penetrate into, transform, and undermine a minority community's ability to maintain its language, culture, and identity. People feel a key part of their traditional culture and identity is lost when that language disappears. As Sir James Henare said of Māori, 'The language is the life force of our Māori culture and mana ['power']. If the language dies, as some predict, what do we have left to us? Then, I ask our own people who are we?' (*Waitangi Tribunal* 1989, 34). When a group feels threatened, its members may resist by emphasizing a number of emblematic culture traits (including language) in order to justify their distinctiveness and promote political claims. Such sentiments provide fertile ground for language revitalization movements.

In 1962, Saunders Lewis, founder of Plaid Cymru (Welsh Nationalist Party) in 1925, delivered a galvanizing speech on the radio titled 'Tynged yr Iaith' ('The fate of the language'). Denouncing the British government's flooding of the valley of Tryweryn in Meirionydd in order to create a reservoir to supply Liverpool at the expense of the mostly Welsh-speaking residents, who were removed from the village, Lewis (1973, 141) contended that 'To defend a language is to defend a community, to defend homes and families. Today, Wales cannot afford the destruction of Welsh-language homes. They are scarce and fragile'. Calling upon his fellow citizens to insist on their right to conduct governmental and local business in Welsh, he proclaimed that 'restoring the Welsh language in Wales is nothing less than a revolution. It is only through revolutionary means that we can succeed'.

The broadcast inspired college students to found Cymdeithas yr Iaith Gymraeg (Welsh Language Society), which launched its first mass protest in 1963, blocking traffic on the Trefechan Bridge in Aberystwyth. Later, they removed or painted over English-only road signs. In 1980,

Plaid Cymru leader Gwynfor Evans was prepared to fast to the death when Margaret Thatcher's newly elected Conservative government revoked plans to establish a Welsh television channel. Thatcher, who declared herself the lady not for turning, turned anyway: S4C (Sianel Pedwar Cymru 'Channel 4 Wales') began broadcasting in 1982.

The struggle for Welsh was inspiring. In the early 1970s, a group of young Māori activists called Ngā Tama Toa 'Warrior Sons' campaigned for a Māori revival, a movement that increased in strength and intensity for the rest of the millennium. In 1984, a programme of Hawaiian immersion preschools, called Pūnana Leo ('language nest'), was modelled on the New Zealand programme Kōhanga Reo (same meaning), begun in 1982 to create a sheltered environment where children could learn Māori. As in New Zealand, activism for the Hawaiian language emerged during a cultural and political renaissance in the 1970s. Concern for Hawaiian went hand in hand with increased activism for land rights, sovereignty, and a heightened interest in traditional art forms, such as hula and long-distance canoe voyaging. Similarly, in Ireland, the project of restoring Irish as a vernacular by establishing an independent Irish state figured prominently in Douglas Hyde's formation of Conradh na Gaeilge (Gaelic League) in 1893. Although most people had already abandoned Irish long before independence, even in the Gaeltacht (i.e., Irish-speaking area), Irish was declared the national language in the constitution of 1922.

Language revitalization is often seen as essential to recovering a threatened group's cultural identity. In their quest to speak in a voice independent of the perceived oppressor's, people are willing to die for different visions of their linguistic identity. Although the term *identity* derives from Latin *idem* 'same', identity is primarily about constructing differences between ourselves and others. Language in(ter)vention in the form of language planning can align linguistic form with ideological preferences and aspirations. The more distinct a language or variety is from some other, the more effectively it serves as an identity marker.

Hence, identity planning goes hand in hand with language planning. For revitalization to succeed, the community must revalorize the very cultural traits and identities that were once despised and stigmatized. Revitalization thus depends crucially on the manipulation of identities. Establishing Modern Hebrew required a deconstruction and reconstruction of identities. Zionists hoped to solve the problem of Jewish identity by creating a secular nation-state whose only legitimate national language was Hebrew. 'Hebrew' became a label for a whole revolutionary package of land, language, and work (Harshav 1993, 135–6). The image promoted of the Sabra as *bne haaretz* ('sons of the land') was the Jew born as a native speaker of Hebrew in an independent Jewish state.

Official ideology therefore condemned retention of diaspora identity, its languages and accents, in particular Yiddish, the language of origin for almost 89% of the world's Jews and nearly 50% of Israeli Jews. The Zionists' struggle against Yiddish was harsh: for the sake of bringing about a shift to Hebrew, nearly all political and ideological forces were directed against anything Yiddish. The Ashkenazim who imposed the revival of Hebrew effectively fought against their own vernacular. From the beginning of the revival, the new standard Hebrew officially rejected Ashkenazic pronunciation in favour of Sephardic's more Semitic sound system. This choice, like that of Hebrew itself, articulated Zionist political ideology.

Language planning and linguistic aspects of revitalization

Turning to the linguistic nuts and bolts of revitalization, the tasks at hand follow closely the lines laid out in language planning textbooks, though such books are generally aimed at modernizing rather than revitalizing languages. In either case the norms to be prescribed must first be selected from a pre-existing set of variants or created, then codified in grammars, dictionaries, usage manuals, style guides, etc., and elaborated. As John Joseph (2004, 225) explains, these tools as well as institutions such as schools, examination bodies, and authoritative texts are necessary to create and sustain the fiction of the standard language. Elaboration may involve expanding vocabulary and extending the stylistic repertoire, so that the language functions in a greater range of circumstances.

However, norms do not become standard solely by dint of codification; their use must be promoted and diffused through media and instruction. Even Klingon has normative agencies such as the Klingon Language Institute and a dictionary (see Appendix 5). Te Taura Whiri i te Reo Māori (Māori Language Commission) was created as part of the Māori Language Bill of 1987, making Māori an official language of New Zealand. In Israel the Hebrew Language Academy's decisions are binding upon all government agencies, including the Israel Broadcasting Authority. Official backing of this sort is critical in disseminating planned innovations, but by no means guarantees acceptance.

Efforts directed at aspects of linguistic form such as spelling, vocabulary, grammar, etc. are examples of 'corpus planning', while those to change a language's societal functions are examples of 'status planning'. Corpus planning activities include, for instance, introducing a written norm where none existed previously, or modifying/modernizing a pre-existing form, creating new vocabulary, etc., so that a language can reclaim lost domains (e.g., restoring Hawaiian as a medium of education or Hebrew as a household language) and/or be extended to new domains in which it has never been used (e.g., Cornish as a language of government administration).

Spelling

Although language planning literature tends to present issues surrounding selection and codification of writing systems as primarily technical matters, spelling systems are not simply convenient, arbitrary yet conventional codes enabling reading and writing. The controversial Cornish welcome mat demonstrates that decisions about spelling are fraught with ideological implications. Disagreement about Cornish spelling divided activists into at least four or more factions. Given only 300 to 400 speakers, this would appear to be too many orthographies chasing too few speakers! Klingon may have more speakers than Cornish (see Chapter 5).

Henry Jenner's (1904) handbook, which founded the revival of Cornish, was based on the last form natively spoken. When Dolly Pentreath, the supposed last native speaker of Cornish, died in 1777, the language had been declining for some time and displayed considerable English influence. This perceived taint would diminish the variety's value for revivalists like Robert Morton Nance, who proposed instead to base the revival on Middle Cornish literary texts from the fourteenth and fifteenth centuries, a golden age when the language was vibrant. Nance introduced a spelling system known as Unified Cornish that was adopted by the Cornish Language Board, founded in 1967, and remained the standard for Cornish learners until the 1980s when Kenneth George developed a competing system. George's orthography, called Kernewek Kemmyn ('common Cornish'), was based on the phonology of the language around 1500, reconstructed from contemporary English dialects in the area where Cornish survived the longest. Although the Cornish Language Board adopted the Kernewek Kemmyn orthography in 1987, not all revivalists did. Richard Gendall proposed his own form, which he called Modern Cornish.

In most, if not all, debates about orthographies, a small subset of written characters is subject to scrutiny. Only minor differences distinguished Unified Cornish from Kernewek Kemmyn (cf. *Kernowek/Kernewek* 'Cornish', *scol/skol* 'school', *nyver/niver* 'number'). Nevertheless, these rival systems, along with at least four others, competed for the loyalties of the handful of speakers of revived Cornish until 2008, when a standard written form was agreed. Likewise, the movement to revitalize Breton has at various times foundered on heated disagreement over rival spelling systems. Much argument focused on the contentious combination <zh> introduced in the 1941 orthography, known as 'the ZH' or 'the unified orthography', which attempted to reconcile regional dialects, some of which used /z/ and others /h/ or /x/ (McDonald 1989, 131). Thus, the spelling <Breizh> 'Brittany' was intended to replace spellings <Breiz> and <Breih> in older orthographies based on different dialects.

Today the unified orthography is associated with the University of Rennes, while the University of Brest adopted a newer orthography excluding the controversial <zh>. A journal called *Hor Yezh* ('our language') published at the University of Rennes 'has been known to decorate its whole cover with triumphant zhs' (McDonald 1989, 133). Meanwhile, to those associated with Rennes, the new Brest orthography 'smelt of French'. Scholars at Brest retorted with accusations of collaboration with the Nazis (McDonald 1989, 211). Nevertheless, supporters of both orthographies attempted to legitimate themselves as representing the 'Breton people' in opposition to French domination.

Another case where symbolic control over definitions of correctness and authenticity plays out in competition between rival orthographies is Hawaiian, recognized as co-official with English in the state of Hawai'i since 1978. Most of the debate focuses on just two new symbols introduced by a group of Hawaiian language teachers at the University of Hawai'i, who restandardized the language in 1978. The Christian missionaries who first wrote down the language in the 1820s did not recognize vowel length and the glottal stop as phonologically distinct and did not include symbols for them. Although the orthography taught in Hawaiian-medium immersion education since 1984 is making headway, current spellings outside that context often present a welter of confusion, as new and old spellings coexist (Romaine 2002).

The typographical distinctiveness of the so-called '*okina*, the symbol chosen to mark the glottal stop in the new orthography, became a focus of public controversy in 1997, when the new Hawai'i Convention Center used an apostrophe instead of the 'correct' symbol on the main marquee outside the Center. Typographically speaking, the '*okina* should look like a backward apostrophe. The typographically incorrect *'okina* quickly gained notoriety as the Convention Center's 'glottal goof' (Burlingame 1997).

Activists regard use of 'correct' spellings and pronunciations as essential to restoring a Hawaiian sense of place. The act of overwriting old spellings such as *Hawaii*, *Waikiki* and *Lanai* with the new ones *Hawai'i*, *Waikīkī* and *Lāna'i* is part of a larger struggle to restore traditional place names and reclaim the land. According to the newer orthography, most familiar place names, including the names of most of the islands and the state itself, are misspelled (and mispronounced). As in Brittany and Cornwall, variant spellings and pronunciations encode conflicting ideologies. Because neither the older nor the newer norm has 'official' status, claims about correctness and authenticity differ among institutions and constituencies. In the case of the missionary orthography, the relevant institution is the church, with the Hawaiian translation of the Bible assuming the role of classical standard; in the case of the new orthography, authority is vested in the newly established immersion schools.

Orthography can also serve to create distance between a minority language and a genetically-related dominant language, or between related varieties of a minority language (Romaine 2005). The goal of differentiating Corsican from Italian has made it important to foreground Corsican sounds not shared with Italian such as voiced palatal affricates. The choice of <chj> and <ghj> to represent them is one of the most visually distinctive aspects of Corsican spelling: compare Corsican *bonghjurnu* with Italian *buongiorno* 'good day' (Jaffe 1999, 217). In the case of Galician, a minority language coexisting with Spanish in the Iberian peninsula, debate has turned on opposing values linked to symbols that would ally the newly standardized written language more closely to either Portuguese or Castilian Spanish, e.g., <ñ> vs <nh>, <ll> vs <lh>, etc.

Although Galician shares a lineage with Portuguese, Castilian has influenced it heavily, as a result of Galicia's union with Castile from the thirteenth century. So Joseph (2004, 16) suggests, if Galician 'is a dialect of any other language, that language is Portuguese'. Nevertheless, the differences between Portuguese and Galician became more marked as each developed in relative isolation from one another on opposite sides of the river Minho, the political border between Galicia and Portugal. After the end of Franco's regime, Galicia became an autonomous region of Spain. Spanish nationalists, however, consider it an inseparable part of the Spanish nation, and Galician a Spanish, not Portuguese, language. The orthographic debate represents one strategy Galician activists deploy to exploit the closer linguistic affiliation of Galician to Portuguese.

Vocabulary

Eliezer Ben-Yehuda was lost for words when it came to asking his wife for a cup of coffee with sugar, and would say in effect: 'Take such and such, and do like so, and bring me this and this, and I will drink' (Fellman 1973, 37–8). Because Hebrew had not been spoken for centuries, it lacked essential vocabulary for performing daily household tasks. Of course, speakers don't wait for language planners to coin new terms for things they talk about every day, especially when words are readily available in other accessible languages. Because Ben-Yehuda was ideologically committed to Hebrew, resorting to his native Yiddish would have been an admission of defeat. Speakers of other languages such as Hawaiian, however, solved similar problems by borrowing English terms for household items such as *pola* 'bowl' and *puna* 'spoon', and new foodstuffs like *kope* 'coffee', *'aikalima* 'ice cream', and adapting them to Hawaiian pronunciation

Although all vocabularies constantly expand to keep pace with technological developments, the process is generally taken for granted and often proceeds without conscious efforts by language planning agencies. English no more than Hebrew or Hawaiian had words for new inventions such as television, microwave, and computer, or concepts like quark. Hebrew's needs were of course quite different from those of languages never used for prestigious functions, or forced to retreat from prestige due to pressure from an intruding language. Though previously used for education and government, by the twentieth century Hawaiian was largely confined to the domestic sphere. Yet the existence of an extensive legal terminology and vocabulary for geography, arithmetic, anatomy, reading, etc. gave it a head start over many other indigenous languages. Also, Hawaiian had a substantial corpus of nineteenth-century texts—newspapers, traditional stories, and a translation of the Bible and numerous other religious tracts. By contrast, Kaurna, once used by Aboriginal people in what is now the area of Adelaide in South Australia, had not been spoken for more than a century. Nevertheless, some people now use it for activities such as greetings, songs, and naming, relying on a very small fragmentary corpus comprising about 3,000–5,000 words. Because there are no sound recordings, even pronunciation was reconstructed from written historical resources (Amery 2001).

Regardless of the language, procedures for coining new words are the same. Barring ex nihilo creations such as *quark* (which are rare), new words are borrowed or fashioned from existing resources. What differs are the extent to which each strategy is deployed and the nature of the existing language corpus. At one point in its history, English borrowed up to half its vocabulary from other languages. Although borrowing has recently become less important as a source for new English words, Greek and Latin elements of English vocabulary are still highly productive resources for new technical and scientific terms, e.g., *kilometre*, *uranium*, *Internet*, etc. A rare instance in which English has borrowed a word from Hawaiian is *wiki* 'quick, fast', which has since spawned a number of compounds such as *Wikipedia*, *Wikimedia*, *Wiktionary*, *wikipages*, etc. Normally, borrowing proceeds from the dominant to subordinate language and speakers of the latter often switch entirely to the language of the dominant culture when talking about things connected with it (e.g., Hawaiian *kelepona* 'telephone').

Attempting to reverse power relationships dictating a largely unidirectional path of influence from majority to minority language, activists generally borrow from the dominant language only as a last resort and prefer instead other strategies for creating new words. In semantic extension, a word already in the language takes a new meaning. The English phrase *surfing the web* contains two such examples: *surfing* as a form of navigating a wave on the ocean's surface is extended to navigating in cyberspace via browsers; *web* is extended from a woven structure to encompass the network of interconnected computers comprising the World Wide Web. Hawaiian has similarly extended *kele* 'navigate' and *mākaʻikaʻi* 'sightsee/tour' to refer to 'web browsing', and *lele* 'fly/leap' to mean 'log out/off'.

In both Hawaiian and Māori, scientific and technical terminology has been coined using native roots and compounding, thus avoiding borrowing from Latin, Greek, or English. (For an interesting fictional analogue to this type of planning, see discussion of Newspeak's 'C vocabulary' in Chapter 3.) A general Māori word for 'metal' was created by compounding *konga* 'fragment' with *nuku* 'earth', then shortening it to create a prefix *konu-*, so that terms for specific metals and compounds could be formed, e.g., *konukura* 'copper' (literally 'red metal'), *konukata* 'lead' (literally 'metal bullet'), *konutai* 'sodium' (literally 'metal sea'), etc. Similarly, Hawaiian created *kōpia* 'carbohydrate' (literally 'sugar cane starch'), just as earlier it coined *mokulele* 'aeroplane' (literally 'flying ship'). Compare also Quichua/Quechua *antahu* 'car' (literally 'metal animal'), and Breton *c'harr-tan* 'car' (literally 'fire cart') and *c'harr-nij* 'aeroplane' (literally 'flying cart').

Some new words derive from loan translation or calquing, i.e., replacing the component parts of the foreign term with native ones of equivalent meaning, e.g., Māori *ngaruiti* 'microwave' (*ngaru* 'wave' + *iti* 'small'), and Hawaiian *pūnaewele puni honua* (World Wide Web, literally 'web around world'). Although many such words have meanings transparently derivable from the component parts (e.g., Hawaiian *hale noho haumāna* 'dorm'; literally 'house live student'), the meaning of *lolo uila* (literally 'electric brain') is not necessarily any more transparent to someone who does not already know what a computer is than the Hawaiianized borrowing *kamepiula*.

Some native speakers find some new creations long and intimidating. Consider Néo-breton *skriverezerez* 'secretary', coined as a replacement for French *secrétaire*, composed of the root *skriv-* plus four suffixes: *-er* 'professional', *-ez* 'machine', *-er* 'professional', and *-ez* 'female' (Jones and Singh 2005, 33). Similarly, English *movie projector* comprises two words (5 syllables) compared to Hawaiian *mīkini ho'olele ki'i'oni'oni* containing three words (13 syllables): *mīkini* 'machine' plus two compounds, *ho'olele* 'cause to fly' and *ki'i'oni'oni* 'moving picture'. Although some Breton and Māori activists have tried to replace borrowings with native coinages, it can be very difficult to dislodge familiar long-established loans, especially if the replacements relying on circumlocution, compounding, or loan translation result in long words or phrases. Māori activists have tried to replace the English borrowing *waea* 'telephone' (literally 'wire') with a native neologism (*kawe reo* 'carry language'). The Néo-breton movement sanctions the use of *tredan*, a neologism from its sister language Welsh, while local Breton prefers French *électricité*.

New words may seem amusing or superfluous to traditional speakers used to borrowings. Dorian (1994) relates how one speaker of a terminal variety of East Sutherland Gaelic in Scotland came across the coinage *guthan* 'telephone' (from the noun *guth* 'voice'). She quizzed every native speaker who phoned, and delighted in stumping them all because none of them knew or used it. We find similar reactions of discomfort with newly created written norms and unfamiliar coinages in other contexts. Basque speakers in the Basque Autonomous Community have been reluctant to use Basque in relations with the administration because a long history of dealing with officialdom in Spanish leaves most ordinary Basque speakers unfamiliar with the newly coined terminology of this domain.

In Hawai'i too the demands of the educational sector and requirements of state and national curricula drive the needs for a standard
written form and many new words. Ke Kōmike Hua'ōlelo Hou (Lexicon
Committee; literally 'new word committee'), a group of self-appointed
language experts formed in 1987 to coin new terms in Hawaiian,
published a dictionary (*Māmaka Kaiao*), containing thousands of new
words created between 1987 and 2000. The committee's stated policy
ranks borrowing last in its ten strategies for creating new words (Ke
Kōmike Hua'ōlelo 2003, ix–x). However, when borrowing is unavoid-
able, loanwords from Polynesian (e.g., *pounamu* 'jade' from Māori) or
other endangered languages are preferred over English, e.g., *penekui*
'Benzoin, a resin used in perfumes and cosmetics' (cf. Old Catalan
benjui) and *kokei'a* 'prairie dog' (cf. Ute *tocey'a*). Words borrowed from
languages related to Hawaiian, like Māori, do not look foreign and
thus do not require a great deal of Hawaiianization. Other borrowings
from other unrelated languages such as Assyrian (e.g., *lalinoka* 'hiero-
glyph'; cf. *rahleenos*), French (e.g., *'ōmā* 'Maine lobster'; cf. *homard*),
and Japanese (e.g., *kaimine* 'Saimin', a kind of noodle soup) require
more adaptation.

Nevertheless, despite this stated policy of prioritizing coinage over
borrowing, and borrowing from languages other than English, English
loanwords or Hawaiianized borrowings are still substantial. So are
calques and semantic extensions that look native but are in fact borrowed because the native word is extended to cover the meaning of
the corresponding English word, e.g., Hawaiian *'iole* 'mouse/rat' for
the hand-held pointing device. For Māori, too, Te Taura Whiri i te Reo
has tried to avoid borrowing, yet vocabulary expansion has relied on
outright calquing from English or extending the meanings of native
words in line with the semantics of their English equivalents (*tuarā* for
the position of 'back' in rugby). Te Taura Whiri i te Reo has also endea-
voured to replace existing English loans, some of which were borrowed early, such as the names for days of the week, and has proposed
restoring traditional names for months from the pre-contact lunar

calendar (e.g., *Kohitātea* instead of *Hānuare* 'January'). Although some speakers have accepted these proposals, the English names are still most commonly used, as in Hawaiian also.

In any case, the extent to which these replacements actually rid Māori of foreign influence is arguable. For example, *Rātū* 'Tuesday' (literally 'day of Tū'), intended to replace *Tūrei*, is a compound whose second component is a shortening of *Tūmatauenga*, the Māori god of warfare (Harlow 2004, 154). This in effect amounts to borrowing the strategy of other languages which name days of the week after deities (cf. French *mardi* 'day of Mars', and English *Thursday* 'Thor's day'). Each month and night of the traditional lunar calendar had its own name, sometimes varying between tribes. Hence, the lunar cycle and the western Gregorian calendar with its twelve months and seven-day week are not entirely commensurate conceptually speaking. In Hawai'i missionaries used English borrowings for the twelve months, but introduced new native compounds for the days of the week. Unlike the newly proposed Māori names for days, Hawaiian retained the Polynesian system of counting nights (rather than days) by using *pō* 'night' as the first element of the compounds, followed by a number (e.g., *pō'akahi* 'Monday'; literally 'evening one', *pō'alua* 'Tuesday'; literally 'evening two'). Nevertheless, the missionaries encoded the Christian idea of Sunday in the compound *lāpule* (literally 'day of prayer').

Pragmatic realities compete with ideological demands for status. This is especially true for scientific terminology, where pressures towards internationalization pose numerous dilemmas. Those who develop science also develop the terminology for discussing it. Due to the dominance of English in the science and technology sector, and the exponential increase in the knowledge created in and spread through English, keeping pace with English will always be an impossible task even for very large languages such as German, the most widely spoken language in Europe, which has retreated considerably as an international language of science.

Vocabulary expansion for much smaller languages such as Hawaiian and Māori would certainly be made easier by adapting existing English terms, particularly where that language is already the first language of students and the revitalized language is acquired as a second language. Recognizing such global realities, Richard Benton has argued against modernizing Māori as a vehicle for science, because a massive infusion of new abstruse technical vocabulary would colonize the language and make it a calque of English: 'Let English remain the language for Geekdom' (1999, 117). Despite resistance to borrowing English generally, Ke Kōmike Hua'ōlelo Hou (Lexicon Committee) has incorporated a great deal of English scientific terminology into Hawaiian, e.g., *sulufura diokesasida* 'sulphur dioxide', *sodiuma bisulapohate* 'sodium bisulphate', *hekokalame* 'hectogram', etc. Such partial transliterations immediately strike the eye as alien because they use letters (e.g., <b>,<d>,<l>, <s>, and <f>) not in the traditional or modernized Hawaiian alphabet. Like most Polynesian languages, Hawaiian has a small inventory of consonants (eight including the glottal stop).

Moreover, choosing between borrowing and native coinage impacts not only the languages concerned, but has consequences for their relatives. Similarities among historically related languages can be consciously enhanced, diminished, or realigned through deliberate manipulation. Consider, for instance, results of cases where Hawaiian and Māori have opted for native coinages, but other Polynesian languages have borrowed from English. Cook Islands Māori has borrowed *nūmero rātinara* 'rational number', while Hawaiian expresses the concept by paraphrase *helu pu'unaue koena'ole* 'number division no remainder'. Hawaiian has coined *pakuhi* 'graph' by shortening *papa kuhi kuhi* 'sheet/surface show', while Tongan and Samoan have borrowed *kalafi*. Differences among modern languages undermine historic similarities due to a common origin.

In other cases, however, efforts are directed at restoring ancestral similarities. Some words lost from Māori in the course of migration to a temperate climate were replaced by English loanwords, e.g., *kokonati* 'coconut' and *panana* 'banana', but are now themselves being replaced with common Polynesian *niu* and *maika*, respectively (Harlow 2004, 154). Modern Hawaiian similarly incorporates material from Proto-Polynesian (e.g., prefix *hika* 'self/auto-' from the indefinite pronoun *kita* 'one'), and a large proportion of Breton neologisms comprises words based on Welsh or obsolete Breton words (e.g., *kaotigell* 'jam'; cf. French *confiture*). Where the 'same' language is spoken in different countries, different choices for forming new words may realign or undermine existing similarities. In the case of Saami, spoken in Norway, Sweden, and Finland, the words for 'police' are all borrowings, but the Saami word *allaoahpahat* for 'university' in Finland is a calque of Finnish *yliopisto*, while in Norway and Sweden Saami has borrowed the international term *universitehtta* used in Norwegian (*universitet*) and Swedish.

Consequences of revitalization

Although language planning addresses itself to solving problems, the previous examples demonstrate how often it ends up creating them. It is impossible to revitalize a seriously eroded language without transforming it in the process, often in unexpected ways with unintended consequences. Although status and corpus planning are 'two sides of the language planning coin', a covert ideological component often underpins corpus planning (Fishman 2004, 80). Hence, selecting a new norm or modifying an old one is often accompanied by conflicts and debates over what constitutes correct usage and thus the most appropriate and authentic basis for the new standard variety —essentially non-linguistic concerns are acted out on the linguistic stage.

While controversies over the choice between <h> and <zh> in Breton or the precise shape of the symbol chosen to represent the glottal stop in modern standard Hawaiian may seem to outsiders like tempests in linguistic teapots, such small details carry a great deal of ideological freight in the communities concerned. Despite the fact that disputes about spelling and borrowing are typically couched in terms of supposedly linguistic issues such as correctness, purity, etc., language serves as proxy for larger moral and political debates. Compromise and consensus in corpus planning has proved elusive precisely because the stakes are so high.

Meanwhile, since, in many places, home and community foundations do not transmit minority languages, immersion schools are creating new speech communities of second language learners who speak varieties different from those of the remaining native speakers. In such contexts, a newly bilingual younger generation distinguishes itself from an older group of native speakers who do not share equally in the social and political process. Newly standardized varieties like Néo-breton and Neo-Galician, which are essentially class-based, may eventually replace traditional varieties, but until they do, their authenticity will be contested. The quest for purity and authenticity, on the one hand, and school-based transmission, on the other, inevitably bring about even more division, as the goals of authenticity and unification often conflict: for some, the most conservative form/variety is the most authentic and correct, for others, it is the newest.

Language revitalization/re-invention and the politics of purity and authenticity

Although purity is no guarantee of survival, purism in its various manifestations has almost inevitably been an especially potent force in revitalization. The notion of a pure language is an invention in which the distinction between foreign and native is ideologically constructed as a marker of group boundaries. Purism may operate at any level, motivating orthographic as well as lexical choices. Just as the Spanish digraph <qu> in the Mayan language Quiché was rejected in favour of <k'> as a way of distancing it from Spanish, loanwords are regarded as alien intruders that undermine the integrity of a linguistic system striving towards autonomy. The discourse of authenticity essentializes and at the same time is oppositional: what is constructed as authentic is about whatever is different from the dominant culture.

A combination of what George Thomas (1991) calls archaizing and reformist purism often accompanies revitalization as a way of re-establishing connections with a supposedly pure and monolingual pre-conquest/contact past. Nevertheless, just as there is no linguistic basis for determining authenticity or the extent to which one variety is sufficiently distinct from another to warrant calling them different languages, there is no going back to an earlier era of monolingualism. In their search for a truly authentic Quechua uncontaminated by Spanish influence, some Peruvian linguists have proposed a newly standardized variety called Quichua Unificado ('unified Quichua') as a basis for school instruction of Quichua as a second language. This national standard, however, contrasts with what is referred to as Quichua auténtico ('authentic Quichua') spoken by many rural, less well-educated, and older people. Paradoxically, Quichua auténtico is considerably influenced by Spanish, and contains many loanwords, while so-called Quichua Unificado is 'purer' technically speaking because language planners attempted to oust Spanish loanwords and replace them with Quichua neologisms. Quichua Unificado is also written with a three-vowel system, replacing the Quechua Language Academy's five-vowel one, which dates from the Spanish colonial period (Hornberger and King 1998). The debate over the competing vowel systems renders even the spelling of the name of the language and people contentious—Quechua in the traditional five-vowel system based on Spanish, and Quichua in the newer three-vowel system.

Invented etymologies are another type of linguistic cleansing and testify to the power of ideology over empirical observation. Such arguments seize upon particular linguistic features as evidence of inauthenticity, e.g., the so-called gheada (absence of word initial and medial voiced velar /g/ in standard Galician). Those who see it as an endogenous development trace its ancestry to the rural dialects believed to be the repository of authentic Galician; others reject it as interference from Spanish, pointing to its low prestige and absence from the literary language. The very term 'interference' is ideologically charged. Divergent genealogies are used to defend different ideological positions about the autonomy of Galician vis-à-vis Spanish (Recalde 2002–3, 47)—whatever linguistic features can be marshalled to distinguish the two languages empowers the autonomy of Galician.

The search for authenticity is nevertheless essentially a futile chase after one's own tail. Exposure to the new purified Breton spoken by outsiders referred to as Néo-bretonnants 'neo-Bretons', who are largely middle-class urbanites, however, has made the locals aware that their own Breton is mixed with French. Meanwhile, many activists, aware of the gap between their school version of Breton and that spoken by the remaining native speakers, actively cultivate regionalisms as a way of authenticating their Néo-breton, but this often results in dialect mixing. Speakers of the revitalized language turn to the dominant language in order to communicate, all the while opposing its influence. Even where the revitalized language attracts new speakers, they will be bilingual in the dominant language, and live under the shadow of its influence. While Māori activists, like their Hawaiian counterparts, insist on the 'correct' pronunciation of Māori words and place names in English, their own Māori inevitably shows the effects of English influence (Harlow 2004, 155–6).

The language of Néo-bretonnants, who have learned Breton mainly at university or in evening classes, is based on standard literary Breton and is distinguished on the one hand by its puristic tendencies (especially vocabulary) but ironically on the other by marked French influence on syntax. Traditional Breton, however, spoken predominantly by working-class people over 50 living in rural areas, displays opposite tendencies, namely more influence from French in vocabulary, but less in syntax. Consider this encounter between an older Breton speaker and a young Néo-breton student (Hornsby 2005, 198).

When the older speaker used French place names such as *Cornouaille*, the student supplied her with the Néo-breton equivalent *Kernev*. However, the student's pronunciation of the Breton name is influenced by French, making it in effect sound more French than the native Breton speaker's pronunciation of the French equivalent.

Changes arising from school-based transmission

Although the emergence of new varieties of some revitalized languages such as School Irish, Néo-breton, School Welsh, or School/University Hawaiian is increasingly reported, the social and political significance of the phenomenon has not been systematically studied. More children are now learning Basque, Irish, Hawaiian, etc., through the education system than learn it at home as a native language. Thus, the notion of 'Basque' or 'Irish speaker' is undergoing a radical transformation: new speakers are very different from older ones with respect to fluency and the density of Basque or Irish speakers in their networks. This has an enormous influence on their language use, as well as on the languages themselves (Romaine 2006). Functional restriction of these new varieties to the classroom has entailed structural loss, simplification, and reduction in variability, change rooted in the transmission process: the most complex and irregular parts of the language requiring the longest time to acquire often weaken or disappear as a result of incomplete or imperfect acquisition.

Immersion schooling appears to have standardizing effects. School Welsh is introducing a new norm based on standard Welsh into places such as Rhosllannerchrugog, a large village in north-east Wales of some 9,000 people, 38% of whom were Welsh speakers according to the 1991 census. Older people's Welsh is mainly dialectal, while younger people's Welsh is more standard. William Haddican (2005) documented similar effects in Basque, with younger speakers showing greater use of new standard forms of Basque as a consequence of the introduction of the newly invented Basque standard (Euskara Batua 'unified Basque') into Basque-medium schools. School-based transmission also leads to stylistic reduction. That is, linguistic markers of informal speech give way to formal ones in all contexts, because the primary domains for use are in the educational sector and media. In the case of French in Ontario, Canada, where school is the main source of exposure, the continuity of vernacular speech from one generation to the next may also be in jeopardy, since it is not spoken extensively in peer groups or at home (Mougeon and Beniak 1991, 137).

In Ireland the variety known as *Gaeilge líofa lofa* 'awful fluent Irish', i.e., fluent but with mistakes, has sparked debate about what constitutes a native speaker and an Irish-speaking community, now that traditional Irish-speaking communities account for less than 2% of the population, and are very scattered and fragmented, with a substantial number of residents using Irish infrequently, if at all. Reg Hindley (1990, 37), for example, refers to *Nua-Ghaeltachtaí* 'New Gaeltachts' or 'primarily Irish-speaking communities in the Galltacht' (i.e., English-speaking area). One such case is the Shaw's Road community in Belfast, where a group of parents, who were not native Irish speakers, established an Irish-speaking community and school amidst the otherwise English-speaking community. Shaw's Road Irish, however, was a new form of Irish, strongly influenced by English. The children's Irish lacked many traditional features of the Irish verbal system, gender distinctions, elements of the phonological system, and borrowed heavily (Maguire 1991). As in Ontario, restricted use of the minority language in the surrounding community had an impact on the variety spoken by children.

Mari C. Jones (1998) predicts that the greater prestige of standard Welsh, to which communities are increasingly exposed through education and the media, will ultimately lead to loss of local dialects. Similarly, the more traditional varieties of Breton seem to retreat, the more Néo-breton appears in public in the forms of immersion schools, bilingual signs, print and broadcast media. Some of the regional variation in Hawaiian, such as that between /v/ and /w/, /t/ and /k/, and /r/ and /l/ still preserved among Niʻihau speakers, may disappear in the long term because second-language learners of Hawaiian seldom interact with native speakers. Learners are taught to pronounce the <w> in words like *manawa* 'time' as /v/, and there is no <t> or <r> in the orthography (Romaine 2002). At the same time, however, reliance on the new orthography has led to spelling pronunciations among learners (e.g., *loaʻa* pronounced with three instead of two syllables).

None of these linguistic changes in and of themselves is unique to languages undergoing revitalization; they are all within the bounds of 'normal' language change. But the amount and rate of such changes are significant and when all the traditional speakers are gone, school-taught speakers will transmit the changes and permanently alter the revitalized languages. Thus, the revitalization setting differs critically from the usual context of second-language learning, where learner errors have no impact on the language because it is otherwise spoken by a community of native speakers.

Shifting the burden of transmission from homes to the educational sector also has social and cultural consequences. As knowledge of languages such as Hawaiian becomes a desirable skill and marketable commodity, those with the advantage of immersion education are better positioned to benefit from the language. However, such schools provide only a small minority of the population with access to scarce linguistic resources. Children attending Diwan Breton immersion schools or Hawaiian immersion programmes comprise less than 5% of each population. As a small elite comes to control a new variety of the traditional language equipped with modern terminology suitable for use in new public domains, the original defining group of speakers meanwhile becomes increasingly removed from its language, while committees of experts coin new terms needed for specialized subject areas. Many of the modern textbooks are not understood by native speakers of the language. Standards of attainment in schools are measured against the new written norms rather than the spoken norms of native speakers. When the few remaining native speakers deviate from the immersion variety, they are said to be either wrong or influenced by the dominant language.

Nevertheless, the net result of the ideological preoccupation with creating native vocabulary for western science is to render the vocabularies of Hawaiian and Māori similar to that of English. Much of the material used in Hawaiian immersion schools consists of the English curriculum with Hawaiian translations pasted over English text. Most reference materials are in English, and students must participate in state-mandated standardized testing in English. Lacking a monolingual Hawaiian dictionary, learners depend on bilingual dictionaries, which equate definition and translation. Hawaiian is thus filtered through English and its conceptual structure rather than learned from the perspective of the Hawaiian world view the immersion programmes seek to instil. Many subtleties and nuances of meaning and cultural content that can be learned only through traditional practice have been lost.

The extent to which the world view underlying traditional varieties is being replaced or 'colonized' by a western conceptual outlook is a concern. Instead of partially Hawaiianizing *sulufura*, Hawaiians could have chosen the pre-existing native compound *kūkae pele* 'sulphur, match, brimstone', literally 'Pele's excrement'. The native term fits into an extensive conceptual network of structurally similar compounds derived from *kūkae* 'excrement or deposit emanating from a person, animal, tree, plant, or substance' that express a rich semantic field of literal and figurative meanings. Consider, for example, *kūkae manu* 'bird dung/guano', *kūkae nalo* 'beeswax' (literally 'fly excrement'), *kūkae hao* 'rust' (literally 'iron excrement'), *kūkae uli* 'octopus ink' (literally 'black excrement') *kūkae 'iole* 'spots on an umbilical cord' (literally 'rat excrement'), and *kūkae akua* 'brownish substance under trees in shape of paste squeezed from tube' (literally 'ghost excrement').

Such terms encode native beliefs and traditions and articulate the conceptual unity of the Hawaiian perspective in which people are intimately connected and genealogically related to the natural environment and spiritual world. The weedy creepy grass native to Hawai'i called *kūkae pu'a'a* (literally 'pig dung') is the plant form of Kamapu'a'a, the pig demigod and suitor of Pele, the goddess of Kīlauea volcano on the island of Hawai'i. Patches of *kūkae pu'a'a* mark Kamapu'a'a's wanderings over the islands just as Pele's eruptions of *kūkae pele* are signs of her activity on the landscape. The number of *kūkae 'iole* on an umbilical cord were thought to indicate the number of children a mother would bear. The compound *kūkae nalo* also means a mole on the body, believed to be deposits of flies during infancy. If *kūkae akua* contained red, it was believed to be the excreta of a dying person or ghost and therefore a sign of someone's impending death. These cultural connections are absent from *sulufura*.

New languages for a brave new world?

This chapter has made a case for regarding revitalized languages as invented languages by examining the kinds of deliberate planning activities undertaken to transform them. Nevertheless, there is nothing unique about the product or process of retooling and refurbishing languages like Hawaiian or Breton so that they can function on a par with 'proper' languages, whose legitimacy is taken for granted. Indeed, the very fact that their legitimacy and naturalness are taken for granted is part of the hegemony of languages like English and French. Created out of the desire for prominent ideological symbols of shared identity, purpose, and nationhood, deliberate intervention in the form of standardization and elaboration has dramatically affected their evolution. Indeed, Eric Hobsbawm (1990, 54) sees such languages as 'the opposite of what nationalist mythology supposes them to be, namely the primordial foundations of national culture and the matrices of the national mind'. Other historians concur in regarding nations and/or languages as inventions involving a significant degree of social engineering and manipulation. Benedict Anderson (1991), for instance, links the rise of national standard languages and the ideology of European nationalism, while Michael Billig (1995, 30) contends that the concept of 'a language' in the sense which appears so banally obvious to us may itself be an invented permanency, a semi-artificial construct developed during the age of the nation-state.

Nation building and language building have gone hand in hand, called forth by 'acts of identity' (Le Page and Tabouret-Keller 1985). Both national and revitalized languages typically owe much to particular individuals, ardent supporters who are frequently cultural nationalists, who labour long and strenuously on their behalf. Eliezer Ben-Yehuda is as much the father of Modern Hebrew as Henry Jenner is the father of Modern Cornish. Tony Crowley (2006, 33) insists that 'only a major historical undertaking created "*the* Irish language" and "the *Irish* language" as it is known today'. The case of Hebrew also reveals how national and ethnic identities can construct languages that in turn can be used to promote these identities. Harshav (1993, 39) goes so far as to say that 'without the revival of the Hebrew language and its domination of the whole social network, it is doubtful that the State of Israel would have come into being'. Land made the language and language made the land. Hebrew of course had a historical territorial link to the land of the Jews (Eretz Israel), and its establishment as the language of the modern nation-state of Israel was viewed as a homecoming to its ancestral land.

The power of identity to imagine and invent both nations and languages is by no means confined to the past. Because national languages, like nations and national identities, are always unfinished projects, they may be challenged at any time. They are continually invented and reinvented, or as Sinfree Makoni and Alastair Pennycook (2006) put it, 'disinvented and (re)constituted'. The enterprise of constructing an Ireland that would be not only free but Irish is not any more complete than is the language symbolically appropriated to accomplish the task. The political tensions ultimately leading to the collapse of Yugoslavia put a formal end to the previous linguistic unity of the language called Serbo-Croatian when Bosnian, Serbian, and Croatian were established as new national languages of independent states.

A similarity of purpose and motivation drives inventors of all new languages, whether in the real or fictional world. The perceived need for them arises from dissatisfaction with the current linguistic state of affairs. Recognition that language can be used for promoting or changing the social, cultural, and political order leads to conscious intervention and manipulation of the form of language, its status, and its uses. In this sense then, the idea of a modern standard Hebrew as the language of a secular Jewish state sprang from the mind of Eliezer Ben-Yehuda, no less than Klingon did from the imagination of its inventor Marc Okrand. Hence the planners of Néo-breton, Modern Hebrew, and other revitalized languages are no less inventors than are authors of speculative fiction like George Orwell or Suzette Haden Elgin, who conceive new languages consonant with their vision of a brave new world. The task is to invent and spread a language to encode it. The project of imagining a world without gender differentiation and inequality gave birth to Elgin's Láadan, invented by women for women, just as much as Modern Hebrew would be conceived as a vehicle for modern Jewish statehood and nationality in the creation of a new land by pioneers, and of a new Jew who would escape the confines of the shtetl. Speaking or narrating in a feminist woman-made language in Elgin's *Native Tongue* (1984) becomes a liberating force for women dominated by a patriarchal society in the twenty-third century, just as Irish became and continues to be a language of resistance in the struggle against British rule.

Nevertheless, Gaurav Desai (1993, 122) reminds us that invention is at once a process of faking and making, which in itself is neither liberating nor oppressive. 'It all depends on who is doing the inventing, how it is being done, in what context, for what purpose, and with what degree of success.' One person's view of the future is another's nightmare. The purpose of Orwell's Newspeak in *Nineteen Eighty-Four*

(1949) was to make it impossible for citizens of Ingsoc to think any thoughts diverging from Ingsoc's ideological principles; hence Newspeak went hand in hand with an oppressive new totalitarian regime. In the real world too, efforts to control language use can advance either libertarian or repressive agendas. Hence the creation of a national hegemony often involves hegemony of language (Billig 1995, 29). In the successor states to the Former Republic of Yugoslavia, the desire to create ethnically pure and homogeneous nation-states went hand in hand with linguistic cleansing as signals of the reorganization of the cultural hegemony. Although the revitalization movements propelling Irish, Hawaiian, etc. aimed to install a new linguistic reality that is democratic rather than hegemonic, revolutions do not always evolve according to the intended plot. The new Norwegian created by Ivar Aasen as symbolic of a more truly Norwegian language has still not replaced the older heavily Danicized variety resulting from centuries of Danish rule over Norway (Haugen 1966). The products of language planning seldom go without contest, but the longer they endure, the more natural they seem. In the case of Basque, for example, opposition to the new standard Basque (Euskara Batua) proposed by the Basque language academy was very bitter, but today the spelling system is seldom questioned.

In the context of Basque, Galician, and Catalan planning, the term 'normalization' refers to a process seeking parity of use and status between the majority and minority languages, all three of which have become co-official with Spanish in the territories where they are spoken. In other words, the goal of language planning was to challenge the dominance of Spanish, to move beyond a supposedly normal historically repressive situation by rendering it discursively abnormal. Nevertheless, some discourses of normalization can be as hegemonic as those they seek to replace. Although the imagined 'normalized' nation of Galicia is in some respects analogous to Tolkien's imaginary Middle-earth, the complete normalization of Galician would entail the disappearance of Spanish, if not traditional varieties of Galician as well. One normative system is replaced by another, but both remain controlled by the hegemonic interests of those in power. As Galician is appropriated and revalorized in a different political climate, power can now be exercised through Galician, but the same process of social control is reproduced through language.

The former functional split between Galician as home and family language and Spanish as a public language of power and social mobility has been transformed into a new one between two clearly differentiated varieties of Galician: old rural traditional and new urban middle-class. In this context rural Galician, once stigmatized and despised by those now controlling Neo-Galician, has become a symbol of resistance. Rural speakers have reacted negatively to the new standard Galician broadcast on television because to them it sounds Castilianized, bookish, false, artificial, and foreign (Iglesias-Álvarez and Ramallo 2002–3, 268–9).

The interests of those learning Galician, Cornish, or other revitalized languages for the sake of identity are not identical with the interests of native speakers. For the local Gaelic-speaking population on the Scottish island of Skye, Gaelic is part of a local identity rooted in everyday practice rather than part of a politicized package of language, heritage, and culture advocated by those outside the community (MacDonald 1997, 238). Most of those choosing the new Gaelic medium programmes at school speak very little Gaelic at home. One 40-year-old man who grew up speaking Gaelic at home said (MacDonald 1997, 218):

> I speak the Gaelic here with my parents and when I go up to the [hotel bar], but I speak it not because I have to but because this is what we speak. I like the Gaelic. But if it is going to become something artificial, then well, I won't feel like speaking it at all. I don't want G to be kept alive by making it artificial … For myself, I'd prefer if it died.

Likewise, the new Breton-speaking world the Néo-bretonnnants are trying to (re)create is very different from the one in which the remaining Breton speakers exist. Not only does it embody different social values, it is also quite different linguistically. As outsiders to the rural communities in which Diwan immersion schools are established, the Diwan movement enthusiasts are far removed from local realities and ways of using Breton. Indeed, outside school it would be very difficult to learn Breton at all, even in supposedly Breton-speaking areas, because locals don't speak Breton to outsiders, or even to their own children. Activists who manage to speak Breton to the locals often find they are misunderstood.

Educated newcomers aspiring to be peasants appear almost as uncomfortable caricatures of the local lifestyle (McDonald 1989). So-called 'neo-Galicians', mainly young, educated, urban professionals whose first language is Spanish and who do not use Galician as their everyday language, are not accepted into traditional rural Galician speaking-circles, either. Traditional rural speakers, who are typically over 50, engaged as homemakers or fishermen, with lower levels of education, interpret the neo-Galicians' use of the language as condescending because they use it only in addressing 'the people' and not at home.

When continuity of traditional language use and cultural identity can be taken for granted, people do not need to talk about it. Kathryn A. Woolard (1998, 17) has underlined the irony that many movements to save minority languages are often structured around 'the same received notions of language that have led to their oppression and/or suppression'. Forms of language activism and language planning that reproduce the dominant language ideology also reproduce structures of domination. Hence, they engender a new standard language culture, and in this way the authoritative becomes authoritarian. Defining, using, and controlling a standard language is always the prerogative of the socially powerful and their hegemonic institutions.

Increasing institutionalization in the revival of Irish, Breton, Galician, etc. has benefited elites able to exploit its potential while it continues to subordinate the active speakers of the language.

The modernization of Hawaiian has generated resentment from some segments of the community who perceive it as a threat to the values embodied in the language's traditional form. 'University Hawaiian' carries a stigma and is thought not to be 'real' Hawaiian (Wong 1999, 100). Older Hawaiians from Ni'ihau in particular regard themselves as preserving Hawaiian in its purest form. They believe the Hawaiian translation of the Bible, which does not indicate vowel length or glottal stops, represents the 'true' form of the language. They see introduction of new spellings as tampering with the language, when in fact they are necessary for today's second-language speakers who can no longer rely on spoken forms.

That the educated middle classes in long-anglicized Dublin moved to revive and modernize Irish made the remaining native speakers along the rural west coast resent the expropriation of their language by wealthy townspeople, who were not native speakers. They were seen as well-off people who had done well out of the language. The idea that Dubliners should determine what is correct Irish aroused utmost disdain. The power of local Irish dialects over their speakers' loyalties leads them not only to reject the 'colorless "Dublin Irish" sponsored by the government' but also to turn off the radio when the authentic dialect of an Irish broadcast does not happen to be their own (Hindley 1990, 41, 60, 63, and 173). Similarly, for traditional rural Breton speakers designation of any one particular language variety for all Bretons is as inconceivable as standardization of costume and dance because they, like rural dialects of Breton, represent expressions of cultural diversity within Brittany. French serves as a common language for speech with outsiders (Kuter 1989, 84).

Because nationalist assumptions about language and identity constitute one of the most deeply entrenched modern ideologies, it is hardly surprising to find state policies as well as challenges to them embedded in them. Cultural survival now depends on the nation-state, which in turn is predicated on ideologies so unquestioned they are taken for granted. Since linguistic identities can be rallying points for furthering the interests (political or otherwise) of a minority group, language activism is often dismissed as 'identity politics', and attempts to replace *téléphone* with *pellgomz* in Brittany branded as outlandish and pointless exercises undertaken by fanatics with an ideological agenda of linguistic cleansing.

Indeed, eminent historian Arnold Toynbee (1987, 508) dismissed the revival of Irish as a 'perverse undertaking [that] has come from the nationalistic craze for distinctiveness and cultural self-sufficiency'. Such accusations miss the point that nationalism is identity politics by another name. Regardless of the political status of the groups on whose behalf such linguistic interventions are undertaken and carried out, they serve a common agenda of validating a language as a 'true' and therefore authentic symbol of national identity. Purism is an inevitable component of such ideology because it assumes that there can only be one authentic language associated with one authentic people.

Because purism always articulates a politics of inclusion and exclusion in which the state of the language functions as a metaphor for the state of the nation, culture, etc., it erupts in response to an ever-shifting set of perceived enemies. Nineteenth-century German nationalists demanded German be purged of French borrowings, just as today France and other countries fight a losing battle against a tide of English loanwords. In March 2003, Walter Jones, Republican congressman for North Carolina, demanded that cafeterias in the office buildings of the US House of Representatives replace the word *French* with *freedom* on their menus so that *French fries* and *French toast* would be called *freedom fries* and *freedom toast*. Even if dismissed by some as a petty culinary rebuke, signs appeared informing customers of the change. Although it is unlikely that the new words ever made any real inroad into everyday speech, they made headlines in media around the world as symbolic of tensions between France and the US. Jones, who intended the new words as a protest against French refusal to support the American-led war in Iraq, got the idea from a restaurant owner in North Carolina, who in turn modelled the new words on ones coined during World War I to replace the German terms *sauerkraut* and *hamburger* with *liberty cabbage* and *liberty steak* etc. Rallying Americans around the new words was meant to foster national unity, patriotism, and identity of purpose.

Fishman (2006, 21 and 48) reminds us that there is and can be no politically innocent or value-free corpus planning. Linguistic decisions are in effect political decisions. Like political decisions, they can be undone and redone. When Danish, Swedish, and Norwegian were standardized, differences between them were consciously exaggerated. Before 1906, all three languages wrote the word meaning 'what' as *hvad*. Now only Danish does; Swedish spells it as *vad* and Norwegian as *hva*. Thus, orthographic differences now disguise what is a similar pronunciation and make the languages look more different in their written form than they are when spoken. Such differences buttress claims about the distinctiveness of the individual languages and their connections to independent nation-states, just as in other cases the use of completely different writing systems serves to create visually unambiguous difference.

Conclusion

If the identity politics fuelling language revitalization are not really different in origin, ideological motivation, or outcome from those underlying the politics of nationalism that created modern languages like French and German, some nevertheless still dismiss non-fluent and/or non-native use of indigenous languages as merely symbolic. Such critics are often surprised to find considerable enthusiasm and commitment the world over to revive and revitalize what may seem to outsiders to be dying and useless languages. Though, as John Edwards (1984, 288) argues, they cannot be either if they serve a vital rallying purpose in nationalistic political movements. While the traditional language seems unnecessary for communication, the strength and persistence of local identities and their transformative power have been consistently underestimated. A new generation of well-educated fluent speakers of world languages such as English, French, and Spanish now view the revitalization and maintenance of their ancestral languages as an idealized expression of contemporary political aspirations, cultural authenticity, and pride.

Such reclamation efforts will become increasingly important as long as there are people who claim a link to a linguistic heritage no longer actively transmitted. Although revitalized and reclaimed languages are likely to be substantially different from the languages historically spoken, they clearly have the potential to serve important community and cultural functions for many minority groups all over the world. This was precisely the point made by Jenner (1904, xi), who answered the question of why Cornishmen should learn Cornish when 'there is no money in it, it serves no practical purpose, and the literature is scanty and of no great originality or value. The question is a fair one, the answer is simple. Because they are Cornish.'

References

Amery, Rob. 2000. *Warrabarna Kaurna! Reclaiming an Australian language*. Lisse: Swets & Zeitlinger.

Anderson, Benedict. 1991. *Imagined communities. Reflections on the origin and spread of nationalism*. London: Verso.

Bentahila, A., and E. E. Davies. 1993. 'Language revival: Restoration or transformation?' *Journal of Multilingual and Multicultural Development* 14.5: 355–73.

Benton, Richard. 1999. *Māori language revitalization*. Wellington, NZ.

Billig, Michael. 1995. *Banal nationalism*. London: Sage.

Burlingame, Burl. 1997. 'Convention Center's glottal goof'. *Honolulu Star-Bulletin* (October 23): A1 and 17.

Cooper, Robert L. 1989. *Language planning and social change*. Cambridge: Cambridge University Press.

Crowley, Tony. 2006. 'The political production of a language: The case of Ulster-Scots'. *Journal of Linguistic Anthropology* 16.1: 23–35.

Desai, Gaurav. 1993. 'The invention of invention'. *Cultural Critique* 24: 119–42.

Dorian, Nancy C. 1994. 'Purism vs. compromise in language revitalization and revival'. *Language in Society* 23: 479–94.

Edwards, John. 1984. 'Language, diversity and identity'. In *Linguistic minorities, policies and pluralism*, edited by John Edwards, 277–310. London: Academic Press.

Elgin, Suzette Haden. 1984. *Native Tongue*. New York: Daw.

Fellman, Jack. 1973. *The revival of a classical tongue. Eliezer Ben Yehuda and the modern Hebrew language*. The Hague: Mouton.

Fishman, Joshua A. 2004. 'Ethnicity and supra-ethnicity in corpus planning: the hidden status agenda within corpus planning'. *Nations and Nationalism* 10.1/2: 79–94.

Fishman, Joshua A. 2006. *Do not leave your language alone. The hidden status agendas in corpus planning in language policy*. Mahwah: Erlbaum.

Haddican, William. 2005. 'Standardization, functional shift and language change in Basque'. *Estudios de Sociolingüística* 6.1: 87–112.

Harlow, Ray. 1993. 'Lexical expansion in Māori'. *Journal of the Polynesian Society* 102: 99–107.

Harlow, Ray. 2004. 'Borrowing and its alternatives in Māori'. In *Borrowing: A Pacific perspective*, edited by Jan Tent and Paul Geraghty, 134–69. Canberra: Pacific Linguistics.

Harshav, Benjamin. 1993. *Language in the time of revolution*. Berkeley: University of California Press.

Haugen, Einar. 1966. *Language conflict and language planning. The case of modern Norwegian*. Cambridge, MA: Harvard University Press.

Hindley, Reg. 1990. *The death of the Irish language: A qualified obituary*. London: Routledge.

Hobsbawm, Eric. 1990. *Nations and nationalism since 1780: Programme, myth, reality*. Cambridge: Cambridge University Press.

Hornberger, Nancy H., and Kendall A. King. 1998. 'Authenticity and unification in Quechua language planning'. *Language, Culture and Curriculum* 11.3: 390–410.

Hornsby, Michael. 2005. 'Néo-breton and questions of authenticity'. *Estudios de Sociolingüística* 6.2: 191–218.

Iglesias-Álvarez, Ana, and Fernando Ramallo. 2002–3. 'Language as a diacritical in terms of cultural and resistance identities in Galicia'. *Estudios de Sociolingüística* 3.2–4.1: 255–87.

Jaffe, Alexandra. 1999. *Ideologies in action. Language politics on Corsica*. Berlin/New York: Mouton de Gruyter.

Jenner, Henry. 1904. *Handbook of the Cornish language*. London: David Nutt.

Jones, Mari C. 1998. *Language obsolescence and revitalization. Linguistic change in two sociolinguistically contrasting Welsh communities*. Oxford: Oxford University Press.

Joseph, John E. 2004. *Language and identity. National, ethnic, religious*. London: Palgrave Macmillan.

Ke Kōmike Hua'ōlelo. 2003. *Māmaka Kaiao: A modern Hawaiian vocabulary.* Honolulu: University of Hawai'i Press.

Kuter, Lois. 1989. 'Breton vs. French: Language and the opposition of political, economic, social and cultural values'. In *Investigating obsolescence: Studies in language contraction and death*, edited by Nancy C. Dorian, 75–89. Cambridge: Cambridge University Press.

Le Page, Robert B., and Andrée Tabouret-Keller. 1985. *Acts of identity.* Cambridge: Cambridge University Press.

Lewis, Saunders. 1973. 'The fate of the language'. In *Presenting Saunders Lewis*, edited by Alun R. Jones and Gwyn Thomas, 141. Cardiff: University of Wales Press.

McDonald, Maryon. 1989. *'We are not French!' Language, culture and identity in Brittany.* London: Routledge.

MacDonald, Sharon. 1997. *Reimagining culture. Histories, identities and the Gaelic renaissance.* Oxford: Berg.

Maguire, Gabrielle. 1991. *Our own language: An Irish initiative.* Clevedon: Multilingual Matters.

Makoni, Sinfree, and Alastair Pennycook, eds. 2006. *Disinventing and reconstituting languages.* Clevedon: Multilingual Matters.

Mougeon, Ramond, and Edouard Beniak. 1991. *Linguistic consequences of language contact and restriction: The case of French in Ontario.* Oxford: Oxford University Press.

Nettle, Daniel, and Suzanne Romaine. 2000. *Vanishing voices. The extinction of the world's languages.* New York: Oxford University Press.

Orwell, George. 1949. *Nineteen eighty-four.* London: Secker & Warburg.

Recalde, Montserrat. 2002–03. 'The Castilianist theory of the origin of the *gheada* revisited'. *Estudios de Sociolingüística* 3.2–4.1: 43–74.

Romaine, Suzanne. 2002. 'Signs of identity, signs of discord: glottal goofs and the green grocer's glottal in debates on Hawaiian orthography'. *Journal of Linguistic Anthropology* 12.2: 89–225.

Romaine, Suzanne. 2005. 'Orthographic practices in the standardization of pidgins and creoles: Pidgin in Hawai'i as anti-language and anti-standard'. *Journal of Pidgin and Creole Languages* 20.1: 101–40.

Romaine, Suzanne. 2006. 'Planning for the survival of linguistic diversity'. *Language Policy* 5.2: 443–75.

Romaine, Suzanne. 2008. 'The Irish language in a global context'. In *A new view of the Irish language*, edited by Caoilfhionn Nic Pháidín and Seán Ó Cearnaigh, 11–25. Dublin: Cois Life. pp. 11–25.

Rosaldo, Renato. 1990. 'Others of invention: Ethnicity and its discontents'. *Voice Literary Supplement* 82: 27–9.

Shohamy, Elana. 2008. 'At what cost? Methods of reviving, maintaining and sustaining endangered and minority languages'. In *Sustaining linguistic diversity. Endangered and minority languages and varieties*, edited by Kendall King, Natalie Schilling-Estes, Lyn Fogle, Jackie Lou, and Barbara Soukup, 205–18. Washington, DC: Georgetown University Press.

Thomas, George. 1991. *Linguistic purism*. London: Longman.

Timm, Lenora A. 2003. 'Breton at a crossroads: Looking back, moving forward'. *e-Kelto* 2: 25–61.

Toynbee, Arnold J. 1961. (1934). *Study of history*. Oxford: Oxford University Press.

Waitangi Tribunal. 1989. *Report of the Waitangi Tribunal on the Te Reo Māori claim*. Wellington, NZ: Government Printer.

Woolard, Kathryn A. 1998. 'Introduction: Language ideology as a field of inquiry'. In *Language ideologies: Practice and theory*, edited by Bambi Schieffelin, Kathryn A. Woolard, and Paul V. Kroskrity, 3–47. New York: Oxford University Press.

Wong, Laiana. 1999. 'Authenticity and the revitalization of Hawaiian'. *Anthropology and Education Quarterly* 30: 94–115.

Zuckermann, Ghil'ad. 2003. *Language contact and lexical enrichment in Israeli Hebrew*. London: Palgrave Macmillan.

APPENDIX 1

Owning Language

This book illustrates various ways in which people invent language, often going so far as to invent *a* language, the whole thing: a sound system (or phonology), processes to form new words (morphology), phrase and clause structure (or syntax), vocabulary, pragmatics (meaning that depends on context), and even orthographies (spelling systems and scripts). Inventing a language, even if it's only on paper, so to speak, is a significant achievement. Someone who invents a better mousetrap patents it. Someone who writes a novel, or, you might say, 'invents a fiction', copyrights the particular language in which it's expressed. Patents and copyright are forms of ownership, and generally we accept that inventors get to own what they invent. They can sell it or license it—they can give it away. But those are choices they make as inventors and owners. So, you anticipate the question, if one can invent a language, can one also own it and by owning it control its development and use?

The question highlights a fundamental difference between alphabets and scripts, on one hand, and language on the other. A language needn't have a written version; it can do without an alphabet. Invented scripts, like type fonts, are particular ways of representing alphabets: they are a matter of visual design. Though an historical alphabet (the Roman alphabet we use in writing English, for instance) may not distinguish all sounds of all languages (for which we have the International Phonetic Alphabet), many languages (Elvish languages invented by Tolkien, for instance—see Chapter 4) can be 'transliterated' or rewritten into it. The scripts, however, are unique. So, in preparing to publish this book, we have applied to owners of alphabets and scripts used in MMPORGs (that is, 'mass multi-player online role-playing games'—see Appendix 6) for permission to use images of alphabets and scripts discussed in Chapter 6. In one case, we were generously given permission to do so; in the others, where both scripted alphabets and samples of the languages in the relevant scripts were concerned, permission was withheld.

Many believe that words and phrases and titles can be copyrighted, too—they can't. On 17 October 2005, the American satirist Stephen Colbert, on *The Colbert Report*, his send-up of conservative television news and opinion programming, pretended to coin the word *truthiness*, which he explained thus: 'We're not talking about truth, we're talking about something that seems like truth—the truth we want to exist.' Colbert is also behind the stunt website *Wikiality*: *wikiality* is another Colbert stunt word, a blend of *wiki*, as in *Wikipedia*, and *reality*, that is, reality by consensus. The entry for 'truthiness' on *Wikiality* includes a sidebar that claims, 'Truthiness is a term invented, copyrighted, and trademarked by Stephen Colbert.' Of course, the whole thing is facetious: later in the entry, a sort of advertisement reads, 'Truthiness Makes The Baby Jesus™ Happy And that Makes Stephen happy, too! [sic]'—it would be difficult indeed to trademark *The Baby Jesus*, because it doesn't name a brand of product or service, a prerequisite for trademarking. And surely, were *The Baby Jesus* a trademark, it would belong to God the Father, or the Church, or Jesus himself, rather than Stephen Colbert.

Not all attempts to own or control invented language are playful commentary on appropriation, ownership, and control. On 27 January 2006, *The Register*, an online journal subtitled 'Biting the hand that feeds IT', reported that the telecommunications company Cingular had applied to patent emoticons — ☺, :-& 'sticking out tongue', 8-) 'happy with glasses', ☹, etc. It will surprise no one that they weren't the first to attempt it. On *Language Log* (31 January 2006), in an article titled 'All your emoticons are belong to Cingular?' (a play on an item of gamer slang—see Appendix 6), Mark Liberman objects. The *Register* article jumped to a conclusion, because Cingular wasn't trying to patent emoticons as such, but 'on any method for entering emoticons via special keys, key sequences or menus'; Liberman argues that 'no one should be able to patent something as obvious as this. It's like asking for a patent on the idea of putting portable mp3 players in a shopping bag so that purchasers can carry them home more easily'. Anyway, all our emoticons are belong to us, the 'speakers' of emoticons.

Part of the problem in the Cingular case is that the cat was already out of the bag: people invented emoticons in everyday discourse, albeit online discourse.

When invented languages are part of a fabricated fictional world like Tolkien's Middle-earth, the issues are quite different. As Tolkien linguist Carl Hostetter writes on the website of The Elvish Linguistic Fellowship (E.L.F.):

> In addition to the general copyright issues associated with the published and unpublished works of any author, legality is further an issue in the study of Tolkien's invented languages because, unlike natural languages, Tolkien's languages are the invention of one man, and thus are his artistic and intellectual property. As such, they, like his writings (published and unpublished), are protected by national and international copyright laws, and by the Estate that Tolkien created expressly for the purpose of ensuring such protections. (Hostetter 2006)

Treatment of Klingon requires similar restraint: Marc Okrand is the primary inventor of the language, but, as an element of television and film scripts, and in authorized elaborations of the language by Okrand (dictionaries and the like), it is owned by Paramount Pictures (see Chapter 5). The Klingon Language Institute (KLI), while deferring to Okrand, is responsible for several translations of classic texts into Klingon (see Appendix 5)—Paramount owns the copyright to the Klingon *Hamlet*, though members of KLI did the translating. All of this brings us back to the question, 'Can you copyright an invented language or just particular texts in that language?' (Davis 2001).

Arguably, the translations are extensions of the Klingon fiction: yet the fiction relies partly on the pretence that Klingon is already a language, for otherwise, it couldn't be a medium of translation. Which is it? Is it a language (what it claims to be), or is it a simulacrum of a language (what most linguists would say it is)? If Klingon or Elvish ever develops a speech community (either as a first language or a natural language of bilingual speakers), it will slough off legislated constraints and speak naturally, conventionally. Regulation of the kind exercised by the Tolkien Estate and ownership like Paramount's of Klingon inhibit language—some would argue that any language thus regulated cannot be a 'real' language. Intuitively, isn't there a difference between regulation of natural languages (claims by teachers and language mavens about what one 'ought' to do) and invented languages tightly controlled by inventors and secondary copyright owners (legal claims about what one 'can' do)? Maybe, but maybe not—the processes and effects of regulation do not distinguish natural and invented languages as sharply as we assume (see Chapter 8).

'Undeterred by the challenge, a group of schoolboys has volunteered for lessons in Sindarin, the "conversational" form of Elvish' (Parkinson 2004). David Salo, who developed Elvish for Peter Jackson's film trilogy *The Lord of the Rings*, cautions, 'We have to be very careful to use words properly, as Sindarin was invented by Tolkien and we should show it respect' (Parkinson 2004). Fans of other languages also try to learn them and find plenty of help: those hoping to learn Klingon turn to the Klingon Language Institute (see Appendix 5); those attracted to Na'vi, the language spoken by the indigenous creatures on Pandora in James Cameron's film *Avatar* (2009), like Klingon created by a linguist (in this case Paul Frommer, of the University of Southern California), can study the materials available at http://www.learnnavi.org, including the file titled 'The Easiest Way to Learn Na'vi—EVER!!'

Encouraging use of artificial languages in natural contexts is incompatible with ownership and control: when real-world speakers employ an artificial language in a real-world conversation (or even an 'interaction', like putting up a flyer in Klingon to advertise a Klingon karaoke party at a club), the language is suddenly no longer artificial, though it may also fall short of being natural. No one, not even Marc Okrand or the Klingon Language Institute, can supervise or authorize a private conversation between Klingon speakers (see the end of Chapter 5): once there are speakers, the language belongs to them. Some authors or creators (or those to whom they have subsequently licensed or sold them) are inclined to assert control over 'their' languages, but they cannot do so, practically or legally, outside of artificial contexts.

The case of Loglan demonstrates how much a language inventor can pursue authorship and control. When I say 'case' I refer to the incident involving Loglan, but also the legal case in which it was resolved, a trademark dispute resolved in the United States Court of Appeals, Federal Circuit (decision dated 28 April 1992; otherwise unattributed quotations below are to this decision). That court's opinion gives a flawless description of Loglan: 'In 1955, Dr. James Brown invented a "logical language" which was designed to test the theory that natural languages limit human thought. [In other words, it tested the Sapir–Whorf hypothesis—see Chapter 3.] It has been described by Dr. Brown as "symbolic logic made speakable" which "derives its word-stock impartially from the eight most widely spoken natural languages and so is culturally and politically neutral as well as suitable for cross-cultural linguistic experimenta-tion". ' It's hard to see how an invented language derived from natural lan-guages, not just natural, in fact, but the most widely spoken, could be copyrighted or controlled, but Brown believed that Loglan could be and that he was its owner.

As Arika Okrent tells the story, 'There had never been any question among the Loglan volunteers that Brown was in charge. It was his language and he had the last word.' But when the Loglan Institute (LI) undertook to 'overhaul … the rules of Loglan word formation … Brown proved unable to relinquish any control, even going so far as to prohibit the members from discussing (in their newsletter) any issues he had not personally approved for discussion' (Okrent 2009, 220). So when Bob LeChevalier and Nora Tansky, dues-paying members of the Institute, attempted to distribute a Loglan flashcard program as shareware, 'Brown informed them they would do no such thing. Loglan was the property of the institute. He would consider letting them distribute the program only if they signed a statement of acknowledgment that the insti-tute owned the copyrights to the language and agreed to pay the institute roy-alties' (Okrent 2009, 224). Brown's controlling tendencies had already fostered schism within the institute, but LeChevalier and Tansky formed a new group dedicated to develop Loglan as Loglan-88 (it was 1988), under the auspices of the Logical Language Group (LLG), which they had formed for the purpose, upon which 'betrayal' Brown attempted to trademark *Loglan*—LLG chal-lenged his right to the mark.

The challenge was first heard by the Trademark Trial and Appeal Board (TTAB) which, on 4 February 1989, rejected LI's claim to *Loglan* as a trade-mark. LI appealed the ruling, but the Federal Circuit also ruled in LLG's favour. The court agreed with the TTAB that *Loglan* is a term 'used generically to designate a language', like *English* or *French*, so could not be used 'as a trade-mark on "dictionaries and grammars"' any more than English can be regis-tered for a dictionary'. *Loglan* is no more a name for a brand of goods or services than *The Baby Jesus*, which is similarly excluded from trademark reg-istration. Unfortunately for Brown, the court found, 'the evidence indicates that Dr. Brown himself has used the term Loglan only in a generic sense', while, for instance, in 1984, 'insisting on moving in the right direction for Loglan whether this means losing control of the institute I founded or not', and thereby losing whatever control he could exercise over the language, legal or otherwise. He would still write books about Loglan, he says; 'Perhaps with my example others will too.' But with that invitation, Brown's control over Loglan was untenable, much as in the cases of conversational Sindarin and Klingon. As the court concluded, Brown's 'encouragement for others to write Loglan books or books in Loglan negates the claim now asserted of proprietary rights in Loglan'.

Okrent asks the question bluntly: 'Can a person own a language? The law is still not really clear on that' (2009, 226). The Loglan case was a trademark dispute and didn't resolve matters of copyright. 'Brown claimed he owned the rights to the *vocabulary* of Loglan. Did he? Brown did have copyrights on his books, including the dictionary [of Loglan which he compiled]. But copyright does not extend to each individual word in a copyrighted work, only to the particular configuration of words' (Okrent 2009, 227). Ludwig Zamenhof, inventor of Esperanto (see Chapter 2), at the peak of interest in the best-known international auxiliary language (see Appendix 2), took a more sensible attitude towards control—he relinquished it. 'If I have passed the best part of my life, freely taking great pains and making great sacrifices without even reserving to myself the rights of authorship—did I do these things solely for utilitarian purposes?' (Zamenhof 1906, 1157). No, of course not: indeed, 'the rights of authorship' are incompatible with language as we know it. If real people use it, an invented language transcends authorship and serves a higher aesthetic, moral, or political purpose. Royalties are beside the point.

In the end, wouldn't owning language be the same as owning culture (see Chapters 6, 7, and 8)? And, Erik Davis (2001) asks:

> What does it mean to own culture? For media companies, ownership means an exclusive right to squeeze dollars out of materials gripped by the ever-growing tentacles of copyright. But fandom [Tolkien fandom, Klingon fandom] is essentially an open source culture, even as it feeds on corporate media. Fan ownership is really stewardship, a commitment that does not center on individual control but on shared imagination and collective process ... fandom harks back to a time when we sat around the campfire and swapped the old, untrademarked tales of heroes and gods.

In natural language systems, speakers own their language, and their free exercise of it is a primary instrument of culture. We can speak of 'human culture', but really we live in multiple subcultures, some natural and some created, and those subcultures depend on the languages in which we swap untrademarked tales.

References

Davis, Erik. 2001 (October). 'The Fellowship of the Ring'. *Wired*. http://www.wired.com/wired/archive/9.10/lotr.html

Hostetter, Carl. 2002. 'Resources for Tolkienian Linguistics'. *Elvish Linguistic Fellowship*. http://www.elvish.org

Liberman, Mark. 2006 (31 January). 'All your emoticons are belong to Cingular?' *Language Log*. http://itre.cis.upenn.edu/~myl/languagelog/archives/002798.html

Loglan Institute, Inc. v. Logical Language Group, Inc., 962 F.2d 1938 (Federal Circuit 1992).

Okrent, Arika. 2009. *In the Land of Invented Languages*. New York: Spiegel & Grau.

Parkinson, Justin. 2004 (4 March). 'Do You Speak Elf?' *BBC News Online*. http://news.bbc.co.uk/2/hi/uk_news/education/3532003.stm

Zamenhof, Ludwig. 1906. 'Aspirations of the Founder of Esperanto: Dr. Zamenhof's Address to the Second Esperanto Congress'. *The North American Review* 183 (No. 604, 7 December): 1153–8.

APPENDIX 2

Esperanto's Zenith

As Arden Smith describes in the complementary chapter, Esperanto reached its zenith in the first decade of the twentieth century, from 1900, when it was exhibited at the World's Fair, into its 'French Period', marked by the first congress of Esperantists in Boulogne-sur-Mer in 1905 and the opening of the Esperanto movement's 'Central Office' in Paris in 1906. Still, it comes as a surprise that when Edwin Davis French, 'America's Foremost Engraver of Book Plates', died, his obituary in the *New York Times* (10 December 1906) observed not only that he was 'a notable figure in American art' but that his 'hobby was universal language, for he was a facile linguist. He was Secretary of the Volapük Society of America, and had a considerable library in that language. Esperanto and Idiom Neutral similarly attracted him'. Surely, it is remarkable that dedication to international auxiliary languages was the stuff of obituaries in 1906, remarkable that French and others were so deeply committed to them, remarkable, too, that some considerable segment of the reading public saw such commitment as a mark of distinction. Thus, a single obituary illustrates quite effectively the status of international auxiliary languages during the last decade of French's life.

In those years, discussion of Esperanto and other auxiliary languages in the *New York Times* had been frequent and even contentious. It was a favourite target of W. L. Alden (1837–1908) in his popular *New York Times* column, 'Mr. Alden's Views'. Alden was sceptical of every enthusiasm not his own, and his breezy, slightly acid style regularly provoked letters from more serious-minded people, people who rarely appreciated Alden's sense of humour. He was living in London while he wrote the column, so his commentary and responses to it are actually of transatlantic interest, thus reflecting much more than merely New York, or even general American, considerations and reconsiderations of the quality and utility of Esperanto and other international auxiliary languages.

Alden reports, on 11 February 1903:

> London is somewhat interested ... in the new international language called 'Esperanto'. So far as I have been able to learn any facts about the new language, it is a great improvement on Volapük, which was preposterous from beginning to end. Volapük was not a simple language, and simplicity is the one thing which is required, if we are to have an international language. Esperanto is far simpler ... but it still is very far from being an ideal language in point of simplicity. Most people fancy that Arabic is a difficult language, and so it is, owing to certain peculiarities in it which are quite unnecessary. But in its main structure Arabic is simplicity itself. A new international language based on Arabic and pruned of the eccentricities of Arabic would meet a great want.

Alden would rather 'purify' a natural language for international use (one doubts that Arabs, or for that matter any other community of speakers, would consent to donating their language to this cause), which is almost the same as 'doing anything' before taking artificial languages seriously.

Alden's column of 15 August 1903 is more caustic. He characterizes Esperanto as the unnatural offspring of wayward, promiscuous languages— 'From the specimens of the language that I have seen, it seems to be a sort of Italian gone wrong in company with some Slavonic tongue'. But he also gets to what many have seen as the illogic of language invention:

> Of all crazes, the scheme of inventing a new universal language is the most preposterous. It recalls those amiable persons who from time to time find the divisions of Christianity intolerable, and so start a new sect and add another to the many divisions which they deplore. There are already too many languages in the world, and it would be far better if every one spoke the same language. How this undesirable state of things is to be cured by adding a new language to those already in existence is not clear.

Resolving mutual unintelligibility is a legitimate desire, but no one language ever satisfies the ideal, so we endure an unending series of invented languages, some of them by serial inventors. From Alden's perspective, that's not the worst of it: 'Conceive of English literature translated in Esperanto! How any one can face such a contingency and still labor for the spread of Esperanto is quite unintelligible.' One can only guess at Mr Alden's reaction to Klingon translations of *Hamlet* or *Much Ado about Nothing* (see Appendix 5).

The story of Esperanto, as Alden tells it on 6 February 1904, is folly heaped on folly:

> At a recent meeting of the National Indian Association, Sir George Birdwood, the Chairman, held up Esperanto as a new variety of terror, and prophesied that if it became popular it would mean that all the modern languages would speedily become as dead as Latin. Sir George did not conceal his dread that this might happen, and his speech will greatly encourage the Esperantists. Nobody was ever afraid of Volapük, but Esperanto is certainly a very great improvement on that ridiculous invention, and if it does come into anything like general use as an aid to commerce Sir George's gloomy prediction may be realized at no very distant day.

And, from the satirist's point of view, it just gets better:

> The French Touring Club, which is the largest body of cyclists in the world, has adopted Esperanto as the means of communication between its members and cyclists from other countries. This would be an excellent plan, provided the other cyclists would also learn Esperanto. ... If the French club wishes its members to be able to converse with English cyclists, why does it not instruct them to learn English? Of course the club would never be so unpatriotic as to promote in any way the study of German. It is an extremely patriotic club, as it proved when it expelled Zola because he asked for justice for Dreyfus.

Readers then as now probably noticed that Alden had little respect for invented languages, perhaps a bit less for their inventors. 'Anyone with any capacity for invention,' he wrote, 'can invent a new language in two hours by the clock'—not, the contents of this book give us reason to believe, the experience of Zamenhof, J. R. R. Tolkien (see Chapter 4), or Okrand and the Klingon Language Institute (see Chapter 5 and Appendix 5). But Alden reserves a special scorn for the enthusiasts, the members of clubs, whether linguistic or touring, the speakers at congresses, the gibbering lunatics at liberty among us.

Alden's columns prompted the enthusiasts to respond. While they are, I suppose, less clever than Alden, they are probably more informative about the fervid interest in IALs generally in those days, but especially Volapük and Esperanto. For instance, in a letter to the editor published on 11 July 1903 (dated 7 July), a certain E. D. F. (who, I think we can assume, is Edwin Davis French) takes exception to Alden's earlier commentary, and his letter is worth quoting at length because it so clearly confirms, in a contemporary voice, Smith's description in the complementary chapter:

> Esperanto was first promulgated in the year 1887, only eight years after the very first appearance of Schleyer's Volapük, at the time that the latter was at the height of its ephemeral popularity. It was first known as 'La Lingvo Internacia', and its author, Dr. Samenhof [sic] of Warsaw, concealed his identity for awhile under the pseudonym of 'Esperanto', i.e., 'the hopeful one', but later on that appellation was more or less appropriately transferred to the language itself, after its author had become better known. Volapük failed to attract a sufficient number of adherents to justify for itself the title of an international language, chiefly because its use and advantages were not understood, and also on account of various dissensions among its chief supporters concerning the structure and amplification of the language, not because of any failure on its part to serve adequately as an international medium of communication. Its chief defects lay in the fact that its radicals, taken largely from existing languages, were often abbreviated and mutilated past recognition, while the elaborate system of arbitrary prefixes and suffixes rendered the whole quite illegible to those who had not learned the system, albeit the learning involved a very inconsiderable fraction of the time to master any one of the existing national tongues. This same defect exists, perhaps to a somewhat less degree, in Esperanto, as well. …

Esperanto fails to utilize the greater portion of these international words [words among several romance languages and English], preferring, as did Volapük, arbitrary combinations of its own elements, ingenious indeed, but more or less of the nature of puzzles to be solved by readers equally ingenious. It has also the serious disadvantage of requiring the use of six letters not in the Roman alphabet, and consequently involving the use of special type. It has an unnecessary special form for the accusative case, an uncouth plural ending in j, and various other eccentricities quite as unacceptable as those which made Volapük the synonym of harsh and unmeaning jargon—to those who judged by sight rather than by hearing.

The nearest approach to a satisfactory international language, as was explained by one of your correspondents a few months ago, is the 'Idiom Neutral', agreed upon by that international organization evolved from the old Volapük 'Academy', under the direction of Woldemar Rosenberger of St. Petersburg. This is made up of words chosen from actual international forms of expression, rejects all arbitrary constructions and artificial combinations, and is certainly a most decided advance upon all preceding systems, even if it may not be destined actually to become the international neutral language of the future. We may boast of the supremacy of English, and rejoice at its ever-extending use in commerce and literature, but as long as other nations and languages exist there is need of an easily learned, simple, invariable, and precise international medium, such as would be afforded by an ideal—and necessarily artificial—neutral tongue.

French addresses Alden's points against Esperanto (and IALs generally) systematically, but temperately and informatively—French is no wild-eyed enthusiast and he often acknowledges the deficiencies of artificial languages he has studied at some trouble and expense, even Volapük, though he was once Secretary of the Volapük Society of America. French never mentions Alden by name, indirection that takes some wind out of Alden's complaints, for humorists are, by their nature, attention-seekers.

Others, however, responded to Alden directly, both to his tone and his arguments. So, H. G. P. wrote to the *New York Times* on 30 August 1904 (published 3 September), 'I note that Mr. W. L. Alden speaks slightingly of

Esperanto and seriously doubt if he has given the subject any serious examination,' while Edward W. Bryant, of New York City, wrote on 2 June 1904 (published 4 June) that 'Mr. W. L. Alden in his London letter takes a little fling at Esperanto, the so-called universal language, with which apparently he has but the most cursory acquaintance'. If one wanted to know the truth about artificial languages, F. R. wrote to the *Times* on 6 February 1904 (published 13 February): 'It is not without interest to compare the critical opinion of authorities like MM Couturat and Lean [sic] with the flippant utterances of certain newspaper writers on the subject.' And F. R. is having none of Alden's nonsense about translation into Esperanto:

> As to translations, your London correspondent took occasion in a previous letter to shudder at the possibility of the gems of English literature being translated into Esperanto! I can assure him that such translations already exist, and preserve to a wonderful degree, as translations go, the charm of the originals. But why more cause for alarm in this than in the long-ago-accomplished fact of 'Hamlet' rendered in French?

Of course, there are those who object to the French translation as well. H. G. P. informs us that, among other texts, *Hamlet* and the *Iliad* had been translated into Esperanto by 30 August 1904.

Respondents had many explanations for Esperanto's supposed defects and many positive defences of it, too, most often emphasizing the ease with which Esperanto can be learned. So, G. W. Wishard, of Irvington, New York, wrote to the *Times* on 4 June 1904 (published 11 June), 'But notwithstanding all its faults, the Esperanto can be learned in far less time and with far less labor than any of the old tongues'; and H. G. P concluded that 'Any one with a liberal education can acquire a good working knowledge of Esperanto in a few weeks'. A few weeks? An article in the *Times* of 8 February 1903, credited originally to the *London Mail*, claimed reassuringly that '"Esperanto" is said by its adherents to be so simple that eight hours' study will enable a man to read any "Esperanto" book with a dictionary of 800 words'. Bryant reminds us that 'Count Tolstoy assures us he learned to read Esperanto with ease in two hours', but ease of acquisition is not limited to literary genius. Advertisements for Esperanto textbooks and instruction were often even more optimistic: 'A NEW UNIVERSAL LANGUAGE. ESPERANTO. POPULAR EDITION 50C. NET.

MASTERED IN AN HOUR. **FLEMING H. REVELL CO., Publishers**' (*New York Times* 17 February 1906). The appetite for self-improvement is not often satisfied by languages that take a lifetime to learn.

Arika Okrent investigated today's Esperanto community and came to this conclusion: 'While Esperanto-land has its share of people you don't want to meet—insufferable bores, sanctimonious radicals, proselytizers for Christ, communism, or a new kind of vegetarian healing—for the most part, the Esperantists I encountered were genuine, friendly, interested in the world, and respectful of others,' but this doesn't change the facts: 'Is it crazy to believe that Esperanto has a chance in the age of English? It's insane. Ask any businessman in Asia, any hotel operator in Europe. Is it ridiculous to believe that a universal common language will bring peace to the world? Of course it is. We have all the brutal evidence we need' (2009, 129–30).

But in the first decade of the twentieth century, some took a different view (and some of the brutal evidence Okrent has in mind was in the future). There was a great deal at stake ideologically in the success of Esperanto. On 24 June 1904 (published 9 July), John Ellis, resident of Keighley, England, wrote to the *New York Times*:

> Those of your readers who have the privilege of attending the St. Louis Exhibition have an opportunity of learning more of Esperanto by visiting the Esperanto exhibit in the French Section of Social Economy, Group 138, (General Progress of the Social Movement). The exhibit is doubtless but an incomplete evidence of the strength of the Esperanto movement, as it was hurriedly put together by the Parisian Groupe of the French Esperanto Society, without any reward but that of serving and helping their fellow-men throughout the world. This broad humanitarian idea has been the sole motive of thousands of ardent Esperantists.

And this earnestness persuaded many quite sophisticated, intellectual people that Esperanto was bound to succeed. George Harvey (1906, 1078) wrote in 'The Editor's Diary' of the celebrated and influential *North American Review*:

> As a result of painstaking inquiries made personally in France and England, and through agents in Germany and Switzerland, we have become convinced that Esperanto will soon be recognized, the world

over, as a language capable of universal use, and that, in consequence of such recognition, it will generally be adopted and acquired. The need of such a vehicle of expression, not for the displacement of any existing language, nor for the purposes of literature [to Alden's relief], but for ordinary service in business, travel, and communication, has long been admitted, and indeed is so obvious [at least, before the brutal evidence piles up] as to render the setting forth of reasons therefor [sic] superfluous.

The Aldens of this world cannot daunt today's well motivated Esperantists, any more than they could their ideological interlinguistic forebears. As the *London Mail* article reported, 'An Esperantist, who was interviewed yesterday said, "Esperantu esperanto sukcesos", which means, "Let us hope it will succeed" ' (*New York Times* 8 February 1903). *Espero saltas eterna.*

References

Material from the *New York Times* has been retrieved through the ProQuest Historical Newspapers database and can be located easily there. Ulrich Becker has recently published *Esperanto in* The New York Times *(1887–1922)* (Mondial, 2010), but as of this writing I have not been able to consult a copy of that book. In addition to the *New York Times*, I have cited the following:

[Harvey, George]. 1906. 'The Editor's Diary'. *The North American Review* 183 (No. 603, 16 November): 1073–88.

Okrent, Arika. 2009. *In the Land of Invented Languages*. New York: Spiegel & Grau.

APPENDIX 3

Nadsat and the Critics

Critics understood immediately that Nadsat was essential to Anthony Burgess's fictional project and obliquely reflected aspects of the dystopian social vision underlying that project. (Most reviews of Tolkien's *Lord of the Rings*, by way of contrast, said little about his invented languages—see Appendix 4). In reviews as well as academic criticism, Burgess is often compared to George Orwell, and *A Clockwork Orange* to *Nineteen Eighty-Four*. The extracts from criticism here barely illustrate that tendency, in favour of other interesting and perhaps less expected comparisons to James Joyce and *Finnegans Wake* (see Chapter 7 for a thorough, astute explanation of Joyce's linguistic inventions).

Nadsat is certainly invented, but where does it lie along the spectrum of invented language? It's not a fully constructed language with grammatical rules and specific phonology, but a vocabulary that evokes a particular register. Those commenting here cannot decide among them whether Nadsat is meant to represent a slang, argot, jargon, or cant; but there is something at stake thematically in knowing which it is, or rather in raising the issue, as it may be some combination of them.

As Julie Coleman works it out, slang 'tends to be used by a closed group of people, often united by common interests. Each generation, for example, has its own slang of approval and disapproval, and its users are able to demonstrate that they are up-to-date and in-the-know. Conversely, those who do not use or understand the appropriate terminology are unfashionable and out of touch'. Jargon 'typically belongs to professions or interest groups, such as doctors or train enthusiasts', and cant (or argot) has as its 'primary purpose … to defraud and to conceal. It is the language used by beggars and criminals to hide their dishonest and illegal activities from potential victims' (Coleman 2004, 4), or the law. Some critics note that Nadsat draws a line between generations, but is also the language of ruthless criminals; youth and criminality are mutually implicated in Alex, the protagonist of *A Clockwork Orange*, 'a teenage fiend incarnate' (Evans 1971, 409–10).

Unlike Klingon or Sindarin Elvish, Nadsat is not the language of a fictional race or nation, even though it is at the centre of a fiction. Rather, it is 'our' language as it might develop given certain historical and moral conditions. So, as Eric Rabkin argues below, it is language invented to stand for language transformed, and should be understood as one version among many of what Walter E. Meyers (1980, 12) calls 'The Future History and Development of the English Language'. The moral condition that shapes the novel is that the world is filled with horrors, and under such a condition, as Bergonzi suggests below, Nadsat is not merely a vocabulary but a pragmatic technique by which both Alex and the reader distance themselves from the horrors, in Alex's case, even as he personifies them.

This function of slang as resistance to the inhuman condition is now more commonly recognized than when Burgess published *A Clockwork Orange*. For instance, it serves a similar purpose for Buffy in the TV series *Buffy the Vampire Slayer*: she is a reluctant teenage hero, rather than a teenage fiend incarnate, who deflects the goriness of her calling with slangy wit, which also serves as 'a means of shrugging off millennial expectations' (Adams 2003, 3). Klingon may interest us, among other things, in the way it imitates and illuminates language structure, as those developing the language attempt to codify it. By way of contrast, Nadsat clarifies the social and psychological dimensions of language, by calling our attention to them in the unfamiliarity of the invention.

The comments that follow do not necessarily reflect the views of the author of the complementary chapter, nor of the editor (and when they do, perhaps not uniformly), nor Anthony Burgess, nor Alex.

> Set, like *1984*, in a terrible, violent yet drab, not-too-remote future prefigured by current events, this story of the reform of a juvenile delinquent has other points of similarity with Orwell's work. One is an invented language, supposedly the argot of the teen-age toughs of future England, significantly compounded more from Slavic roots than American hip talk. … The ideas presented are thought-provoking, but the brevity of their treatment and the invented language—for which,

unlike Orwell, the author provides no glossary or explanation—often distract from the narrative and will act as a barrier to the general reader. … For inclusive fiction collections only.

> John F. Morgan, reviewing *A Clockwork Orange* for *Library Journal*
> (15 February 1963)

In *A Clockwork Orange*, Anthony Burgess has written what looks like a nasty little shocker but is really that rare thing in English letters—a philosophical novel. The point may be overlooked because the hero, a teen-age monster, tells all about everything in nadsat, a weird argot that seems to be all his own. Nadsat is neither gibberish nor a Joycean exercise. It serves to put Alex where he belongs—half in and half out of the human race.

> Unsigned, reviewing *A Clockwork Orange* in *Time*
> (15 February 1963)

Written in a pseudo-criminal cant, *A Clockwork Orange* is an interesting tour-de-force, though not up to the level of the author's two previous novels.

> Martin Levin, reviewing various novels in
> *The New York Times Book Review* (7 April 1963)

Burgess is anything but a slick or careless writer; he has a Joycean preoccupation with language, particularly in his later books where it plays a large and active role, such as the Russianized teen slang in *A Clockwork Orange*. … *The Right to an Answer* [Burgess's novel of 1960] gains a good deal when it is read in conjunction with one of his blackest books, *A Clockwork Orange*, a superb tour-de-force of impersonatory writing. The narrator is a teenage hoodlum who is morally but not mentally stunted: he writes an alert, witty narrative in a teenage slang that uses a large number of Russian root-words plus a variety of home-made idioms. The construction of this language—which is hard to read at first, but becomes successively easier as one goes on, especially if one uses the glossary that Stanley Edgar Hyman compiled for the Norton Library edition—is a brilliant achievement on Burgess's part. It serves a number of functions: one is to stress, by implication, the Americanization of current English teenage speech; by imagining the importations as Russian instead they become more noticeable (in another novel, *Honey for Bears*, the main character sees Russia and America as equally alien to English culture). Another function of this dialect is to keep at a distance the horrors that Mr. Burgess's narrator so cheerfully describes: to say 'we gave this devotchka a tolchok on the litso and the krovvy came out of her rot' is less immediate than the equivalent, 'we gave this girl a blow on the face and the blood came out of her mouth.'

> Bernard Bergonzi, reviewing Burgess's novels retrospectively for
> *The New York Review of Books* (20 May 1965)

The story is about juvenile delinquents in that nearish future English novelists often choose to write about, when the world is apparently under an American–Russian condominium and is an extremely disagreeable place to live in. The book is written in 'nadsat', the local slang of the delinquents, since it is supposed to be the autobiography of Alex, the j.d. described in both the English and American blurbs as 'genial'. Readers with a smattering of Russian will find minor philological enjoyment in recognizing 'horrorshow', 'droog', 'the old moloko', 'devotchkas', 'rot', 'slovo', etc. 'Horrorshow', which means wonderful, is the most successful invention in 'nadsat'; most of the others are straight transliterations without bilingual punning. Other elements of the invented language are scientific-futuristic or simply valueless substitutes in the manner of much real slang, e.g., 'viddy' with 'glazzies'—to see with eyes. 'Cancers' for cigarettes is rather good. The English blurb suggests that 'it will take the reader no more than fifteen pages to master and revel in the impressive language of "nadsat"'. Since, beginning even on page two, the author cheats, as it were, by providing a glossary as he goes along—'rooker (a hand, that is) ... litso (face, that is)' instead of forcing the meaning by context as the game would seem to call for, mastery may be said to be simultaneous with exposure.

> Diana Josselson, reviewing *A Clockwork Orange* in *The Kenyon*
> *Review* (Summer 1963)

Very relevant is the English novel, *A Clockwork Orange*, experimental in a double sense. The teen-age narrator Alex is a murderous Holden

Caulfield, ingenious and witty in a horrid way, who lives in a controlled, badly controlled, society of the very near future. Alex and his pals and most of the young people around him are totally alienated. They devote themselves to sex, violence, and drugs and—significantly—music of all kinds, Beethoven as well as rock-and-roll. Nearly every night, like the rather more aristocratic Mohawks in eighteenth-century London, they go out stealing, raping, smashing up homes and shops, just for the sport of it, and fighting other gangs with knives and chains. All of this is described in detail and with relish. The author, Anthony Burgess, maintains distance by using a strange argot, partly slang but mostly made of what seem to be Russian words, 'tashtook', 'ptitsas', 'litsos', 'britva', 'devotchka', 'slovos', 'goloss'. There are two or three to a sentence often, and the reader has gradually to learn them from context. Russian words are chosen because Russia suggests a brutal statism. The novelty of the terms and the slight effort required to find and remember their meanings keeps from being too monotonously gory the chronicle of meaningless brutalities described by their perpetrator.

Robert Gorham Davis, reviewing various novels in *The Hudson Review* (Summer 1963)

Anthony Burgess, in *A Clockwork Orange* (1962), is in the Huxleyan (rather than the Orwellian) tradition: in his society conditioning is used to remove moral choice by programming people to choose good over evil. The unconditioned protagonist, Alex, chooses evil and is, significantly, portrayed as one of the few remaining creative people in the society, not least in his use of language. Alex's subversive language, Nadsat, is virtually incomprehensible to the conditioned members of society, and, after he has been subjected to conditioning, Alex no longer uses it. For Burgess, creativity necessitates the freedom to choose evil.

Noel Dorman Mawer, reviewing David W. Sisk's *Transformations of Language in Modern Dystopias* (1997) in *Utopian Studies* (1999)

The novel is not, however, filled with linguistic pyrotechnics in the same way that Joyce's *Finnegans Wake* is. Joyce is attempting, however successfully, to delve beneath the conscious levels of speech; Burgess is playing with ordinary speech conventions. It is as if he were testing our ability to read. ... [C]learly there are times when the words ran away with him and his intention, so far as one can ascertain, was simply to amuse the reader in the way that puns or nonsense verse amuse us. ... But what has this to do with the special argot of youth, which ... will inevitably change as new youths replace those who have passed into the ossifying adult world? Why should three per cent, or so, of the words be Anglicized Russian words instead of, say, Arabic or French? ... [I]n fact neither French nor Arabic would do. There is a real sense in the novel in which, to borrow Marshall McLuhan's terminology, the medium becomes the message. For the Anglo-American reader the Slavic words connote communist dictatorship ... without moral value and without hope. How the young people in the novel learn the argot is never explained. It seems to come to them through the air somehow. Their parents, the police, the psychiatrists know about it, but they cannot speak it. The writer is of course describing a common enough linguistic phenomenon. ... But Burgess is exaggerating beyond all reasonable bounds this sort of linguistic process.

Robert O. Evans, 'Nadsat: The Argot and Its Implications in Anthony Burgess' *A Clockwork Orange*', in the *Journal of Modern Literature* (March 1971)

The best known example of an apparently new language [in science fiction] is the nadsat style of Anthony Burgess' excellent *A Clockwork Orange* ... Much has been made of the fact that a great deal of this style can be traced to Russian ... Indeed, 'nadsat' is a Russian affix for the numbers eleven through nineteen, roughly equivalent to the English 'teen', and hence this juvenile delinquent's language is known as 'nadsat'. But this doesn't really offer us an alternative ideology, not even if we equate nadsat in part with Russian communism, because the language does not oppose our old language. Instead, the metalinguistic function here— which is admittedly impressive—primarily makes a reality claim about the narrative world being a possible future state of our own world ... This apparently new language is actually transformed language.

Eric S. Rabkin, 'Metalinguistics and Science Fiction', in *Critical Inquiry* (Autumn 1979)

References

Adams, Michael. 2003. *Slayer Slang: A Buffy the Vampire Slayer Lexicon*. New York: Oxford University Press.

Coleman, Julie. 2004. *A History of Slang and Cant Dictionaries. Volume I: 1567–1785*. Oxford: Oxford University Press.

Evans, Robert O. 1971. 'Nadsat: The Argot and Its Implications in Anthony Burgess' *A Clockwork Orange*'. *Journal of Modern Literature* 1.3 (March): 406–10.

Meyers, Walter E. 1980. *Aliens and Linguists: Language Study and Science Fiction*. Athens, Georgia: University of Georgia Press.

APPENDIX 4

Tolkien's Languages: A Brief Anthology of Commentary

As E. S. C. Weiner and Jeremy Marshall argue in the corresponding chapter, 'Tolkien invested at least as much of his expertise, ingenuity, imagination, and time in constructing his languages as he did in devising his narratives'. So it comes as some surprise, looking through early reviews of *The Fellowship of the Ring* (1954), *The Two Towers* (1955), and *The Return of the King* (1955), collectively republished later as *The Lord of the Rings* (1965), that Tolkien's languages are barely acknowledged in them. Of course, the depth of Tolkien's linguistic invention was barely apparent until readers (like Jenny Turner, quoted at the outset of the chapter) encountered Appendix F in *The Return of the King* and linguistic marvels later revealed in *The Silmarillion* (1977), *Unfinished Tales of Númenor and Middle Earth* (1980), and Christopher Tolkien's twelve-volume edition of *The History of Middle Earth* (1984–96). Some critics saw the value of Elvish and other languages to the mythological enterprise, however, and noted, as had Tolkien, how the reality of fantasy relies on cultural history implicit in languages that must be invented as though they were found.

The comments that follow do not necessarily reflect the views of the authors of the complementary chapter, nor of the editor (and when they do, perhaps not uniformly), nor of Tolkien, of course, except in those instances where the comments are his. It seemed appropriate to give him the last word.

> Of any imaginary world the reader demands that it seem real, and the standard of realism demanded today is much stricter than in the time, say, of Malory. Mr. Tolkien is fortunate in possessing an amazing gift

for naming and a wonderfully exact eye for description; by the time one has finished his book one knows the histories of Hobbits, Elves, Dwarves and the landscape they inhabit as well as one knows one's own childhood.

> W. H. Auden, reviewing *The Fellowship of the Ring* in the
> *New York Times* (31 October 1954)

Mr. Tolkien is a distinguished British philologist, and the language of his narrative reminds us that a philologist is a man who loves language. His names are brilliantly appropriate; the tongues he has devised for the elves and orcs perfectly express, just by their rhythms and phonemic systems, the natures of these races; his style is full of joy, the joy that follows the making of a perfect gesture.

> Donald Barr, reviewing *The Two Towers* in the
> *New York Times* (1 May 1955)

If, as I believe, Mr. Tolkien has succeeded more completely than any previous writer in the genre by using the traditional properties of the Quest, the heroic journey, the Numinous Object, the conflict between good and evil while at the same time satisfying our sense of historical and social reality, it should be possible to show how he has succeeded. To begin with, no previous writer has, to my knowledge, created an imaginary world and a feigned history in such detail. By the time the reader has finished the trilogy, including the appendices to this last volume, he knows as much about Mr. Tolkien's Middle Earth, its landscape, its fauna and flora, its peoples, their languages, their history, their cultural habits, as, outside his special field, he knows about the actual world.

> W. H. Auden, reviewing *The Return of the King* in the
> *New York Times* (22 January 1956)

I first became acquainted with the Tolkien books in the spring of my senior year at college, just before final exams. ... Every afternoon during that exceptionally balmy May I would take my notebooks and textbooks and reference books out onto the college lawn and arrange them around me in neat piles on the grass. Then I would open a volume of Tolkien and lose myself in its pages for hours and hours until I fell asleep— to wake up in time for dinner, completely refreshed and convinced that

I had put in a good day's work in the hot sun. I don't remember any exam questions that dealt specifically with Hobbit-history, or the inter-relations of all the languages of Middle-Earth, or the origin and destiny of the Kings of Westernesse, but I still believe that the trilogy was an excellent preparation for finals.

> Gerald Jonas, reviewing the first American paperback edition of
> *The Lord of the Rings* in the *New York Times* (31 October 1965)

The obsession of the author with his own creation has become profound—he has invented languages (giving details in his huge appendices of pronunciation, spelling, and writing), histories and family trees for the imaginary peoples of his epic. ... The book's obsessive quality, its mysticism, its layers of incomprehensible allegory, its confusing variety of names, the tedium of much of the purely descriptive writing, would make it no more than a scholar's whimsy were it not for Professor Tolkien's inventive brilliance and tremendous narrative power.

> Elizabeth Leigh Pemberton, reviewing *The Return of the King* in
> the *Spectator* (25 November 1955)

Professor Tolkien has, indeed, used all his ingenuity in inventing the various languages of elfs, orcs, hobbits and dwarfs, together with their histories and family trees which, in this last volume, form an appendix of a hundred pages; and perhaps one has to be a 'very leisured boy' [Edwin Muir's criticism] to appreciate them, or, of course, to invent them. The action of the history, however, has nothing in common with such mechanical inventions; it has not been contrived, it has arisen, like all true mythology.

> Francis Huxley, reviewing *The Return of the King* in *The New
> Statesman and Nation* (5 November 1955)

A map, embodying this type of geography, unfolds at the end of The Fellowship of the Ring by Professor Tolkien. Much of the book is translated from Elvish and Dwarvish, from the Red Book of the Hobbits and from various runes of a type unfamiliar to most, if not all students of Runic, but available to Professor Tolkien who, after all, has inspired generations of early medieval historians at Oxford. He has no trouble at all with these languages. If now and then the names seem vaguely

Saxon, vaguely Gothic, surprisingly Afghan or somewhat Icelandic, that is because their original language corresponds to the language in these parts of the hitherto known world. Doubtless the inhabitants of the Ice Bay of Forochel, to the north of the map, speak something akin to the Lapp or Esquimaux languages, since their inevitably similar ways of life would tend to introduce a similar grammatical structure. The Ice Bay comes into the map but not into the first volume. Never mind: it is there in the map, in the mythology; it is there on purpose; we shall know about it one day, even if we have to wait for the third volume or even beyond.

> Naomi Mitchison, reviewing *The Fellowship of the Ring* in
> *The New Statesman and Nation* (18 September 1954)

Though the historian and the romancer alike need imagination, the faculty of invention is proper only to the latter. Dr. Tolkien's inventiveness is of that order which, because it challenges the credulity of us ordinary mortals, we call genius. He has invented another Earth, with its geography of rivers, mountain ranges, and seas set forth circumstantially in the maps that accompany these volumes. He has invented new languages with their philological apparatus, their special alphabets, their rules of pronunciation, and the principles that apply to their translation—all developed in extended and scholarly appendices at the end of the last volume.

> Louis J. Halle, reviewing *The Lord of the Rings* in the
> *Saturday Review* (28 January 1956)

At last the great edifice shines forth in all its splendour, with colonnades stretching beyond the ken of mortal eye, dome rising behind dome to hint at further spacious halls as yet unvisited. Before inviting the public to view his construction the author has furnished it completely, providing even appropriate documents to fill the pigeon-holes in the muniment-room; as the maker of a model railway might lavish unneeded skill on the advertisement hoardings. The book ends with more than 100 pages of pseudo-philology and pseudo-genealogy, dealing with the imaginary languages and imaginary pedigrees of this invented world. Such amazing energy of fancy, in a work already on a scale that would astonish Dugdale and Leland, must earn the wondering respect of every shortwinded writer of this degenerate age. ... On the whole the charm of the embroidery more than consoles for some incoherence in the main pattern. Such a timeless story must be told in timeless prose. Dr. Tolkien manages this very well, buttressing the idiom of Nordic saga with the melody of fantastic proper names, fantasies which must have given great pleasure to the learned philologist who invented them.

> Review of *The Lord of the Rings* in the
> *Times Literary Supplement* (25 November 1955)

The remark about 'philology' was intended to allude to what is I think a primary 'fact' about my work, that it is all of a piece, and fundamentally linguistic in inspiration. The authorities of the university might well consider it an aberration of an elderly professor of philology to write and publish fairy stories and romances, and call it a 'hobby', pardonable because it has been (surprisingly to me as much as to anyone) successful. But it is not a 'hobby', in the sense of something quite different from one's work, taken up as a relief-outlet. The invention of languages is the foundation. The 'stories' were made rather to provide a world for the languages than the reverse. To me a name comes first and the story follows. I should have preferred to write in 'Elvish'. But, of course, such a work as *The Lord of the Rings* has been edited and only as much 'language' has been left in as I thought would be stomached by readers. (I now find that many would have liked more.) But there is a great deal of linguistic matter (other than actually 'elvish' names and words) included or mythologically expressed in the book. It is to me, anyway, largely an essay in 'linguistic aesthetic', as I sometimes say to people who ask me 'what is it all about?'

> J. R. R. Tolkien, notes to his American publisher,
> Houghton Mifflin Co., for use in publicity (30 June 1955),
> in *The Letters of J. R. R. Tolkien* (1981)

Qenya thrived in the same soil [as soldier's slang, in the trenches of the First World War], but not in the same mood. Nothing could be further removed from the unbeautiful inflexible practicalities Tolkien was being taught than the invention of a language for the joy of its sounds.

John Garth, Tolkien and the Great War (2003)

Later, in A Secret Vice, [Tolkien] talks of his creation, Quenya Elvish, as a 'language that has ... reached a highish level both of beauty in word-form considered abstractly, and of ingenuity in the relations of symbol and sense'. The 'phonetic fitness' and resulting beauty, therefore, are also to be found on a scale vastly larger than that of individual words, namely the level of an entire language. The foundations are again the same: 'sound pattern + meaning', 'symbol and sense'. For Tolkien, language without sound-symbolism would have been a lifeless thing.

Ross Smith, 'Fitting Sense to Sound: Aesthetics and
Phonosemantics in the Work of J. R. R. Tolkien', in
Tolkien Studies (2006)

Rather the same phenomenon of superficial similarity and deeper opposition appears if one widens the scope of the argument to considering the whole phenomenon of 'modernism', of which <i>Ulysses</i> is accepted as a definitive work. Authoritative recent accounts of modernism ... often seem immediately applicable to Tolkien. Modernist style, we are told, is characteristically local, limited, finding beauty not in abstractions but in 'small, dry things' ... Modernism was said furthermore, by T. S. Eliot, to have made it possible to replace narrative method by 'mythical method'; and the whole drive of Tolkien's work, as one can see, was towards creating a mythology which his major narrative was there to embody. When one reads also ... that modernism is distinguished by experiments with the representation of time; by rejection of the 'realist illusion'; by the use of multiple narrators; and by experiments with language ... the deliberate creation of unknown languages and unrecorded dialects ... Why is it unacceptable to see Tolkien, then ... as a modernist author parallel to Joyce? [NB: Shippey goes on to explain why it is unacceptable, but it seems interesting, in the context of Chapter 7 and its appendix, to raise the question.]

Tom Shippey, J. R. R. Tolkien: Author of the Century (2000)

The linguistic faculty—for making so-called articulate noises—is sufficiently latent in all for them (caught young as they always are) to learn, more or less, at least one language with merely or mainly practical object. It is more highly developed in others, and may lead not only to polyglots but to poets; to savourers of linguistic flavours, to learners and users of tongues, who take pleasure in the exercise. And it is allied to a higher art of which I am speaking, and which perhaps I had better now define. An art for which life is not long enough, indeed: the construction of imaginary languages in full or outline for amusement, for the pleasure of the constructor or even conceivably of any critic that might occur.

> J. R. R. Tolkien, 'A Secret Vice' (1931), in
> *The Monsters and the Critics and Other Essays* (1983)

APPENDIX 5

Advanced Klingon

Marc Okrand took Klingon language as far as the various television series and films demanded and beyond in books like *The Klingon Dictionary* (1985; second edition 1992) and *Klingon for the Galactic Traveler* (1997). Some linguistically-minded fans of Klingon formed the Klingon Language Institute (KLI), with headquarters in Flourtown, Pennsylvania, in 1992, in order to further develop and promote interest in the language. KLI publishes *HolQed*, a peer-reviewed, quarterly journal about Klingon, as well as *jatmey*, a more or less annual volume of original poetry and fiction written in Klingon, and an online journal published in Klingon only, *Qo'noS QonoS*. Each year, KLI awards the Kor Memorial Scholarship to an undergraduate or postgraduate student 'to recognize and encourage scholarship in fields of language study'—not Klingon specifically. KLI certifies aspirants at various levels of Klingon proficiency; even first-level certification is parsecs of cool better than a decoder ring. One can find more about KLI's activities at its website: http://www.kli.org.

A few literary classics have been translated into Klingon under the auspices of KLI: Roger Cheesbro translated the Babylonian epic *ghIlghameS* and Nick Nicholas restored the original Klingon version of Wil'yam Shex'pir's *paghmo' tIn mIS* (literally, 'The Confusion is Great because of Nothing', but *Much Ado about Nothing* in English), both published in 2003; more recently, Agnieszka Solska has translated the *Tao Te Ching* as *pIn'a' gan paQDI' norgh* (2008). Translations of texts so generically various and so thematically and stylistically sophisticated obviously require a much more developed Klingon than had film or television. In *Star Trek VI: The Undiscovered Country* (1991), the Klingon Chancellor Gorkon opines, 'You have not experienced Shakespeare until you have read him in the original Klingon.' The best evidence of Klingon's eventual structural complexity and consistency is Nick Nicholas's and Andrew Strader's translation (or, from the Klingon point of view, 'restoration') of *The Klingon Hamlet* (2000)—rather, *Khamlet*.

In order to illustrate this fully elaborated Klingon, I have chosen a number of brief quotations from the *Hamlet* most readers of this book will know best (the English one) and matched them to their Klingon equivalents in the table below. I have selected some famous English lines and some less famous, but filled with words hard for the Modern English speaker to understand ('Let the galled jade wince, our withers are unwrung' or 'he galls his kibe') without an annotated text, so especially challenging, I assume, to translate into Klingon. Unless one is a native speaker of Klingon, has a certificate in ultimate-level Klingon, or has actually invented aspects of it, one cannot figure out how some of the grammatically complicated and lexically obscure English passages work in Klingon, at least not completely—translators must invent, or ask Marc Okrand to invent, as yet unknown Klingon words in the course of their work, and these words are presented to readers as *faits accomplis*.

But with the phonological and grammatical information provided in the corresponding chapter in mind, and with help from *The Klingon Dictionary* (1992) and the glossary of previously unattested words in *Klingon for the Galactic Traveler* (1997), as well as the glossary of new Klingon words at the KLI website, one can recognize (often, not always) enough elements of a Klingon passage to match it with its English counterpart. While attempting to unravel the less obvious elements, one begins to grasp Klingon in all of its structural integrity. For that reason, as Arika Okrent notes in *In the Land of Invented Languages*, Klingon 'is completely believable as a language, but somehow very, very odd' (2009, 271).

For instance, Nicholas and Strader translate 'There is no ancient gentlemen but gardeners, ditchers, and grave-makers; they hold up Adam's profession' as 'ben negh chaH pochwI', lamwI', molwI' je heH. Qu' naMpu'Mogh qeng lutaH': *pochwI'*, *lamwI'*, and *molwI'* are literally 'one who plants', 'one who dirts', and 'one who graves', respectively, according to the entries for their bases in *The Klingon Dictionary* (1992). All three forms share the verb suffix -*wI'* 'one who does', and comparison of the English and Klingon shows the constructed system of Klingon, with the verb suffix predictably parallel to the noun suffix -*er* in English. One can also see the metaphorical turn in Klingon, as 'graves' stands for 'makes graves' and 'dirter' stands for 'ditcher'—as in all languages, the adapting lexicon of Klingon relies on continual metaphorical extension, not always inventing new words, then, but packing more meanings into the already existing words. The Klingon 'qaboQmeH neH qabuq' suggests something about the relations between sound and meaning in Klingon: *qaboQ* is 'cruel' and *qabuq* is 'kind'. The formal similarity of the words emphasizes their semantic opposition, and one speculates that they may be etymologically related.

There is much to explore and even appreciate about Klingon. It is a brilliant achievement of imagination, and, as Okrent points out, 'those who can hack it feel a haughty pride in their linguistic accomplishments, despite the fact that no one who hasn't attempted to hack it can understand what they have to be proud of' (2009, 271). Most English speakers in the Federation of Planets will nonetheless continue to believe that *Hamlet* is best in English, the ideas more profound, the language play sharper, the poetry more beautiful than in Klingon. Just as surely, and rather more aggressively, Klingons will insist on the superiority of the Klingon version. Both should remember Khamlet's observation, 'QaQbe' 'ej qabbe' ghu' 'a QaQ, pagh qab 'e' tu' qelwI' neH,' or, as Hamlet would say, 'There is nothing either good or bad but thinking makes it so.'

Hamlet in English and Klingon

You come most carefully upon your hour (1.1)	bImatlhba', quarqu'mo' bIcholmeH poHllj.
Not a mouse stirring. (1.1)	vIHbe' je ghew.
This bodes some strange eruption to our state. (1.1)	Vaj wo'vaD qaS Qugh taQ 'e' pIHmoHlaw.
In the most high and palmy state of Rome,	tIQtaHvIS, chepbogh romuluS wo' quvDaq
A little ere the mightiest Julius fell,	poSchoH Hoch mol, loQ pumpa' yulyuS Dunqu'.
The graves stood tenantless and the sheeted dead	'ej chlmchu'. romuluS vengHeDaq jawchoH
Did squeak and gibber in the Roman streets. (1.1)	'ej jach lom'e' wej luqtHa'lu'bogh.
A little more than kin, and less than kind. (1.2)	qorDu'Hom 'oH. 'ej puqvaD qorlu'law'.

How weary, stale, flat, and unprofitable
Seem to me all the uses of this world. (1.2)

Frailty, they name is woman! (1.2)

He was a man, take him for all in all,

I shall not look upon his like again. (1.2)

The friends thou hast, and their adoption tried,

Grapple them to thy soul with hoops of steel. (1.3)

Neither a borrower, nor a lender be;

For loan oft loses both itself and friend. (1.3)

But to my mind, though I am native here,

And to the manner born, it is a custom

More honoured in the breach than the observance. (1.4)

Something is rotten in the state of Denmark. (1.4)

Murder most foul, as in the best it is;

But this most foul, strange, and unnatural. (1.5)

These are but wild and whirling words, my lord. (1.5)

There are more things in heaven and earth, Horatio,

Than are dreamt of in your philosophy. (1.5)

POLONIUS: What do you read my lord?

HAMLET: Words, words, words. (2.2)

Though this be madness, yet there is method in't. (2.2)

O, what a rogue and peasant slave am I. (2.2)

The lady doth protest too much, methinks. (3.2)

Let the galled jade wince, our withers are unwrung. (3.2)

I must be cruel only to be kind. (3.4)

va, jIHvaD Doy'law', raghlaw',
qetlh 'ej lI'be'law' qo'vam Hoch malja'!
be' 'oH ponglIj'e!
loDna' ghaH jay'. Hoch laHmeyDaj vIchovDI',
vaj not ghaH rurbogh latlh vIleghqa'laH.
Hoch jup Daghajbogh tobchugh ghu'mey poH je,
Vaj qua'lI'Daq DabaghmeH mIr tIlo'.

ngIpwI' nojwI' joq yIDaQo'. bInojDI',
pIj tugh loj Doch Danojpu'bogh, juplI' je.
toH, wo'vam Sung jIH. jIHvaD motIhtaH tIghvam,
jIboghpu'DI'. 'ach vuDwIj tlhoblu'chugh,
vaj tIghvam'e' wIquvmoHqu' wIbIvDI'.

Hu'tegh, DaH Qo'noS wo'Daq nonlaw' vay'.
quvHa'qu' chotDI'. reH quvHa' chotwI'.
'ach chotDI' Hujqu', wemqu', 'ej quvHa'qu'.

Maw' neH 'ej taQqu' mu'meyvam, joH quv.
chalDaq, ghorDaq je law'bej Doch, Horey'So.
'ej puSqu' Dochmey'e' neH najbogh QeDlIj.

POLONYUS: nuq DalaD, joHwI'?

KHAMLET: mu', mu', mu'.

maw'bej, 'ach meqlaw'taH.

baQa', Qovpatlh, toy'wI''a' qal je jIH!
wejpuH Hoch 'Iprup be'.

chut DIlobbogh maH'e' nujoy'laHbe'
pe'vIl nov Div DISmoHbogh tuQDoq'e'.
qaboQmeH neH qabuq.

When sorrows come, they come not single spies,

But in battalions. (4.5)

There is no ancient gentlemen but gardeners, ditchers, and grave-makers; they hold up Adam's profession. (5.1)

The age is grown so picked that the toe of the peasant comes so near the heel of the courtier, he galls his kibe. (5.1)

Alas, poor Yorick. I knew him, Horatio; a fellow of infinite jest, or most excellent fancy. (5.1)

There's a divinity that shapes our ends,

Rough-hew them how we will. (5.2)

Now cracks a noble heart. Good night, sweet prince

And flights of angels sing thee to thy rest. (5.2)

nucholDI' lot, nIteb ghoqwI' DaQo' bIH.

nawloghDaq ghomlaw' jay'!

ben negh chaH pochwI', lamwI', molwI' je neH. Qu' naMpu'Mogh qeng lutaH.

'Itlhqu'mo' Nugh, chuQun quvDaq Sumqu'mo' tlha'bogh rewbe' Qut, movDaq yaDbutlh ngoH.

va Do'Ha' yorIq. yIntaHvIs vIsov, Horey'So. HaghmoH not 'e' mevqang. tIvmoH reH 'e' tob.

Nemmaj raQbogh San'e' reH tu'lu'bej,

biH wIteyHa'taHvIS je.

DaH ghor tIq quv. Qapla', joH quv. Qapla'.

bIleSmeH DaH DuDorjaj yo' qIj Dujmey!

References

Cheesbro, Roger. 2003. *Gilgamesh: A Klingon Translation*. Rockville, Maryland: Wildside Press.

Okrand, Marc. 1985. *The Klingon Dictionary*. New York: Pocket Books.

Okrand, Marc. 1992. *The Klingon Dictionary*. Second edition. New York: Pocket Books.

Okrand, Marc. 1997. *Klingon for the Galactic Traveler*. New York: Pocket Books.

Okrent, Arika. 2009. *In the Land of Invented Languages*. New York: Spiegel & Grau.

Shakespeare, William, Nick Nicholas, and Andrew Strader. 2000. *The Klingon Hamlet*. New York: Pocket Books.

Shakespeare, William, and Nick Nicholas. 2003. *Much Ado about Nothing: The Restored Klingon Text*. Rockville, Maryland: Wildside Press.

Tzu, Lao, and Agnieszka Solska. *Tao Te Ching: A Klingon Translation*. Flourtown, Pennsylvania: Klingon Language Institute.

APPENDIX 6

L4ngu4ge G4m35 in G4ming L4ngu4g35

Online games, especially games with multiple players set in fantastic worlds (or MMPORGs), often require their own languages, as James Portnow describes in the complementary chapter. From the outside, MMPORGs are often seen as arcane and escapist—people who think so generally aren't attracted to games or fantasy and would like all of us to keep our noses to the proverbial grindstone—and those who play them are often characterized as 'geeks', which some take as a disparaging term, though many of the so-called geeks consider *geek* a term of honour. Regardless, in the public imagination, the geek is a socially isolated person—whether cut off by others or self-isolating or a bit of both is an open question. Nothing could be further from the truth, at least in the universe of MMPORGs, which are intensely social activities.

Social groups are bound to adopt in-group language, slang, or jargon, some of which is 'invented' more or less consciously. In the case of gaming, the slang is often quite consciously made, because communication among players is mediated by the hard- and software of games, which slows things down and gives game players time to think about how they want to represent themselves. In this, the language of online gaming resembles other vocabularies invented for a fiction, like Orwell's Newspeak and Burgess's Nadsat (see Chapter 2), except that, although gaming language is part of participating in the fiction, it is not per se 'within' the fiction, like Gargish or D'ni (see Chapter 6). Gamers speak their slang while role-playing: they are game players temporarily inhabiting game characters, and the personae overlap.

Whether what gamers say in the course of gaming is jargon or slang depends on whether the word or phrase in question serves primarily social purposes or is focused on the 'work' of playing the game. Words like *abandonware* and *joystick* (see the glossary further down) are terms for gaming equipment and are pretty clearly jargon; *BG* 'bad game, no fun', on the other hand, is just as clearly slang, not part of playing a game, but bonding speech among players that follow on the game. Items like *camper* and *carebear*, however, are more difficult to categorize, because they describe types of players and play, but at the same time evaluate players and their approaches to gaming on social terms and often draw lines between players who are 'in' and those who are, in social terms, 'out', though they may nonetheless be playing the game. For more on the distinction between jargon and slang, with a generous allowance for grey areas, see Adams (2009, 16–42).

Gamer slang, like so much language in computer-mediated activities, tends towards abbreviation. So we find initialisms like *BG*, *DPS*, and *FMCDH*, or clippings like *grats*, *sim*, or *ventrilo*, the sorts of words we would find in everyday slang, whether texted (*B4N*, which is also gaming slang) or face-to-face (as in *props* 'propers' or *rents* 'parents'). But it isn't all so commonplace: *griefer* adds the agent suffix *-er* to an unusual base; nouns for emotions aren't usually *-er*ed, so no *angerer*, *gladder*, *sorrower*, or *wistfuler* 'one who does the wistful'. Some items of gamer slang are half initialized, half phonetically compressed, as in *orly*. One of the most famous gamer terms derives from a QWERTY-driven misspelling: *pwn*. And some, like *All your base are belong to us* and *Leeroy Jenkins*, rely, in a way at first inaccessible to outsiders, on the popular culture of online gaming.

One especially interesting aspect of gamer slang is Leetspeak or Leet, which Portnow discusses at the end of his chapter. The name for the slang is an item of the slang, which forms words from number instead of letter symbols, in whole or in part. Advanced Leet is quite complicated—the example Portnow gives is overwhelming. Three items in the glossary below are elementary Leet, namely *leet*, *noob*, and *woot*, originally *1337*, *n006*, and *w007*. This innovation is different from words *B4N*, where the numeral name is used like letter names in initialisms (*FBI*, *ACLU*).

The origins of Leet are disputed. One version of Leet's rise in the 1930s goes as follows: 'The major developments of leet came out of filter evasions (e.g., strings like 10tt3ry cannot be easily detected), securing passwords, gaming, or computer hacking. The rationale of using leet is that it employs a visual encryption code that allegedly can be easily read by any human reader … but would foil most search engines' (Perea, Duñabeitia, and Carreiras 2008, 237).

Some, though, are sceptical of this origin, including Portnow, who proposes that hackers developed Leet for the sheer fun of it, because they could (see also Dent 2004, 59, though the basis of her scepticism is not clear). The hackers who developed Leet were, in fact, elite—*1337* was originally a shortening of *elite*—so elite that they conceived Leet.

Empirical research suggests, however, that 'words can be readily accessed in their leet form for readers with no prior knowledge of leet' (Perea, Duñabeitia, and Carreiras 2008, 240). You have to be elite to invent Leet and to use it in hacking, but not to use it as gaming slang. The degradation of *1337* is evident in the following glossary entry: '*L337* or *l337 h4xx0r(z)*: elite hacker(s), anyone possessing above average skills with HTML or programming' (LeBlanc 2005, 72). Someone whose programming skills rank in the 20th percentile, well above average, is really good, but not elite. The people most likely to notice this are the truly elite, who will avoid use of Leet and turn to something infinitely cleverer to promote their group solidarity and mark the social territory of their in-group. Beginner's Leet has been absorbed in the less exclusive lexicon of gamer slang. Beware the following, very selective glossary of that slang: if I can collect it and define it, then it may be obsolete or at least much diminished in currency and value.

abandonware	'obsolete software, neither developed, sold, nor supported'
AFK	'away from keyboard' (used when one leaves a game temporarily)
All your base are belong to us	geeker in-group marker (a mistranslation from Japanese into English in the game *Zero Wing* (1991))
B4N	'bye for now'
BG	'lit. bad game; no fun'
buff	'game character augmentation, of power or ability'
camper	'game player who maintains one position for a long time' (sometimes a strategic advantage, but often looked down on by other players)
carebear	'online game player who plays in the least challenging way possible'
DPS	'damage per second' (for the damage a weapon or character in a game can inflict per second of play)
dupe	'trick a game into supplying a duplicate weapon or other item important to the game; a form of cheating' (the etymology of this item appears to be mixed, from both *dupe* 'cheat, trick' and *duplicate*)
epic	'one in a million; extraordinary' (thus, in the second sense, *epic fail* 'amazingly bad')
FFA	'free for all' (game play in which everyone competes against everyone else)

FMCDH	'from my cold dead hand' (a way of drawing the line with opponents in a game)
FTW	'for the win' (indicating end of game; alternatively, to announce that one is about to lose the game, **FTL** 'for the loss')
GG	'good game' (for subtleties of use and meaning, see Portnow's chapter)
grats	'congratulations'
griefer	'player who acts up and intentionally causes problems during a game'
guild	'permanent group of players who join forces while playing'
hardcore	'more experienced, more capable' (what a CAREBEAR is not)
hit points	'total number of hits required to defeat an opponent in a *role playing game* or *RPG*'
IC	'in character; also, "I see"'
joystick	'input or control game hardware'
KOS	'kill on sight' (injunction from one online game player to others, about what to do if they encounter yet another)
KS	'kill stealing; joining in on a kill already initiated by another player, in order to gain whatever benefit (for instance, LEWT) accrues to a kill in a particular game'
LAN party	'party of game players and their computers, during which they play games and exchange files' (Usually small and local, LAN parties occasionally involve thousands of participants.)
Leeroy Jenkins	'NOOB who leaps into conflict in games without thinking, strategy, a sense of the consequences for himself or other players'; cf. CAREBEAR and GRIEFER; also the catchphrase **Don't be such a Leeroy** and the verb **Leeroy** (Derived from the name of a character in the MMPORG *World of Warcraft*, created by Ben Schulz; in a video of a guild playing the game, 'Leeroy' leaves the game, misses a strategy session, and disrupts the game by blasting away on re-entering.)
leet or **1337**	(1) 'elite'; (2) 'elite hacker'; (3) 'hacker slang' (The form of this word was originally alphanumeric, because elite hackers could avoid detection by using unexpected alphanumeric code, so the practice migrated to their slang; now that *leet/1337* is widely known, those who declare themselves *leet* clearly are not—elite hackers have figured out new ways to identify themselves. In sense (3), *leet* may by a clipped form of **Leetspeak**, but *Leetspeak* might just as easily be an expansion of *leet*.)
loot or **lewt**	'virtual items or currency earned or transferred among players in an online game'
MMORPG	'mass multiplayer online role playing game' (MMORPGs, also called **MMOG** or even **MMO** for short, can involve thousands of players and continue for long periods, as players enter at a low level of status ability (within the game) and continue to play until, through their game exploits, they achieve the highest level of status and ability.)

mt	'mistell; information accidentally given to someone for whom it was not meant'
nick	'online alias or **handle** (from *nickname*)'
noob or n00b or n3wb	'newbie; inexperienced newcomer'
orly	'oh really'
party	'ad hoc group of players who play cooperatively in a game'; see also GUILD and LAN PARTY
PvP	'player versus player' (describes a game in which participants are human, or at least humanoid, not computers)
pwn	'humorous misspelling of *own* 'dominate'' (One player can assert that she *pwnz* (present tense) or *pwned* (past tense) another.)
rawr	''loud' self-satisfied exclamation, from *roar*'
RvR	'realm versus realm' (In some MMORPGs, players can aggregate into 'teams' called *realms*; *RvR* is the group version of *PvP*.)
sim	'simulation, simulated'
speed hacker	'player who uses software external to a game in order to exploit the game'
twinking	'application of higher-order abilities or items in order to accelerate the rise of a game character'
teleport hacker	'SPEED HACKER who can vanish and reappear from a game'
ventrilo	'trademarked name of a voice communication program that enables multiple players to talk and listen to one another while playing'
woot or w00t or w007	'happy or pleased exclamation'
xp	'experience' (Experience is what you gain by doing what games require; as a player gets more *xp* and achieves more, their status or level rises correspondingly.)
yrly	'yes, really'; appropriate response to ORLY

References

Adams, Michael. 2009. *Slang: The People's Poetry*. New York: Oxford University Press.

Dent, Susie. 2004. *Larpers and Shroomers: The Language Report*. Oxford: Oxford University Press.

LeBlanc, Tracy Rene. 2005. *'Is There a Translator in teh House?': Cultural and Discourse Analysis of a Virtual Speech Community on an Internet Message Board*. M.A. thesis, Louisiana State University.

Perea, Manuel, Jon Andoni Duñabeitia, and Manuel Carreiras. 2008. R34DING W0RD5 W1TH NUMB3R5'. *Journal of Experimental Psychology: Human Perception and Performance* 34: 237–41.

APPENDIX 7

The Case for Synthetic Scots

In the complementary chapter, Stephen Watt eloquently describes ways in which Joyce, Beckett, and Muldoon invent language when natural languages (Standard English, Hiberno-English) aren't up to the task of expressing either Irishness or modernism, or (and we can understand why this might burden natural language) both at once. The practice of these and similarly inventive writers pushes the issue of what we mean when we say 'a language' is 'invented': we speak of a particular literary style as 'a language' metaphorically, but it certainly isn't a language in the sense that English or any other natural language is, nor is it 'invented' in the same sense as Tolkien's languages or Klingon. The invention is unsystematic, also is continuous and characteristic, which is to say that it might be a bit systematic, for all that. Literary invention of this kind rests at one end of the spectrum of linguistic invention; full-blown language creation is at the other end of the spectrum. And there is a lot in between.

Lallans, or 'synthetic Scots', was 'invented' in the early twentieth century by a group of nationalist poets, primarily Christopher Murray Grieve (1892–1978), who is better known by his pseudonym, Hugh MacDiarmid. Lallans is a literary 'dialect' based on but not identical to the natural Lowland Scots dialect, for which the term has also long been used; it was a significant feature of literature of the twentieth-century Scottish Renaissance, of which MacDiarmid was the instigator. Unlike the inventions of Joyce or Beckett or Muldoon, Lallans is not idiosyncratic; unlike reconstructed languages (see Chapter 8), it need neither aspire to nor achieve the structural consistency and completeness of a language per se. MacDiarmid argued that Scottish literature needed 'a synthetic

Scots... in harmony at once with distinctive Scots psychology and contemporary cultural functions and requirements' (Grieve 1926, 193).

English was far outwith such harmony. MacDiarmid argued:

> It is insufficiently realized that the very nature of the English language is directly and incurably anti-Scottish. It has enhanced its vocabulary by tremendous borrowings from practically every other language in the world—but not from Gaelic. The genius of the two tongues is utterly incompatible. English has not even borrowed to any extent from Braid Scots [the historical Lowland dialect of English], though Braid Scots has hundreds of admirably expressive words for which English has no equivalents at all or no precise equivalents. Why has it all along eschewed Scots in this way? It means that it has similarly eschewed those qualities of the Scottish spirit which made the words in question. English ascendancy necessitates the suppression of these Scottish elements. It depends upon the stultification of all that is most vivid and vitally Scottish. (1934, 180)

A revitalized Scottish literature, then, would require a revitalized Scots, in order to express vividly and vitally something supposedly essential to the Scottish character.

The Scottish literary historian G. Gregory Smith specified the 'distinctive Scots psychology' or the 'qualities of the Scottish spirit' to which MacDiarmid pointed: 'in the very combination of opposites—what either of the two Sir Thomases, of Norwich [Sir Thomas Browne] and Cromarty [Sir Thomas Urquhart], might have been willing to call "the Caledonian antisyzygy"— we have a reflection of the contrasts which the Scot shows at every turn, in his political and ecclesiastical history, in his polemical restlessness, in his adaptability' (1919, 4). MacDiarmid acknowledged its relevance to his own linguistic practice in a poem titled 'The Caledonian Antisyzygy' (1948): 'I write now in English and now in Scots/ To the despair of friends who plead/ For consistency ... Fatal division in my thought they think' (MacDiarmid 1993, 230), but, of course, they are wrong, unless Scottishness itself is fatal.

Smith certainly predicted MacDiarmid in the phrase 'polemical restlessness', which is evident throughout his prose and poetry, for instance, in the following passage from 'The Kind of Poetry I Want' (1943), which was not written in his synthetic Scots:

> Is not this what we require?
> Coleridge's esemplasy and coadunation
> Multeity in unity—not the Unity resulting
> But the mode of its conspiration
> (Schelling's *In-eins-bildung-kraft*)
> Of the manifold to the one,
> For, as Rilke says, the poet must know everything,
> Be μινδεδνεος (a phrase which I have borrowed
> From a Greek monk, who applies it
> To a Patriarch of Constantinople),
> Or, as the Bhagavad-Gita puts it, *visvato-mukha*.
> 　　　　　　　　　　　　　　(MacDiarmid 1943, 122)

This is, however, a performance of 'Caledonian antisyzygy', as well as a manifesto. Obscure and allusive, lexically international and historical, it argues for a tropic inclusivity and nearly shares Joyce's interests and methods. The Greek μινδεδνεος means 'myriad-minded', but the Scots, as Watt proves, are not the only myriad-minded ones. For MacDiarmid, though, paradox was more than an intellectual and emotional facility—it was a programme. As Robert Crawford concludes in *Scotland's Books*, 'Throughout his career, he would attempt to fuse ideas of national language, culture and Scottish independence with an intense enthusiasm for the international modernist avant-garde' (2007, 542).

　　MacDiarmid's 'synthetic Scots' was suggested by similar linguistic inventions. 'But to get the whole matter into better perspective.' MacDiarmid suggests, 'it is necessary to go back to Dante's "De Vulgari Eloquentia". Dante's conclusion was that the corruption common to all the dialects made it impossible to select one rather than another as an adequate literary form, and that he who would write in the vulgar must asemble [sic] the purest elements from each dialect and construct a synthetic language that would at least possess more than a circumscribed local interest: which is precisely what he did. ... He wrote a vulgar ... which, in fact, was certainly not spoken, nor ever had been' (1934, 184). MacDiarmid frequently mentions the recent revival of Irish

Gaelic, as well as Nynorsk, the nineteenth-century synthesis of Norwegian dialects intended by its inventor, Ivar Aasen, as a standard that could replace Danish as the written language of Norway. Both of these examples were of political as well as linguistic significance to MacDiarmid and others who started writing in synthetic Scots. Burns' example also influenced MacDiarmid, who quoted the Scottish novelist John Buchan to this effect:

> Burns is by universal admission one of the most natural of poets, but he used a language which was, even in his own day, largely exotic. His Scots was not the living speech of his countrymen, like the English of Shelley, and—in the main—the Scots of Dunbar; it was a literary language subtly blended from the old "Makars" and the refrains of folk poetry, much tinctured by the special dialect of Ayrshire and with a solid foundation in English. (1926, 192)

In his New Lallans, MacDiarmid reinvented a wheel of which Burns was the original wright.

The English of his day, MacDiarmid believed, was 'suffering from a kind of Imperial elephantiasis … The future of English—otherwise than as a kind of esperanto [sic] for mere commercial and industrial use—is in the melting pot'; this development 'accounts for the vast amount of experimentation that is going on in English literature to-day. Meredith, Hardy, Doughty, Joyce—scarcely a writer of English in recent times who has not been brought hard up against this problem and compelled to try all kinds of verbal innovation' (1934, 181). But the problem was more complicated than anything due to the history and structure of English alone: experience of the modern world requires a new language, MacDiarmid thought: 'Our needs to-day are immensely more complex and extensive; and what Dante did falls far short of what Joyce is doing. Lewis Carroll's inventions were merely telescopings of English words; Joyce has drawn upon the whole world … more extensive foreign borrowings, synthese [sic] from dialects, use of archaic forms, exact phonetic reproductions, technical vocabularies, and so on' (1934, 184). MacDiarmid's enthusiasm for Joyce here particularizes his 'enthusiasm for the international modernist avant-garde', or, in fact, the international avant-garde of any period. In an immodest modesty that expresses the Caledonian antisyzygy, MacDiarmid admitted, 'My synthetic Scots has not touched the fringe of Joycean experimentation; it has been limited to the sort of thing Dante did' (1934, 184).

Here is 'Adam', a sample of poetry in synthetics Scots, by Tom Scott, from his *The Ship and Ither Poems* (1963, 21–2):

I **cannae mind** the **wrang** they say I did,   cannot recall/wrong
The **screiver lee'd**, **but ken** that but for it   writer lied, and also claimed
Our kind had ne'er been born. Could it **no** be   not
That birth **itsel** was **aa** the crime, the **bairn's**   itself/all/infant's
Rebellion at the womb? And **syne** expulsion   thereupon
Intil the **tuim** anxietie **o** space,   into/empty/of
Dependent on the undependable,
The soil accursed, and me cursed **intil** toil,   into
A sword **forbiddan ilka** wey led back.   forbidding every

Lanely we wander, cursed for an **unkent** sin,   lonely/unknown
The wound in my side **caaed** Eve at my **shouder** tall,   called/shoulder
The **Faa til** life her life-lot aye to bear,   Fall to
My love **o** her to begin and end in pain,   of
And **aa** a joyous sorrow in between.   all

Wes this rejection meant, or **duis** the **saul**   was/does/soul
Miscaa every gain **frae** sense **o** loss?   disparage/from/of
I **canna** think that life **itsel's** a sin   cannot/itself's
Wi death **nocht** but the **wey** that we atone.   with/nothing/way
I think that God **intendit nae sic** thing,   intended no such
But we **oursels** misdreamed our progress **sin**   ourselves/afterwards
Because we moved **frae** pleasure **intil** pain.   from/into

And **nae wey** back, **aa** roads **a leadin** on.   no way/all/a-leadin'
Lang, lang, I **cuist** myself **agin**   long, long/cast/against
Thon adamantine **yet, thon fleeran** sword,   that/gate/that flaming
And fell back aye in bluid **melled** aye **wi** tears,   mingled/with
The terrible rejection **sair** to bear,   sore
My **ain** sword **uisless** by yon awesome blade,   own/useless
Yet by dependence forced to try to win
Re-entrance **til** my paradise again.   to

Sae my story's been. **Hevin** on my mind,   so/Heaven
Rejectit for my **pouerlessness**, I planned   rejected/powerlessness
To seize the **pouer o** God, to Satan **doun**   power/of
The Author **frae** his lordship **owre** the **warld**,   from/over/world
Omnipotence the key **til** Eden's **yet**,   to/gate

And dragged in pain my past-**tormentit** mind	tormented
Throu centuries **o** earthly **darg** and sweat,	through/of/toil
Gleg to see in some sun-lightened plain	happy
The place that I had come **frae sae lang syne**,	from so long ago
Yet **scarcelins noticean** the comely earth's	scarcely noticing
Likeness **til itsel** — its **guidness** in **itsel**.	to itself/goodness/itself
Until it broke **intil** my **sicht**, the **licht**	into/sight/light
O day **dispellan** Eden's **muinlicht glaumour**,	of/dispelling/moonlight/spell
And I **surrendrit aa thon** vain pretence,	surrendered all that
Wes nae mair God, **nae mair** afraid to be	was no more/no more
Alane, shut out, nor envied God possession	alone
O **whit** he'd made his **ane** — **nae langer** strove	of what/own/no longer
Wi angels to return, nor feared their sword,	with
And **fand whit** peace I could in **bein** man.	found what/being

References

Crawford, Robert. 2007. *Scotland's Books*. London and New York: Penguin.

Grieve, C. M. 1926. *Contemporary Scottish Studies*. London: Leonard Parsons.

MacDiarmid, Hugh. 1934. *At the Sign of the Thistle*. London: Stanley Nott.

MacDiarmid, Hugh. 1943. *Lucky Poet*. London: Methuen.

MacDiarmid, Hugh. 1992. *Selected Poetry*. Ed. Alan Riach and Michael Grieve. New York: New Directions.

Scott, Tom. 1963. *The Ship and Ither Poems*. Oxford: Oxford University Press.

A Reconstructed Universal Language

In Chapter 2, Arden Smith notes that Neo-Latin was, in the minds of some, a more likely universal language than any of the Early Modern invented language schemes he describes in detail, not to mention the many more for which there wasn't room in the chapter. Latin was a more efficient universal language, one might argue, because it was already in use. Neo-Latin, however, involved a degree or two of invention along lines Suzanne Romaine, in the corresponding chapter, lays down for renewed and reconstructed languages. Like Néo-breton, Māori, Neo-Galician, Modern Hebrew, Cornish, or Hawaiian, renewal of Classical Latin into Neo-Latin required some purification, codification of norms, and expansion of the vocabulary to encompass phenomena undesignated in earlier forms of the language.

As Anthony Grafton explains, Neo-Latin functioned as an international auxiliary language among the European elite: in 'the period that stretched from the Black Death of the fourteenth century to the Enlightenment of the eighteenth ... thousands of learned Europeans saw themselves as citizens of a second country as well: a republic of letters, which stretched at its height from Rekjavik [sic] to Kiev, and whose citizens spoke and wrote Latin' (2001, 5). In their project of language reform, Neo-Latinists, as Romaine puts it, expressed 'dissatisfaction with the current linguistic state of affairs' represented by the Babel of vernaculars and the supposed inadequacy of Medieval Latin. Today, dispassionately removed from Early Modern linguistic controversy, we might see Medieval Latin as a collection of 'unclassical but useful dialects of the ancient language—historians sometimes refer to them as "pragmatic" forms of Latin' (Grafton 2001, 6). But 'Humanists condemned the useful, sophisticated, modern language of the medieval universities as "barbarous"' (Grafton 2001, 7).

Neo-Latinists, then, would need to purify Latin of barbarisms: 'Its programme,' writes James Hankins, 'was to reverse the linguistic effects of the fall of Rome ... and renew the noble, refined intercourse of the ancients' (2001, 22). The fall of Rome left Europe to the vernacular languages, some of them 'foreign' and outside Roman influence (Germanic languages, for instance), but many of them Romance languages derived from Vulgar Latin. The fall of Rome—that is, the fall of the Western Empire in 476, in turmoil well before that year—was like another fall from grace, and once Europe was expelled from the garden of empire, it was Babel all over again: the Neo-Latin attempt to recover Classical Latin as a pure, intellectually robust, descriptively unambiguous language for Early Modern Europe was, in a sense, an attempt to recover the language of Adam—well, Adam's language had he been at a good school.

Neo-Latin's reform was not primarily structural: classical declensions, conjugations, phrase, and sentence structure were maintained, indeed, had been maintained throughout Medieval Latin (IJsewijn 1977, 246–247). But Neo-Latinists saw ways of ordering and regulating Latin more thoroughly than their predecessors, for instance, by developing a system of diacritics. Piet Steenbakkers aptly describes the problem Neo-Latinists wished to solve: 'The Latin alphabet has relatively few letters and must therefore be used efficiently. This frugality is one of its strengths: it accounts at least in part for the unrivalled dissemination of this alphabet. On the other hand, it necessitates the introduction of diacritical marks, when distinctions are to be represented for which the existing letters do not suffice' (1994, 930). Diacritics were not new with Neo-Latin, but their use was expanded and regulated with new vigour.

Latin (like other languages, English among them) includes many homonyms (words spelled and pronounced the same but different in meaning) and homographs (words spelled the same but different in pronunciation and meaning), which arguably confuse listeners and readers and beg for differentiation—at least, in the purist's mind. For instance, the Latin pronoun/demonstrative adjective *hic* 'this' (of *hic, haec, hoc* fame) and the adverb *hic* 'here' are homographs.

Neo-Latin not quite introduced, but generalized, use of the circumflex ^ to indicate vowel length and resolve the supposed confusion: adverb *hîc* with the vowel of *seek* as opposed to pronoun *hic* with the vowel of *sick*. (Nowadays, the circumflex is often replaced with a macron, thus *hīc* for the adverb in my Latin primer.)

Neo-Latin also used the circumflex to mark contractions, as when the genitive plural *deorum* 'of God' becomes *deûm*, much as Modern French uses the circumflex to mark an etymological /s/ lost in pronunciation of a word, so Old French *crouste*, Modern French *croûte*, and English *crust*, borrowed from French in the fourteenth century, before the /s/ went missing. Neo-Latin had uses for grave and acute accents, too, but the details cause many eyes to glaze over, not least because 'usage differs considerably from author to author and from printer to printer' (Steenbakkers 1994, 927)—best leave them to experts. Neo-Latin interest in consistent, systematic orthography is akin to that of modern language reformers, amply illustrated in the complementary chapter.

In contrast with its structural restraint and orthographic adjustments, Neo-Latin greatly expanded and enhanced Latin vocabulary, another parallel with Romaine's examples of revitalized and reconstructed languages. 'Even when [Latin was] described as an eternal language,' Hankins writes, 'the world did not stand still, of course. Neo-Latin writers, however traditional in their outlook, recognized that if Latin were to remain a living language it would need to adapt itself to the extraordinary changes occurring everywhere in the early modern world' (Hankins 2001, 26). Neo-Latin created words in astronomy, botany, chemistry, medicine, zoology. Vernacular reflexes of these once pristine words (English *telescope* from Neo-Latin *telescopium*, for instance) are so common and familiar that we easily overlook the role of Neo-Latin words in world scientific vocabulary today, without any regard for their role in the Early Modern universal language of science and public affairs.

In the Early Modern period, printing was a new technology and it required a new or at least renewed vocabulary to support it, given the international nature of writing, editing, printing, publishing, and selling books during the period, especially those written in Latin. Thus, from a minute examination of early printed English books, James Binns has isolated 'Latin terms used in describing the printing process, for of necessity Latin words had to be coined or extended in meaning to describe this after the invention of printing' (1977, 1). Binns' glossary includes such Neo-Latin terms as *collector* or *corrector* 'proofreader', *compositor* 'compositor', *folium* 'sheet', *libraries* 'publisher', *pericula* 'proofs', *typographicus* 'printing', so *typographica errata* 'printing errors' (1977, 25–6), a list subsequently amplified by others with *castigator* 'corrector, proofreader', *efformator* 'printer', *emissio* 'edition', *officina libraria* 'bookshop, printing shop' (Shaw 1989, 229–30). Similar lists for all of the other sciences and technologies are easy enough to compile if you know Latin particularly well and have plenty of time, access to the right books, a genius for research, and infinite patience.

Neo-Latin also had to adapt to new social and political thinking in Early Modern Europe. According to Michael Silverthorne, Thomas Hobbes (1588-1679) 'attempted some contributions of his own to natural philosophy (e.g., optics and ballistics)... but also felt that he could make a major contribution to the improvement of moral and civil philosophy' by focusing on 'the clarification of the basic terms of discourse' (1996, 499). Neo-Latin was essential to this process of disambiguation: 'The fluidity of natural languages, for Hobbes, is in conflict with the aspirations of science to reason accurately, since true reasoning has to be based on stable definitions. The fixing of the meanings of words in every area of discourse is therefore of the first importance' (1996, 500). So, modern moral as well as natural science required a turn away from natural languages (that is, language after Babel) to one in which meanings were 'fixed' (something like the language of Adam), in which words behaved more like names.

Whereas *jus* 'right' and *lex* 'law' overlapped in Latin before Hobbes—*jus* could mean 'law', but *lex* did not mean 'right'—he argues in *Leviathan* (1651), his foundational work in political philosophy, that they should be used exclusively, one meaning per word, one word per meaning. In similar ways, and in pursuit of the same philosophical position, *civitas* is extended to the modern meaning 'state', *curia* and *senatus* are specialized to 'council', and *concilium* not to 'council' but 'assembly', since the *concilium plebis* of classical Rome is a public meeting of 'the people'—a large gathering, not a *curia optimatum*, or council of the elite. These examples are all taken from Silverthorne (1996) and show how old words can be redefined for a new age; as Romaine points out, this is as true of natural as of planned languages, but we can detect the motives for change in planned languages.

There is no better example of a Neo-Latin vocabulary maker than the Swedish scientist Carl Linné (1707–1778), better known as Carolus Linnaeus — his very identity was and remains Neo-Latin. Linnaeus was a taxonomist, one who classifies living things by discerning their characteristics and relationships. Classification entails naming, and Linnaeus is responsible for many scientific names and for the basic process of scientific naming. Anyone who has studied biology, looked up an animal or plant name in a good dictionary, or walked through a zoo or botanical garden has encountered these names: the jaguar is *Panthera onca*, the rabbit is *Oryctolagus cuniculus*, the cultivated strawberry is *Fragaria ananassa*, and the lumpfish *Cyclopterus lumpus*, and so on, to all intents and purposes ad infinitum.

Originally, Linnaeus' 'polynomial phrase names served two functions that were ultimately incompatible: (1) to serve as a label and (2) to serve as a diagnosis of the species' and the names, though very specific, proved cumbersome. 'An example of such a polynomial [for a variety of plantain] is: *Plantago foliis ovatis glabris* … . Further study increased the number of species recognized, forever necessitating an emendation of the name so that it might adequately summarize the growing list of characters needed for unambiguous differentiation. Thus in 1753 this same species was renamed: *Plantago foliis ovatis glabris, nudo scapo tereti, spica flosculis imbricatis*'. So, 'In 1745 Linnaeus separated these functions: he started to give his species two names, one a one word epithet (*nomen triviale*), the other a polynomial diagnostic phrase; the generic name plus a trivial name form a Linnaean binomial (*binomen*). In 1753 in his *Species Plantarum* he applied binomials to the whole vegetable kingdom. The species mentioned twice above was given the trivial name *major* and the binomial *Plantago major*' (Jansonius 1981, 439). We have benefited from Linnaeus' method ever since.

Linnaeus' method was not beyond controversy, however, and the controversy was not about the classification so much as the ethics of naming. Early in his career, Linnaeus had used Greek for his botanical names, rather than Latin, and his renowned colleague, Johann Jakob Dillenius (1687–1747), complained about his naming practice. (All of this is laid out brilliantly in an article by John Considine, without which I would know none of what I relate here.) On 18/29 August 1737, Dillenius wrote to Linnaeus, in Latin, of course, "'You rush upon it and wreck everything. I do not object to Greek words, especially in compound names; but I think the names of the ancients ought not rashly and promiscuously to be transferred to our new genera, or those of the new world. The day may possibly come when the plants of Theophrastus and Dioscorides may be ascertained; and, till this happens, let us leave them their names'" (qtd. Considine 2009, 333; the translation is Considine's). The issue was not modernity, not the methods of science, but the relationship of past and present, the plasticity of words and meanings, and how the universal language of science ought to develop. In future, Linnaeus used Latin rather than Greek and left Theophrastus and Dioscorides to fend for themselves.

As Karen Meier Reeds writes in a review of a recent translation of Linnaeus' *Philosophia Botanica*, 'Linnaeus loved a list. He could turn out eloquent essays about Nature, but lists and outlines were clearly the cheapest and most efficient way to accomplish the enormous task God had set him (so he saw it) of naming, describing, and classifying everything in Creation' (2007, 369). Of course, everything had already been classified and named, when everything was a garden and not the universe as we know it, here and now. As long as everything gets bigger and more complicated, some of us will be dissatisfied with the current linguistic state of affairs and probably with the past ones, too. We will strive to reconstruct the language of Adam until we get it right—we won't, of course, but that makes no difference, because the dissatisfaction, the striving, the aspiration, the ingenuity, the obstinacy are all in our nature.

At the outset of this book, I proposed a spectrum of linguistic invention on which one can locate fully invented languages, but clearly, as we come full circle, a spectrum is not the only nor even the best metaphor to explain linguistic invention and invented languages, as the preceding chapters, in their unexpected variety and unaccountable detail, so amply prove. Language renewal, revitalization, and reconstruction and all of their structural, historical, and ideological implications invite us to reconsider the revolution of invented language.

References

Binns, James. 1977. 'STC Latin Books: Evidence for Printing-House Practice'. *The Library* (5th series) 32.1: 1–27.

Considine, John. 2009. 'Ancient Greek among the eighteenth-century languages of science: Linnaeus, Dillenius, and the lexicographical record'. *International Journal of the Classical Tradition* 16.3-4: 330–43.

Grafton, Anthony. 2001. 'Latinland'. *Harvard Library Bulletin* n.s. 12.1-2: 5–12.

Hankins, James. 2001. 'A Lost Continent of Literature'. Harvard Library Bulletin n.s. 12.1-2: 21–7.

IJsewijn, Jozef. 1977. *Companion to Neo-Latin Studies*. Amsterdam: North-Holland.

Jansonius, Jan. 1981. 'Linnaean Nomenclature — Universal Language of Taxonomists — and the Sporae Dispersae (with a Commentary on Hughes' Proposal)'. *Taxon* 30.2: 438–48.

Reeds, Karen Meier. 2007. Review of *Linnaeus' Philosophia Botanica*, translated by Stephen Freer (Oxford University Press, 2003), in *Journal of the History of Biology* 40.2: 369–71.

Shaw, David. 1989. '"Ars formularia": Neo-Latin Synonyms for Printing'. *The Library* (6th series) 11: 220–30.

Silverthorne, Michael. 1996. 'Political Terms in the Latin of Thomas Hobbes'. *International Journal of the Classical Tradition* 2.4: 499–509.

Steenbakkers, Piet. 1994. 'Accent Marks in Neo-Latin'. In *Acta Concentus Neo-Latini Hafniensis*, edited by Ann Moss and others, 925–34. Binghamton, New York: Medieval and Renaissance Texts and Studies.

Index

Index

Index

Index
*

Index

*

Paramount Pictures 119, 121, 229
Parma Eldalamberon (Elvish
    journal) 76
Parsons (*Nineteen Eighty-Four*) 55
patent 227
Patrick, Peter L. 128
Pavlov, Ivan 65
Peano, Giuseppe 40
Pemberton, Elizabeth Leigh 251
Pennycook, Alistair 214
Pentreath, Dolly 195
Permanent Commission of the
    Délégation pour l'adoption d'une
    langue internationale 39
Perry, Katy (musical artist) 147
P., H. G. (editorial letter writer) 238–9
Philosophia Botanica (Linnaeus) 277
philosophical languages 23–5, 30
phonology, *see* particular languages
Pig Latin 149
pIn'a' gan paQDI' norgh (Klingon
    translation of *Tao Te Ching*) 256
Plaid Cymru 191–2
*Plea for an American Language or
    Germanic-English* (Molee) 44
poetic competence 9
Polari 8
Polish 31
political correctness 60–1, 220–1
'Politics and the English Language'
    (Orwell) 58–9
Polynesian 202–5
    Proto-Polynesian 205
Portnow, James 14–15, 261–2
*Portrait of the Artist as a Young Man,
    A* (J. Joyce) 165–6
Portuguese 42, 197–8
Powers, Mary Farl 181
Pragmatics, *see* individual languages
'Preface to Politicians' (Shaw) 163
Price, Glanville 187
Primitive Elvish 91, 100

Primitive Qendian 93
Protoss 140
Pure Saxon English (Molee) 45

Qenya 92–3, 97–102
    etymology 101–2
    and natural languages 98–102
Quechua 207
    Quechua Language Academy 207
Quenya 77–9, 81–2, 84–93, 97, 99,
    103–5, 254
    derivation 87–9
    etymology 76, 79, 88–90, 93
    euphony of 77–8, 82–3
    inflection 83–6
    and natural languages 76, 93–5, 104
    orthography 79
    phonology 77, 81–3, 86–8, 90, 93
    and Qenya 92
    syntax 78, 87
    vocabulary 93–5
Quiché 206
Quichua 207
    Quichua auténtico 207
    Quichua Unificado 207
Qo'noS QonoS (Klingon journal) 256

Rabkin, Eric 243, 247
real character 14, 20, 24
realism 61
reconstructed languages 10–11, 15
Red Cross 37
Reeds, Karen Meier 277
Register, The (online journal) 228
regulation 273
Rembrandt 11
revitalization 185–225, 272–8; *see also*
    language planning
    and borrowing 188, 198–203
    and covert ideologies 205
    folk etymology 207
    functional restriction of 209, 217

Index

Index